Ingrid Nebe

ACTA UNIVERSITATIS UPSALIENSIS
BOREAS Uppsala Studies in Ancient Mediterranean
and Near Eastern Civilizations
20

D1730798

THE RELIGION OF THE ANCIENT EGYPTIANS

COGNITIVE STRUCTURES
AND
POPULAR EXPRESSIONS

**Proceedings of Symposia
in Uppsala and Bergen
1987 and 1988**

Edited by
Gertie Englund

Uppsala 1987

ACTA UNIVERSITATIS UPSALIENSIS

BOREAS. Uppsala Studies in Ancient Mediterranean
and Near Eastern Civilizations. 20

Editors: Rostislav Holthoer
             Tullia Linders

Editor's address: Gustavianum, S-752 20 Uppsala, Sweden
English text revision: Lana Troy
Computer aided layout: Bengt Mattsson
Distributors: Almqvist & Wiksell International, Box 638, S-101 28 Stockholm

Published with the aid of a grant from Vilhelm Ekmans Universitetsfond, Uppsala

Abstract

Englund, G., (ed.), 1989. The Religion of the Ancient Egyptians, Cognitive Structures and Popular Expressions. Proceedings of Symposia in Uppsala and Bergen 1987 and 1988. Acta Universitatis Upsaliensis. Boreas.
Uppsala Studies in Ancient Meditarranean and Near Eastern Civilizations 20. 146 p. with illustrations. ISBN
91-554-2433-3

This volume contains nine articles by five Scandinavian scholars, historians of religion and egyptologists, on
Egyptian religion presented at two symposia, one in Uppsala, Sweden in 1987 and one in Bergen, Norway 1988.
The first symposium focussed on the Egyptian religion in its theoretical and cognitive form as presented by the
temple philosophy; whereas the second concentrated on expressions of the popular model of this theoretical
system.

ISBN 91-554-2433-3
ISSN 0346-6442

Printed in Sweden by
Tryckeri Balder AB, Stockholm 1989

Contents

VI

Preface

This volume consists of edited versions of papers presented at two symposia on Egyptian religion held at the University of Uppsala, Sweden, Department of Egyptology, in March 1987, and at the University of Bergen, Norway, Department of History of Religion, in May 1988.

These symposia assembled Scandinavian scholars from two different disciplines, egyptologists interested in Egyptian religion and historians of religion interested in Egyptology, for stimulating and fruitful discussions. The theme of the Uppsala symposium was "Cognitive Structures". The participants were Ragnhild Bjerre Finnestad from Bergen, Paul John Frandsen and Jørgen Podemann Sørensen from Copenhagen, and Jan Bergman, Gertie Englund, Rostislav Holthoer, Torgny Säve-Söderbergh, and Lana Troy from Uppsala. The second meeting in Bergen focussed on our knowledge of the popular aspects of Egyptian religion. This symposium was attended by Ragnhild Bjerre Finnestad and Richard Holton Pierce from Bergen, Paul John Frandsen and Jørgen Podemann Sørensen from Copenhagen, and Jan Bergman, Gertie Englund, and Lana Troy from Uppsala.

Unfortunately it was not possible for all the participants to contribute to this volume, but it is our hope that the articles which appear here will mirror the themes of the two symposia and be of interest for our colleagues from other countries.

Uppsala in June 1989
Gertie Englund

VIII

PART ONE

Uppsala 1987

Jørgen Podemann Sørensen

Introduction

The search for the Egyptian mind or 'la pensée égyptienne' has a somewhat discouraging parallel in the idea of a 'primitive mentality' or 'savage mind', which haunted anthropological thought during the first decennia of the twentieth century. The pre-logical, collective thought, postulated and richly documented by Lucien Lévy-Bruhl[1] was no doubt the most famous exponent of the idea of a mode of thought which was peculiar to primitive peoples and responsible for their mythology, their rituals, and their social life as well. The basic shortcomings of the whole pre-logical idea were shown in anthropological discussions following the publications of Lévy-Bruhl and even to some degree realized by his own work.[2] Yet both the idea of a primitive mentality and the **law of participation** formulated and amply exemplified by Lévy-Bruhl continued to exert a considerable influence, especially in History of Religion and in Egyptology. A heavy portion of the shared responsibility for this 'survival of the primitive mind' rests on **Gerardus van der Leeuw.**[3]

The law of participation - and to a certain degree also the principles of sympathetic and contagious magic of Sir James Frazer[4] - were meant to account for the deficiency of the primitive mind - or at least its deviance from modern European logical standards. In a European context, however, words like logic and thought always have epistemological connotations, and to get an idea of modern European thought one should consult philosophical and scientific literature. Nobody would base an account of European logic on an analysis of the Lord's supper or, say, the use of fireworks on Guy Fawkes' day. But such was exactly the procedure of Lévy-Bruhl and others: taking their point of departure and their examples almost exclusively from the **rituals** of non-literate peoples, they constructed their pre-logical laws to account **in general** for the strange ways of strange peoples. Van der Leeuw's recasting of Lévy-Bruhl's primitive mentality within the framework of a **phenomenology of religion** was therefore essentially a rectification - even if the new framework, as conceived by van der Leeuw, presented a host of other problems not to be considered here.

The great modern renewer of the study of ancient Egyptian religion, **Henri Frankfort,** rejected the idea of pre-logical thought for reasons very much akin to those stated above. He did so, however, in a book called *The Intellectual Adventure of Ancient Man*, in later printings to be entitled *Before Philosophy*.[5] Strongly opposed to evolutionist ideas about the intellectual inferiority of primitive man, Frankfort wanted to trace the pre-philosophical or implicit philosophy of ancient man and to show the logical consistency of his thought. To account for this consistency, in what seemed to a modern observer a mess of unrelated symbols and sayings, he coined his famous principle of **multiplicity of approaches**:

"Ancient thought - mythopoeic, 'myth-making' thought - admitted side by side certain **limited** insights, which were held to be simultaneously valid, each in its own proper context, each corresponding to a definite avenue of approach. I have called this 'multi-plicity of approaches' ...".[6]

The principle here offered still describes ancient thought in terms of its deviation from modern standards. It is somewhat qualified by a passage in Frankfort's *Kingship and the Gods*:

"Abstract nouns, adverbs, and conjunctions which enable us to modulate meaning were relatively little used by the Egyptian. His mind tended towards the concrete; his language depended upon concrete images and therefore expressed the irrational, not by qualifying modifications of a principal notion, but by admitting the validity of several avenues of approach at one and the same time."[7]

Ancient and modern thought is seen by Frankfort to differ on the level of expression and cultural context only, not in intellectual quality. His implicit or pre-philosophical philosophy anticipates the idea of a 'logic of the concrete' so prominent in the works of Claude Lévi-Strauss. If a faint note of Lévy-Bruhl's **mentalité primitive** is also heard in the first chapter of *Before Philosophy*, this is not to be wondered at, since Frankfort's main source of inspiration in these general matters was undoubtedly van der Leeuw.[8]

To the study of ancient Egyptian religion Frankfort's ideas, and their utilization in the first modern book treating Egyptian religion as a whole, were seminal and even revolutionary. They marked the end of the kind of separatist interpretation of Egyptian religious texts that would construct a complicated text history and refer to political attempts towards religious primacy to account for the joint presence of Osirian, Heliopolitan, and Hermopolitan elements in one single text. Given the courage to look for the unity of thought expressed by the multiple approaches Egyptologists found with Frankfort that it was possible to make sense of religious texts formerly considered as more or less corrupt or devoid of meaning - and not just a Theban or a Herakleopolitan sense, but an Egyptian one.

We shall not, however, content ourselves or loose sight of our subject by enumerating the merits or measuring the impact of Henri Frankfort. Even though he may be said to have established the modern study of 'the Egyptian mind' his initial and general formulations of the central principle of 'multiplicity of approaches' are not without difficulties. They are not, as it were, ideologically, but rather methodologically akin to the idea of the primitive mind: they claim to be universal as far as 'ancient man' is concerned; they describe ancient thought in terms of its deviations from modern thought, which is believed to allow for only one avenue of approach at a time; and they are based primarily on ritual texts, yet speak in "epistemological" terms like 'insights' and 'avenue of approach'. Even if Frankfort's central principle is quite justified - and it has indeed proved useful in the study of Egyptian religion - it is obvious that there is much more to do along the path he has blazed.

Erik Hornung's *Der Eine und die Vielen* in many ways marked another revolution in the study of ancient Egyptian religion. In connection with the main theme of the book, Egyptian conceptions of God, Hornung had to deal with 'the problem of logic'.[9] Considering both Frankfort's 'multiplicity of approaches' and Jan Zandee's ideas about 'complementary thought' he ends up with a somewhat sharpened reformulation of Frankfort's central principle: **mehrwertige Logik**. In contradistinction to modern European binary logic (zweiwertige Logik) Egyptian mehrwertige Logik will permit that both 'A' and 'not A' is predicated about the same subject. Within this logical framework it becomes possible and meaningful to regard 'the one and the many', the unity and the multiplicity of God, as complementary statements towards the total conception of God. The somewhat problematic nature of a logic not defined by rules of its own, but by the one European logical law that it violates, is clearly realized by Hornung:

> "Solange die gedankliche Begründung einer mehrwertigen Logik fraglich bleibt, können wir nur Perspektiven aufzeigen, aber keine gültigen Lösungen. Scheitert die Begründung, dann bleibt ägyptisches Denken, "vorgriechisches" Denken überhaupt, weiterhin der logischen Willkür oder Verschwommenheit ausgesetzt....".[10]

What is needed in order to proceed from the point to which Frankfort and Hornung have led us, is exactly some kind of 'gedankliche Begründung'. Whether we speak about 'multiplicity of approaches' or about mehrwertige Logik, we shall have to examine the rules or the preconceived structures governing Egyptian religious expression. Without such rules or structures, both principles are nothing but a logical **carte blanche**, a licence unrestricted by syntactic rules.

It is the aim of the present dossier of studies to examine such rules or structures. We shall try to characterize ancient Egyptian thought not by the manner in which it differs or deviates from modern European scientific thought, but by positive rules of its own. We shall do so with a view to what has, within the subjects of Anthropology and History of Religion, replaced the idea of the primitive mind. Since van der Leeuw, who was both an Egyptologist and a historian of religions, is ultimately responsible for the way the primitive mind entered the study of ancient Egyptian religion, it is only fair that Egyptologists and historians of religion **together** try to adjust our ideas about the 'Egyptian mind' to keep pace with the achievements of the comparative study of religion and culture.

If old slogans like 'the part equals the whole' and 'like produces like' are no longer heard in the fields of Anthropology and History of Religion, it is probably because progress in these disciplines have shown such rudiments of the pre-logical construction to be superfluous or even misleading. To account for the strange ways of strange peoples recourse is no longer had to logical deviations, but to systems of symbolic classification. To understand the symbolic statements of a given culture, to gain access to its cultural codes, means to the modern anthropologist first and foremost to map its classificatory systems. Although cross-cultural parallels have been pointed out, systems of classification are basically culture-specific. And once such a system of native categories is established, the logical consistency of native thought is also perceived.

On the whole, careful study of the structure of native religious expression has replaced the interest in reconstructing exotic logical laws and aberrations that might have made it plausible in the eyes of native logicians.

The importance of such structural studies within the field of mythology needs hardly be pointed out. The 'logic' appealed to in 'mythological' studies is a logic of systematic relations within the material studied, not an epistemological device or a norm of argumentation.[11]

Perhaps there is still room for pre-logical notions of causality in the study of ritual - especially in ancient Egypt, where belief in ritual efficacy is confessed in virtually every heading of a magical or mortuary formula. But again, closer examination has shown limits to logical licence. The more detailed studies of ritual suggest that its cosmological references are important. The 'like' that produces like and the part that equals the whole do so in accordance with cosmological principles; a ritual subjects its case to ritual control by reducing it to its cosmological significance.[12] It has therefore become a major objective of the study of ritual to describe the various ways in which cosmology is put to work in ritual - and, once again, this means that a logic of systematic relations must be studied.

It is in this sense, of a logic of systematic relations specifically Egyptian, yet accessible by comparative methods, that the question of 'the Egyptian mind' may still be posed. And it is in this sense that the following papers are going to treat the question.

NOTES

1. Notably in *Les fonctions mentales dans les sociétés inferieures*, Paris 1910 and *La mentalité primitive*, Paris 1922.

2. *Les carnets de L. Lévy-Bruhl*, Paris 1949, p. 129 sq.

3. Cf. G. VAN DER LEEUW: *Phänomenologie der Religion*, Tübingen 1956, § 83,2; id. *La structure de la mentalité primitive*, 1928.

4. J.G. FRAZER: *The Magic Art* I, London 1936, p. 52 sqq.

5. HENRI FRANKFORT et al.: *The Intellectual Adventure of Ancient Man*, Chicago 1946; later edited as *Before Philosophy*, Harmondsworth 1949.

6. HENRI FRANKFORT: *Ancient Egyptian Religion*, New York 1948, p. 4.

7. HENRI FRANKFORT: *Kingship and the Gods*, Chicago 1948, p. 41.

8. Cf. e.g. *Ancient Egyptian Religion*, p. 4 sq.

9. ERIK HORNUNG: *Der Eine und die Vielen*, Darmstadt 1971, p. 233 sqq.

10. ibid. p. 238.

11. EDMUND LEACH: *Culture and Communication: The Logic by which symbols are connected*, Cambridge 1976, esp. p. 69 sqq.

12. Cf. J. PODEMANN SØRENSEN: The Argument in Ancient Egyptian Magical Formulae, *Acta Orientalis* 45, 1984, p. 17.

Gertie Englund
Gods as a Frame of Reference
On Thinking and Concepts of Thought
in Ancient Egypt

1. Introduction

1.1 The essence of Egyptian religion

The essence of Egyptian religion is not easy to grasp. This has been a problem for scholars almost as long as Egyptology has existed. Different generations of scholars have tried different appellations: **monotheism, polytheism, pantheism, and henotheism.**

In 1869 the French Egyptologist Emmanuel de Rougé expressed his opinion that it was a monotheistic religion and during the 1870s this was the accepted opinion among scholars not only in France. In 1880 another French Egyptologist, Maspero, declared that Egyptian religion was polytheistic. And then the fight began.

During the first half of the 20th century the conflict between the monotheists and the polytheists gradually ceased. From 1905 when Adolf Erman published his book on Egyptian religion up to and including the writings of Kees in the 1940s, scholars did not bother about this old controversy but devoted themselves to other aspects of this very rich material. The question did not, however, disappear altogether. Herman Junker presented his theory about the 'High God' *Wr* in 1930 and Abbé Drioton in France communicated, in the 1930s and -40s, his ideas about a neo-monotheism. By this expression he meant a secondary monotheism arisen out of an older polytheism, that functioned as a monotheism for the learned and the wise. (For a detailed discussion, see Hornung 1971, pp. 1-19.)

The source material of our subject is thus very ambiguous and far from evident. Both the unity and the plurality of the godhead is strongly stressed in the Egyptian material and this puts the Western observer in an embarrassing situation. This combination of two appararently opposed notions is exactly what Eric Hornung choose as a title for his book on Egyptian religion: 'Der Eine und die Vielen' (1971). In order to solve the conflict he experiences when confronted with the Egyptian religious material and its coexistence and simultaneousness of unity and plurality he suggests that the reason might be that we are facing a different logic, a different structure of thought, and that logic would have to be called 'eine mehrwertige Logik'.

1.2 The insufficiency of Western concepts

It is actually so that we can fight with each other and with the material forever if we want to force it into the concepts we are used to. We will certainly have to refrain from these concepts as they have proven insufficient and do not allow us to get at the reality that the Egyptian gods describe. Hornung also points this out in the final chapter of his book (1971, p. 248).

Why are our concepts insufficient?

The answer to this question is probably that the word 'religion' is too narrow a concept to cover the whole field in question in the Egyptian material. I believe that it is actually only out of traditon and in want of a better expression that we keep on talking about 'Egyptian religion'.

What then was this 'religion' of ancient Egypt?

There are definitely similarities with our own. Take personal piety for instance. It is striking how great the similarities between piety in modern society and in ancient Egypt are in the mentality and the way of expression, even in the choice of the words.

Nevertheless the differences between religion here and religion there are greater than the similarities.

There was no common worship in the Egyptian temples, people did not have access to the temples, except for the outer parts, and the execution of the ritual did not concern anybody but the priests.

The theologians there did not study and interpret a basic text but they kept on creating new texts that were the results of a continual speculation over the world and the new texts were of the same importance as the older ones.

Egyptian theologians were first and foremost interested in cosmology. The thoughts that emanated from the temples and the temple schools were all-embracing and explicating. They constituted a systematic thinking and this system of thought was normative. Those thoughts represented the Egyptian way of thinking. Actually it represented the thinking of the elite and it is still an open question to what extent it permeated the entire society. The main lines of it must have been part of the common heritage of age-old thinking shared by the population as a whole. All the subtleties and details of this elaborate thinking were, however, probably of less or no importance for the people (cf. Baines 1984, p. 35-37).

This way of thinking does not correspond to what we in every day language call religion. It embraces not only matters of faith but also philosophy, psychology, and theories about the functioning of the world and society. It has also sometimes been called 'the Egyptian science' (Hornung 1972, pp. 11-12), and that is perhaps a better designation of the field of knowledge in question. The Egyptian civilization is actually situated in a period when science, philosophy and religion were not yet separate activities taken over by different disciplines (Bateson 1972, p. XXII).

1.3 Models of interpretation

Is it possible for us to understand and to interpret a civilization and a way of thinking that is so far from us in time and space? Is it reasonable to think that we can get at the essence of it? Yes I believe it is and I think that our status as outsiders can even help us to understand. It can be something positive and useful. Thanks to the fact that we are alien observers, not sharing the socio-cultural programming we can see the phenomena from outside, we have the possibility to see the main structures, the system within the plurality of data in a way that the members of that civilization could not and had no need for. They above all needed an understanding that made it possible for them to live in the reality that their civilization represented. For them the system of thinking had a practical purpose. It was a means to orient themselves in life and to handle the events of the day.

Thus what we can do is to build up research models in order to understand the cultural phenomena that interest us. These models are then investigations of the material in modern terms according to our ways of thinking. We need not get bogged down by the outer form in which the thought is presented in the source material. We have the chance to see what is actually happening in what seems to happen. This is particularly important when dealing with a foreign and to us rather strange material like the Egyptian where practically every thought is cast in the mould of myth. The mythic expression of thinking is no longer ours and we don't understand it. We have to transform it into the language of the observer, into the mental form that is ours i.e. we have to present it in an abstract, systematic, and analytical manner (Baines 1984, p. 39).

1.4 A research model of a research model
What the Egyptologist is facing is, however, in my opinion, the task of constructing a research model of a research model. The reason for this is that those who were working in the Egyptian temples belonged to an elite group of scholars and the material that we mainly deal with is the opinion of this little, dominating and normative group.

It is a truism to say that the group was small. On reading the article of Baines and Eyre entitled 'Literacy in Ancient Egypt' (1983) one realizes very strongly how small this group actually was. The authors calculate that 1 % of the Egyptian population was literate and they suggest that there were different levels of literacy. The majority of this one percent probably had a limited degree of knowledge restricted to hieratic for business and office purposes. Only a minority of the literate population is likely to have been able to read both hieratic and hieroglyphic script. As time passed and a new variant of script appeared, Demotic, and furthermore the language changed so that it was necessary with language studies in order to understand older text material, the number of those able to read Egyptian in all different scripts from all periods must have diminished considerably.

It was this very small minority in Egypt that created the textual and pictorial material that form the basis for what we call the old Egyptian religion. That is why I mean that what we study is a research model. What this elite created was not accessible for every one. It can hardly have been intellectually accessible for the average Egyptian and it was definitely not physically accessible, hidden as it was in the temple libraries and temple sanctuaries where only the scholarly elite were allowed to enter or in graves where it was intended to be inaccessible for everyone. What the people were taught was the information that the temple wanted to transmit and we don't know very much about that. Certain aspects of the thinking that were elaborated in the temple and the temple schools and the moral and ethic values that it involved do, however, seem to have been part of the cultural heritage.

We are priviledged to have access to so much material from all different periods and from so many different places all over Egypt and furthermore in all different scripts. This position may be unique. It is possible that not even the highest level of Ptolemaic scholars shared this advantage. What we don't have, however, and what we will never have is the native insight but I still believe that we have a fair chance of building a good modern model of the thinking of the old Egyptians.

1.5 The folk model

If I am right in saying that there was a scholarly model of thinking in ancient Egypt concerning the field of knowledge that we for want of a better designation call 'religion' then there must also have existed a popular variant of the knowledge in question. It is, however, much more difficult to discover. The illiterate part of the population did not have the same possibility to account for their thoughts and ideas.

2. The Intellectual Aspect

Let us start with the intellectual aspect of this field of knowledge and talk about how the pantheon can be interpreted as representing a systematic thinking and how the concepts of this system are used in different contexts, religious and others.

2.1 The theoretical model of thought

The intellectual aspect is clearly perceptible in many texts although a theoretical approach is not characteristic for the Egyptian way of writing. Even without theoretical analyses it is, however, quite obviously so that the texts emanating from the *House of Life* of the temples present models of reality on a structural level.

Let us take the teachings about the creation of the world as an example, those that are attributed to Hermopolis, Heliopolis, Memphis, and Thebes. Generally these teachings are considered to be variants of the creation myth, variants due to historical events and the competition for supremacy among the different regions and their princes and priesthoods. They can, however, also be regarded differently. Herman Junker was of that opinion as early as 1917 (p. 69) when, talking about the consistency in the transmission of the Onuris myth, he wrote: "Das alles kann nur seine Erklärung darin finden, dass auch noch in der Ptolemäerzeit eine gewisse systematische Theologie existierte, die in den einzelnen Tempelschulen gelehrt wurde, die über viele Behelfe, Listen, Kopien usw. verfügte und die sich keineswegs auf die heimischen Traditionen beschränkte, sondern auch mit den anderen Tempelschulen in Verbindung stand." The opinion that there is a systematic thinking behind all the local systems of gods and the whole plurality of gods is still now and again put forward (e.g. te Velde 1967, p. 117).

With regards to the teachings about the creation they can be seen as variants that intentionally stress different aspects of the problem concerning the origin and the genesis of the world. The Egyptians were just like us very much interested in "the big bang". They pondered very much as we do on what happened, how it was possible that a state of absolute unity, totally homogeneous, differentiates and is transformed into the plurality that constitutes our world.

This process of transformation comprises several problems to be considered.

2.1.1 What is the original unity like?

The first problem to be dealt with is the origin. What is the origin like? If the absolutely homogeneous unity of the origin is to differentiate and give rise to plurality, it must contain a potential heterogeneity. The Egyptian scholars present their model for the potentiality of the origin in the Hermopolitan teaching. There they describe the unity of the origin as a potential duality. The symbols that they chose in order to describe what is absolutely different from all we know, the origin inconceivable for the human intellect, all appear in two variant forms. If we in the West today want to describe two variants of one and the same thing we are in the habit of calling the variants 'alpha' and 'beta', 'one' and 'two', or 'zero' and 'one'. These scholars , however, choose a designation much closer to human experience in order to express their thought and as the human being appears in two variants they called the variants of the origin 'male' and 'female'. It must, however, be kept in mind that the origin is elsewhere described as "before two things existed" so this duality of male and female is only latent, only exists as a predisposition, as a germ of the realization to come.

The symbols by which they tried to grasp and describe the character of the metastate were water, darkness, concealment, denial, and searching/impulse. A few more characteristics are sometimes added to this list. The symbols are carefully selected in order to describe what is completely different, what is actually indescribeable, unreachable for human thought but that one has to try to grasp somehow and to explain. They choose the amorphous water, *Nw*, as there are as yet no forms; darkness, *Kkw*, as the sun and the light have not yet come into existence; concealment, *Imn*, as the origin cannot be seen or perceived by any human senses; denial, *Niw*, as the metastate of the origin is nothing in relation to the plurality of the created world; and finally searching/impulse, *Ḥḥw*, as the metastate must contain the ignition mechanism that has obviously once triggered off the process of transformation so that the world known to mankind was created.

2.1.2 What are the rules for the transformation from the potential to the manifested state
The next problem is of course to find out how the potential energy is transformed into manifested energy, to try to understand and describe what happens when the ignition triggers

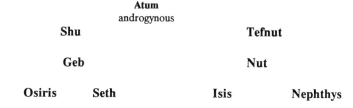

Fig. 1. The Ennead of Heliopolis.

off the transformation. That process means that the unity of the origin must split and this is taught in Heliopolis. The teaching of Heliopolis can be considered as a theoretical model of the process of dualisation. What the scholars of Heliopolis were particularly interested in was how the potential duality of male and female contained in the metastate is hypostasized (Fig. 1).

The origin is as said neutral. The potential forces balance each other. This state is inert or as the Egyptians expressed it themselves *nny* (Fig. 2). Therefore the process of dualisation also has to disrupt this inertness and bring in a polarisation. The two poles are the passive/static and the active/dynamic or to put it in Egyptian terms: *ḏt* and *nḥḥ*.

All the gods of the Heliopolitan Ennead are hypostases of the androgynous Atum and they represent intradivine projections of the androgynous potential of male-female and dynamic-static. It is said in the Coffin Texts (spells 75-80) that they are integrated in the creator, not differentiated from him. Now, if one thinks that they are representations of the

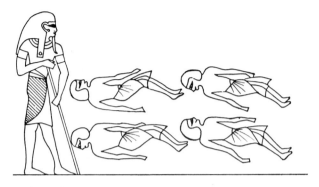

Fig. 2. The inert ones. From *The Book of Gates*, 2nd hour.

intradivine process, then it is natural that they are all androgynous. It is also possible to imagine that he or those who elaborated the system wanted to work with different combinations of androgyny and the gods of the Ennead are actually an explicit example of that.

The potential duality male-female was actualized as the duality **Shu-Tefnut.** In the passage referred to of the so called Shu theology (CT spell 75-80), Shu is described as completely integrated in Atum and is presented as the active element that starts the process of transformation. In this passage it is further said in way of an additional explanation that he is *nḥḥ* while his twin sister and partner, Tefnut, is said to be *ḏt* (CT II 28d). Another passage where these terms are used as explicative notions exists in the famous Chapter 17 of the Book of the Dead where it is stated in one of the glosses: "Re is *nḥḥ* and Osiris is *ḏt*, the day is *nḥḥ* and the night is *ḏt*". W. Westendorf in Göttingen has presented the theory that these terms are to be regarded as categorizing notions, while other scholars consider them to be expressions of time, expressions for two aspects of eternity. When presenting his theory (1974, s. 136-141) Westendorf showed how *nḥḥ* and *ḏt* polarize creation and give rise to a division of the sphere of perception (Fig. 3).

To sum up the information given in Figure 3 one can say that *nḥḥ* is dynamic/mobile/active and at the same time protruding/penetrating and *ḏt* static/at rest/passive and at the same time enclosing. In this context there are also two more terms that are very useful phallic

nḥḥ	*ḏt*
männlich (Vater/Gatte/Sohn)	weiblich (Mutter/Gattin)
Zeitablauf (dynamisch)	Raum (statisch)
Tag/Sonnenlicht	Nacht/Dunkelheit
Diesseits/irdisch	Jenseits/ausserirdisch
Ordnung	Chaos
Widerkehr	Dauer
Re/Horus/lebender König	Osiris/Königsmumie
Bai-Seele	*ḥ3t*-Leichnam/Leib

Fig. 3 The categories *nḥḥ* and *ḏt*.

Fig. 4 The lions of the border line and the birth of the new life. Coffin of Khonsumes, Uppsala.

and uterine, coined by L. Troy in her dissertation 'Patterns of Queenship' (1986), two terms that are very expressive when it comes to interpreting iconography and metaphorical expressions.

Let us now after this excursus return to the Ennead of Heliopolis. According to the text passage just referred to and also according to pictorial representations (Piankoff and Rambova, 1955, Fig. 47) Shu is *nḥḥ* and Tefnut is *ḏt*. They represent the two potential aspects of the androgynous Atum. The process of differentiating, leading from unity to plurality, has started with this duality that is, however, not separated from Atum, but integrated in him (CT spells 75-80 passim). It is said about Atum, Shu, and Tefnut that they create their godhood themselves (PT 447b). They form together a triune creative unit. It is interesting to note here that the coming into existence of the triune creative godhead does not mean that the absolute unit of the origin comes to an end. They co-exist as it is stated in Pap. Bremner-Rhind (27.1-2): "After I had come into being as sole god, there were three gods in relation to myself." From this quotation we see, moreover, that the sole god does not come into being before the differentiation has set in and that the two aspects of the godhead, the absolute and the triune unity, are not only coexisting but also interdependent.

After having passed over the border that the coming into existence of Shu and Tefnut means - they are, as we all know, the lions of the border line (Fig. 4) - the process of differentiation continues. What comes next is a clear-cut number two, a real couple: **Geb** and **Nut**. Even though they are represented as a man and a woman, they are both androgynous. Geb is a man with predominant *ḏt*-character, lying indolently (Fig. 5) hardly beginning to get out of the pre-creation state of inertness (cf. Fig. 2), even though sometimes represented ithyphallic. Nut is a woman with predominent *nḥḥ*-character shown through her dynamic movement. It is to be noted here that they, although separated and differentiated, function as a unit - the picture indicates the very moment of separating them. This unit is the enclosing *ḏt*-element for the separating Shu. There is another interesting thing to notice here - an

Fig. 5 Shu separates Geb and Nut. Coffin of Khonsumes, Uppsala.

inversion. Even though the texts speak of Shu and Tefnut as the parents of Geb and Nut, it is Geb and Nut who fulfill the function of parents and who are elsewhere always representatives of parenthood while Shu and Tefnut are most of the time representing childhood. These earliest intradivine processes can only be expressed in paradoxes. Everything is simultaneous. The human language is not conceived to express such processes and the images chosen work all the time with inversions.

The process of differentiation then goes on. This is expressed by stating that Geb and Nut give rise to four children. This new generation works with further combinations of androgyny. The mummyformed **Osiris** who according to the myth looses his phallus is a typical masculine *dt*-element, while the dynamic **Isis** is a female *nhh*-element. In **Seth** we find a combination of masculine gender and dominating *nhh*-character. He is, however, not a hundred percent male for according to the myth he is bereft of his testicles. And then as last member of the Ennead we have **Nephthys**. As the counterpart of Seth who is male with *nhh*-character, Nephthys is presented as a female with *dt*-character. But again it is not a question of a hundred percent, for it is said about her: "Imitation woman who has no vagina" (PT 1273). Also these two are androgynous. In the burlesque story about the adventures of Horus and Seth it is said that Seth swallowed the semen of Horus and that he gave birth to the sun disk out of his forehead. And in the Pyramid texts (1154) it is said about Nephthys that she begets the king, expressed with the verb *wtt* that is generally followed by a phallus as determinative.

Thus the Ennead is a description of nine facets of androgyny. Through this androgynous medium creation comes into being, a creation that is not essentially different from the origin, that is manifested godhead, that is the son, the new unit, identical with the father. These hypostases are necessary for the differentiation of the original unity, i.e. for the passage from one to two, so that the process can reach the new unit, the son, the other.

According to the myth, the Ennead gives birth to two son figures: Nut gives birth to Re and Isis gives birth to Horus. The two son figures merge into one another under the name of Re-Hor-akhty, Re-Horus-of-the-border-passage, the rising sun, the new unit, the source of energy for the creation.

If the only concern had been to hypostasize male-female and active/dynamic-passive/static then it would of course have been possible to stop after Geb and Nut but there were certainly also other viewpoints to be considered. The symbolism of numbers is surely important in this connection. It is only when the Ennead has come into being that the process reaches the new unit 'ten'.

It is not difficult to find references in the text material proving that the Egyptians themselves speculated like this. As for the Ennead as hypostases of Atum this is confirmed by epithets and statements in the texts that are otherwise difficult to explain. It is said about **Geb** that he is 'at the head of the Ennead' (PT 1919, 2103, 2226), that he is 'the only great god' (PT 1616), that he is 'the essence (*k3*) of all the gods' (PT 1623), that he is 'the one who nourishes Atum's heart and gathers together those very weary limbs of his' (CT II 35), and that he is 'Atum's father' (CT IV 37). And it is said about **Horus** that he is 'Atums son' (PT 874). The identity between the father and the son is confirmed by the name combinations Atum-Re and Re-Atum. One can further cite Atum's words in the Book of the Gates, 2nd hour: "I am the son who emanated from the father, I am the father who emanated from the son", a passage that clearly states the essential unity and the interdependence in the coming into being of both - without a father there is no son, and without a son there is no father. In the same passage Atum also calls Re his father.

The words chosen always come directly from the every day experiences of man even in order to express abstractions. That is why relationship and causality are phrased in terms of family relations.

The Heliopolitan teaching about the Ennead became the normative model of thinking as far as transformation was concerned. It can be called a metamodel, a model of all models (Bateson 1979, p. 20) or 'a paradigmatic cycle of perfectly ordered change' (Eliade 1978, p. 91). The interplay of male and female, active/dynamic and passive/static creates the world and maintains the creation. The Heliopolitan teaching found many subtle applications in the Egyptian culture and in the conceptions and iconography of the Egyptians. These applications have recently been described in detail (Troy 1986).

2.1.3 The transformation of energy into substance

Let us now go over to the teaching of Memphis. Hermopolis dealt with the character of the origin and Heliopolis with the rules that govern the big bang. Now the Memphitic teaching concerns the coming into being of substance and material forms. As the rules for the transformation process are given and apply to everything, the Memphitic Ennead is identical with the Heliopolitan. The context in which the energy works is, however, another. The images come from man's close surroundings and the human experience of designing and creating. As the artist starts out with an idea about the final product, Ptah, the god of arts and crafts, feels an idea being born in his heart that rises up to his mouth and lips and is pronounced and gives rise to substance. Here thought and the power of the pronounced word carry the creative energy.

Let us for a moment compare the teachings of Heliopolis and Memphis. Heliopolis wants first and foremost to show the dynamics of the transforming process and how the process leads to a dynamic state of energy, Re. As stated above, in all transformation the two poles active/dynamic/*nḥḥ* and passive/static/*ḏt* must be present and the Heliopolitan teaching takes this into account in the detailed analysis of the Ennead and in the fact that the Ennead as a whole functions as a *ḏt*-element for the final outcome of the process, Re, the

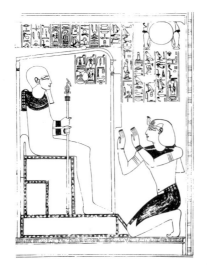

Fig. 6 The god Ptah with the sceptres of stability, life, and prosperity in his hands. From Calverley 1935, The Temple of Sethos I at Abydos, Pl. 22.

Fig. 7 Nefertem, the son of Ptah. From Michalowski, Ägypten p. 560.

representative of *nḥḥ*. In the Heliopolitan teaching it is, however, the *nḥḥ*-side that is stressed. The act of creation is sexual, the phallic aspect is dominating. The Memphitic teaching stresses on the contrary the *ḏt*-aspect. The uterine side is dominating. Bandaged and with bound limbs (Fig. 6) Ptah is a typical representative of the passive and stationary *ḏt*-side. He is a figure that encloses vital forces indicated by the sceptres he holds in his hands: *ḏd*, *'nḫ*, and *w3s*. Ptah is, as it were, pregnant with creation and material forms come out of him. "Ptah is called 'He who created the all and brought forth the gods'. ... The gods entered into their bodies of all kinds of wood, all kinds of minerals, all kinds of clay, and all kinds of other things that grow thereon, in which they had taken shape." (Sandman-Holm-

Fig. 8a and b The lotus carrying the young sun god at his birth.

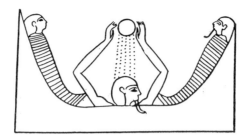

Fig. 9 Osiris as the border land from which the sun goes forth. (An Amduat papyrus from Cairo, Piankoff-Rambova, Mythological Papyri, Fig 7a).

berg 1946, p. 22). The son figure in Memphis also belongs to the *ḏt*-side - the lotus flower god Nefertem (Fig. 7). Think of how the sun is carried by, and born out of the lotus (Fig. 8 a and b). Thus the two teachings of Heliopolis and Memphis are complementary, representing the male/active and the female/passive respectively: *nḥḥ* and *ḏt*.

2.1.4 Maintenance

Another problem that is as great and important as the very act of creation, when the inert energy is transformed into active energy and substance, is the question of the regeneration of energy so that the whole work does not come to a standstill, i.e. the problem that we treat under the terms thermodynamics and entropy.

The Egyptians treated this problem in the **Kamutef**-motif (Jacobsohn, 1939) and in their continual discourse on the relation between **Re** and **Osiris**. Kamutef, which means 'the bull of his mother' is the technical term for self-generation and describes how the son units himself with his mother in order to give rise to himself again. A few of the great gods like Amon, Min, Horus have this epithet and the roles of the divine prototype are taken up within the royal family (Jacobsohn 1939, Troy 1986). The other motif of regeneration is the

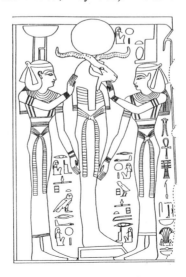

Fig. 10 The united figure of Re and Osiris. (Tomb of Nefertari).

relation between Re and Osiris and that motif is treated in all funerary texts from the Pyramid texts and onwards. The nuances of this relation are modulated more and more as time goes on changing from the very shortcut statement about Osiris in the Pyramid Texts: "You are the border land (*3ḫt*) from which Re goes forth" (PT 585a, 621a-b, 636c; exemplified in the New Kingdom iconography, see e.g. Fig. 9) to the thorough textual and pictorial penetration of the relation in the texts from the royal tombs of the New Kingdom. This long discourse is then synthesized in the fantastic icon in the tomb of Nefertari where the two are one, one resting in the other (Fig. 10). Thus it is, according to the Egyptians, in meeting and merging with the inert passive *ḏt*-element that the active life-spending *nḥḥ*-energy is regenerated so that the world endures. It is in a cyclically repeated encounter that reinforced energy enters creation. This regeneration prevents creation from running down, prevents the state of entropy from coming about.

The process of regeneration as it is presented in the relation Re-Osiris follows completely the rules for transformation that were presented in the Heliopolitan Ennead. It is the power of the androgynous creator that is at work in the two who act one against the other in the same manner as the power worked within Atum himself. What we have in this relation is the interplay between the manifested and the potential, Re the manifested and Osiris the potential.

Also the Theban teaching deals with the maintenance of the creation. The Theban teaching about Amon presents a great god comprising four generations that synthesize all the aspects of the problem with the world, its origin and its coming into existence that have been dealt with separately in the other teachings. Amon is the father of the fathers of the primordial eight gods of Hermopolis, he is also the father of the eight and is in this aspect equal to Ptah-Tatenen. Further Amon is one of the eight and finally he is the heir of the eight (Sethe 1929, p. 60). And this god, Amon, is the hidden unity of existence. Despite the apparent plurality life is one coherent unity.

2.1.5 *The geographic distribution*

It seems thus that the larger temples of the country represent the same way of thinking, one might even call it a common philosophy. The temple teachings, each of them in their way, represent a total view of ontological, religio-philosophical kind and each of them concentrated on one aspect or one angle of approach. It seems that all particular cults of all temples were facets of the same comprehensive view. And this is something one notices when studying Egyptian thinking: "... plus un phénomène est complexe, plus il laisse de possibilités d'énonciations, de constatations à son sujet, sans qu'elles s'excluent mutuellement" (Hornung 1987b, p. 115).

There is, however, something rather bewildering about it. That is the fact that this all-embracing way of thinking was locally distributed. What might the reason have been to split this comprehensive view of the world geographically? One can of course look at the unity of the world differently, consider different aspects of it, but they could have taught all the aspects together at every temple school. And even if they did so in the oral teaching everywhere, the different aspects of the system were distributed over the temples of the country officially. According to what criteria was this done and why? A reason why this was done might have been a wish to stress the different aspects. The geographic distribution has an emphatic effect on the various approaches, which could otherwise easily be overlooked. It is a way of drawing attention to what is considered to be important. This way of emphasis resembles that used in the royal tombs of the New Kingdom where certain text passages appear both in normal and in enigmatic writing in order to stress their significance (Hornung 1987a, p. 226).

2.1.6 The further ramifications of the system of thought

If now the major schools give the main lines of a coherent system of thinking, a little more is needed for the system to be complete and to cover the whole field of human experiences of life.

According to the Egyptian world view creation thus emanated from a state of potential energy. As this energy was differentiated, each differentiated part of it obtained its particular character and had a field of activity and a name attributed to it. The differentiation of the energy kept on and thus a field of forces came into being, a more and more fine-meshed network of forces that constituted the world. Everywhere where man became aware of a part or a point of this field of forces in nature, in social or cultural phenomena, be it by speculation or other forms of experience, the force was given a name. Every such point of the network was personified. Logically the concept precedes its personification (Baines 1985, p. 68) and the personification then functions as an animated version of the concept (Baines 1985, p. 24). In this way we get a lot of gods who all represent one side of the unique divine energy and we are faced with a system of thinking that works with unity and plurality at the same time, which has been, and still is, a stumbling stone for the modern observer.

2.1.7 Scholar and folk models

Many of the endless number of gods appearing in Egyptian texts and iconography were never the object of a cult and knowledge about them probably never passed the gates of the temple. They existed as concepts in the metalanguage of iconography and the metaphors of the temple texts. However, the lack of cult does not mean that a god is a purely speculative philosophical creation. The popular god Bes did not have a cult and no temple was dedicated to him. It is on the whole very difficult to decide where the division line lies between that which was the knowledge reserved for the temple and that which was part and parcel of the popular stock of information. The temples were not at all separated from the surrounding area but were centres for the life of the region to a large extent. The temple staff came from the surrounding area and one section of the priesthood, the so called wab-priests were part-time working priests, active in the temples for about two months a year and for the rest of the time exercising other professions. On the other hand it is, however, always strongly stressed that knowledge is secret and must remain secret. To be secret and hidden is a mark of quality as far as knowledge is concerned.

It is thus very difficult to come to an unequivocal conclusion about the form of the supposed folk model of the system. One way of grasping which gods of the pantheon the people knew and were familiar with would be to investigate which divine names occur in private personal names, names of public feasts, and in literary texts. It might be so that a divine name in those contexts means that the god was known. As for personal names one must, however, also reckon with the possibility that those names were just names, arbitrary designations where the divine name was not obvious to the user as can be the case after centuries of use that allow the original meaning to be forgotten. Changes in the pronunciation so that the original phonetic form is no longer preserved and the original meaning thereby vanishes may also have occurred. Let us, however, suppose that a personal name containing the name of a god means that the owner of the name knows that god.

A consultation of works concerned with theophorous personal names (Ranke 1935-1976, Helck 1954, Kaplony 1963, Lüddeckens 1985) shows that the names of the gods of the Ogdoad are completely lacking in the material, that the names of the gods of the Ennead can occur from the Middle Kingdom and onwards but are very rare at all periods except names with Isis. Further one notices that, among the names related to the Memphitic teaching, Ptah and Sekhmet are frequent, as for Ptah, however, only from the end of the 4th dynasty (Helck 1954, p. 32), whereas that of Nefertem is always rare. Among those related to the Theban teaching, Amon and Mut appear in the Middle Kingdom and become very frequent from the New Kingdom and onwards, whereas that of Khonsu is attested as early as the Old Kingdom. The scarcity of the names of the Ennead is in contrast with the fact that the gods of the Ennead are very frequent in the iconography of the temples and in funerary contexts. From this state of affairs one might conclude that the teaching about the Ennead was, and mainly remained, a matter of temple discourse and that popular beliefs draw on other sections of the pantheon, on the gods of the many facetted network of the manifested divine power.

The feasts constituted occasions for the people to get in touch with things divine. A considerable number of gods had their own feasts celebrated on local or state level but here again the gods of the Ennead are lacking except Osiris and Isis who had their local feast and were also celebrated on state level together with Nephthys and Seth during the epagomenal days.

The literary texts are likely to have been known not only by the scholarly elite but also told by the story tellers thus reaching out to a broader public. The number of gods mentioned in each story is mostly very restricted, generally between two and five, occasionally more. Only two stories, 'Sinuhe' and 'Horus and Seth' mention a great number of gods. In the stories the gods of the Ogdoad are never mentioned. The Ennead is often mentioned as a group whereas the individual members are seldom referred to and then mostly in 'Sinuhe' and 'Horus and Seth'. Only a few gods like Amon, Amonrasonther, Re, Rehorakhty, Seth, Thot, and the Ennead as a group are mentioned in several different stories.

The trend that comes out of a brief survey of the material thus shows that a considerable number of the innumerable Egyptian gods that appear in funerary and temple contexts are not mentioned in the contexts that seem likely to reflect the popular knowledge of the pantheon.

The gods belonging to the scholarly sphere and those belonging to the popular sphere do not, however, make up two different sets of gods but those who enjoy the fate of being more widely known also belong to the scholarly model. They are just a selection out of the pantheon probably mostly representing those aspects of the divine that are related to daily experiences and most easily discernable.

2.2 The model of thought as a general frame of reference

Parts of this pantheon, which in itself is an explanation of the structure of the world and of society and civilization and represents animated concepts, were actually used as concepts of thought outside the group of initiated people. The gods became a general frame of reference and the qualities of individuals and their activities and their position in society could be linked to this frame of reference.

Let us take a few examples.

There are surprisingly few adjectives in the Egyptian language. In order to describe their world they have recourse to nouns and the description is given the form of an expression of identity. What one identifies with or identifies oneself with is gods. The gods who are personified concepts are used as concepts.

"Worship king Nimaatre, ever-living, in your bodies,
cleave to his Majesty in your hearts!
He is **Sia** in your hearts,
his eyes seek out every body,
he is **Re** who sees by means of his rays,
who lights the Two Lands more than the sun-disk,
who makes verdant more than great **Hapy**.
He has filled the two lands with vital force ...
Khnum is he for every body,
begetter, who creates mankind,
Bastet is he who protects the Two Lands,
he who worships him is protected by his arm,
Sekhmet is he to him who defies his command,
he whom he hates will bear distress."
(From Sehetep-ib-res stela, Dyn. 12)

In this example we see how the identifications function. As for the translation we might just as well have said: 'he is **a Sia, a Re, a Hapy, a Khnum, a Bastet**, and **a Sekhmet**. Nothing prevents such a translation (cf. Hornung 1982, p. 505-506). The divine names give a description of pharaoh. He is discerning and enlightened (**Sia**), great, mighty, and radiant (**Re**), life-spending and propitious (**Hapy**), creative and formative (**Khnum**), mild and vigilant (**Bastet**), and powerfully intervening (**Sekhmet**).

This way of describing is used not only about the king but also about private persons, both living and dead. The funerary texts abound in examples where the dead identifies himself with gods and entities in order to show and prove the insight he has reached, the position he has attained, and the powers he disposes over.

This frame of reference is, however, not only used to express qualities through identity but also to express status. Status is then asserted by alleged family relationship with the gods. The power that makes the cereal grow and multiply was called **Nepri**. If everything grows well, one can have stocks of grain, one gets rich. The Egyptians could express this idea by saying 'he is the son of Nepri' (Posener 1960, pp. 11-12). Causality was expressed by means of words for a family relationship which is close at hand. Now if one has also grown flax with a good result and has stocked linen material then the goddess of flax cultures and weaving, **Tait,** has contributed to the riches and the lucky person can be said to be 'the husband of Tait' (Posener 1960, pp. 11-12).

It is evident that priestly titles were linked to the name of the god in whose service the priest was. But even civil servant titles were linked to the names of gods (LÄ Priester for ex.) and then the word 'servant' was used as part of the title. This habit in combination with the projection of the pantheon on the country resulted in rather strange titles sometimes. If a caravan started from the town of Mesen whose main god was Horus then the caravan leader could be entitled 'divine servant of Horus of Mesen' (LÄ Priester col. 1085).

This reference system does certainly not mean that they had this linking to the world of the gods continually present in mind in everyday life. Generally we are not conscious of the language we use. Actually the language wants to be overlooked. There is a rule which the linguists call repression of sense (Henriksen 1986, p. 23) and that means that the user of a language does not realize the basic and original meaning of a word that is used in a metaphorical sense, he only sees what the sentence intends to communicate. As an example Henriksen cites: 'monkeys are bad guinea pigs' where the basic meaning of 'guinea pig' is immediately repressed.

Thanks to this particularity of the language that the users do not pay attention to the metaphors of their mother tongue the very theoretical model of thought that the pantheon constitutes found an application with the people.

It is probably the fact that this repression does not function with Egyptologists but that we see the concrete meaning of all words that has made Egyptologists say that the Egyptians could not think in an abstract way and that they lacked abstract words.

3. The Emotional Aspect

In the intellectual system the gods were the points of reference. They were intellectual concepts that had been animated and given an anthropomorphic or zoomorphic form or a combination of the two. We meet these concepts particularly in the temple and tomb iconography and in the metaphors of the texts but also in the language of everyday life. This means that the elaborate intellectual system of thinking, or at least part of it, was known also outside the temple circles of literate people and was integrated in the general cultural heritage. As this rather high-brow thinking survived for thousands of years it must also have had possibilities and qualities that corresponded to the religious needs of the Egyptian society. However, the faith of the people in their gods is not so well documented as the thinking of the temple. The cultural pattern that the individual follows in his everyday life and by means of which he interprets the world and which is the basis for his actions is embedded in his unconsious. Normally these unconsious contents are not brought up to the conscious level and intellectualized and are thus inaccessible for us.

The Egyptian system must have offered the possibility for people to get in close personal contact with their gods. It seems obvious to me that there must have been a living faith in the gods of Egypt at all different periods of Egyptian history even though the abundant information about personal piety is limited to a rather short lapse of time of the Ramesside period.

From prayers and thanksgiving addressed to the gods it is obvious that people could turn to the gods when they were in distress in order to get consolation, help, guidance, and grace. There were thus ways of direct personal contact between mankind and the divine just in the same way as we are used to see piety function today. There was also another way in which this need for contact with, and help from, superior beings was satisfied. There were the saints. We have for instance the cult that grow up around Heqa-ib in Elephantine and we have Imhotep and Amenhotep, son of Hapu, and many more. They were mediators and their everincreasing importance had its root in emotional needs. Apparently Amenhotep, son of Hapu, who was a member of the inner temple circles was aware of this need and placed himself consciously as a mediator by means of the statues of himself that he allowed to be placed at Karnak.

4. The Social Aspect

Religions also have a social aspect. There is a need in man to be together with the fellow-members of his group. This need for social contact within the frame of the religion is important. From our point of view, seen with this long distance in space and time, it might seem that there is a weak point in the Egyptian system in this respect, as there was no congregation assembled to assist at the divine services. The services were entirely the business of priesthood. It might seem that people were deprived of an essential experience by being excluded from the inner temple ceremonies. As far as we know the right to be present in the inner temple was, however, never contested. So it seems that this lack was sufficiently compensated by the right to enter the outer court and to participate in the many feasts when the holy statues were brought out for processions.

5. The Behavioural Aspect

As has been said, when man is in difficulty and when he is suffering he turns to the gods in prayer. But he also feels the need to try to avert evil before it has come, he desires to interfere with the way the world turns or might turn. Could an Egyptian do that? Did the system allow man to influence the gods and man's relations with the divine?

The gods of Egypt made up a system that described and explained the world, they were the knots of a network of forces. The governing idea of this network was **Maat**. This word stands for order, harmony, balance, justice, and truth.

Life is thus not chaos and hazard. Life is system and order. That is the message of this theology. Order is the first thing that comes about in the act of creation, expressed in the family terms, typical of the Egyptian way of expressing ideas, order is the daughter of the creator. As the daughter of the creator is the one through whom the genesis starts, order becomes the generative principle of the universe.

Now human experience tells us, however, that states of order, harmony, and balance are fragile and impermanent. That is the way it has always been. Life is composed of constructive and destructive forces. Life must be carefully looked after in order to subsist. The care was the task of the *House of Life* and of the temples as a whole.

The *House of Life* had to give life (*s'nḫ*) to creation and society. It was the task of this institution to protect life and keep the threatening catastrophy away, and to put straight again what had gone wrong.

What means did the scholars of the *House of Life* have to handle this task? How did they go about it?

Their possibilities to intervene were both spiritual and material - but perhaps mostly spiritual. All the knowledge that was the essence of the Egyptian culture was assembled in the *House of Life*. Culture belongs in itself to the order of the world and culture is in itself ordering, it creates Maat. P. Salt 825 describes the *House of Life* and we are told there that the building itself was considered to be a microcosm. In its library there were scrolls that described the world. The scholars working there knew the rites by means of which the order of the world could be supported and maintained. They were the priests who carried out the daily cult of the temples whose aim it was to keep the world in balance through a series of symbolic acts where mankind and gods met in exchange of gifts. These gifts to the gods are very interesting. Mankind presented offerings to the gods so that the gods in their turn presented gifts to mankind. *Do ut des.* It is carefully indicated what kind of gifts were presented in one direction as well as in the other. Man offers what he has produced: food-stuffs, wine, oils, perfumes, jewellery, etc., etc. In return man receives life, stability, strength, joy, victory, and the like. If one analyzes these gifts in both directions, one notices that there is a symbolic play enacted and repeated daily in the temples in order to maintain and sup-port the constructive forces of life (Englund, 1987 pp. 57-66). In this symbolic enactment the greatest gift of all was a small statue of Maat. One can say that the temples thus func-tioned as a sort of power central where the energies were connected and directed (Der-chain, 1965, p. 14).

As the temple cult was the task of the priestly elite and there was no participating crowd, then this way of acting belonged to a very small, limited scholarly group and it represents their way of handling their knowledge in order to influence the powers that govern exist-ence.

As usual we are not so well informed about the relation of the people to these powers that direct the events of the world. Nor do we know how the people tried to influence these powers to intervene in the way the world turns. There will probably have been some kind of cult and rites in front of the altars with an image of a god that existed in Egyptian houses. The amulets representing different gods and goddesses that were worn on necklaces and bracelets also constituted connecting links between man and the divine. In wearing an amulet one put oneself under the protection of the god in question, it was a means of in-fluencing that particular god to interfere in favour of that person. The amulets can give us a clue as to which gods out of the pantheon elaborated in the temple were known outside the temple and thus part and parcel of the cultural heritage of the people. The people had also another possibility to find out the will of the gods and to communicate with them. I am thinking of the possibility to establish a contact with the god that was brought out in pro-cession. On these occasions people had the opportunity to formulate a question about the problems that tormented them and to get an oracular answer. There also existed the possi-bility to get in contact with the divine through dreams (Vernus 1985, col. 746, note 18). Fur-ther they had the myths. The myths offer as it were key scenarios of typical difficulties and problems. Man can recognize these scenes as being similar to his proper situation and by going into the roles of the myth man has the possibility of entering into a dialogue with the governing divine powers and of receiving consolation and guidance in order to get through the personal crisis thanks to the mythical solution of the problem. The most important of these key scenarios is probably the story of Isis and Horus that is constantly evoked in magical contexts to avert all evil.

6. The Comprehensive World View

The system of thought that we come across in ancient Egypt is comprehensive and explicative of the whole universe. It comprised both the primordial nothingness and the created universe, and the rules governing the transition from chaos to cosmos, as well as the rules that govern cosmos, the powers that control life.

What characterizes this system is that there is no hiatus between the potential and the manifested. On the contrary, there is full identity between them - they are, as it were, the two sides of the same coin. The coming into existence of the cosmos does not put an end to the chaos but both co-exist. This is clearly expressed through the terms chosen : the potential metastate and that which manifests itself in creation have the same name - Atum. And the meaning of this term is 'nothingness' and 'all'.

The essence of the system is thus:
- Being and existence, i.e. life, is one,
everything is a unity, a whole, everything is connected,
- creation is a field of forces,
order reigns in this field,
- man lives in an ordered system.

This could be called 'ecology' for it is of course an ecological outlook to see everything as integrated in the same system, to see life as a dynamic weave where everything is interconnected and interacting with everything else, where a change or an action in one point of the network has consequences for the whole system. I believe that that is exactly how the Egyptian temple cult and magic were supposed to function. Through a serious of symbolic actions directed towards one point of the system they intended to contribute to the balance of the whole and to maintain the balance between the constructive and the destructive forces of the system as a whole i.e. of the cosmos. The condition for such cultic actions to be effective and also for intercessory prayers and magical declarations is a sort of ecology of thought and mind (Bateson 1972; cf. also Baines 1984, p. 40).

7. Conclusion - Characteristics

In order to characterize the system of thought in Ancient Egypt the most fitting term would then be **monism**. According to the Egyptians there is unity and coherence throughout creation. Existence itself forms a unit, a whole, with the primordial state. Existence is manifested Being, manifested godhead. Despite this unity, there is, however, a difference between the Absolute Unity of potential Being and the manifested created plurality. This insight is brought forth in the fact that all units within creation are presented as dualities as the Two Lands, the double crown, the Two Ladies, etc.

In this monistic thinking everything in life is interrelated in a large all-embracing network. In this network certain evolutionary patterns are continually being repeated. They are those describing the coming into existence of the world the first time, *sp tpy*. Everything that is experienced as similar or homologous to the event *sp tpy* is considered to be related to and connected with the prototype and not only with the prototype itself but with every other reiteration of the same prototype. This thinking in **homologies** is the 'logic' of the system. This sometimes comes into collision with our thinking in causalities. The homology thinking leads for instance to the fact that one can have recourse to the creation myth in any crisis. As a crisis is homologous to chaos the energy that has proven itself to be efficient against chaos must once more be able to subdue the evil forces, to solve the problem, and put an end to the crisis. Moreover, the interrelationship of all homologous situations leads to what we are wont to call 'multiplicity of approaches', to the fact that several different assertions about one and the same thing are valid simultaneously as the fact that Re is the son of Atum, of Nun, of Nut, of Hathor, of Neith, of Osiris, of the sun disk, and may be of a few more. The undescribable can not be comprehended in one single image, term, or sentence but by means of a multitude of convergent angles of approach man reaches an approximation of reality.

A system of thinking based on homologies might seem incoherent to us. The system is, however, able to organize the totality of an agent's thoughts, perceptions, and actions by means of a few generative principles (cf. Bourdieu 1977, p. 110). The generative principles involved are, as seen, reducible to a fundamental dichotomy, the age-old dichotomy of male and female that is likely to have characterized all prehistory thinking as might be concluded from the rock drawings and objects (Leroi-Gourhan 1964). The androgyny of the original unity, the dichotomy in male and female, and the androgynous character of all created units, whether male or female, are the dominating generative principles that will permeate all the causal powers that come about and all creation.

It is an economical and simple system that does not make use of a lot of theory, not more than is needed for praxis. Can it be the reality or is it a fancy of the investigator when the same simple pattern is seen everywhere over and over again? The information transmitted is thus really redundant. But isn't it so that it is actually this redundancy that is the important vital factor of the system, that preserves the system and allows it to continue. It is the redundancy from all channels of the culture system that confirms the pattern for the members of the society and integrates it in their ways of perception and thinking. It is this very redundancy that "helps to combat noise and other kinds of variety tending to distort the system's distinctive information" (Clarke 1968, p. 91).

Further it seems that Egyptian thinking, as might be expected and as is the case in all cultures, operates on several levels and that we, as modern observers and investigators, can discern at least two of them: the discourse level and the level of praxis - within which there are certainly many sub-levels that we are going to leave out of this discussion. The discourse level corresponds to the sophisticated thinking of the temple scholars who, throughout the Egyptian civilization, were working on a given set of problems and themes. The answers and solutions to these gradually evolved and became more and more elaborate. Parallel with this we have the level of praxis found among the people. The two levels are not in contradiction with each other. They have the same origin, they are variants of the same age-old thinking inherited from prehistory. The distinctive factor of the levels is the degree of systematisation and conscious analysis. They work, however, with the same themes and the same principles, although sometimes under different names. That is why they so easily intermingle and integrate, why there is no opposition, why we come across so many equations of one god with the other, why there are so many overlappings. The level of praxis comes close to the notion of *habitus* (Bourdieu 1977, pp.72-87), "systems of durable, transposable *dispositions*, structured structures predisposed to function as structuring structures, that is, as principles of the generation and structuring of practices and representations which can be objectively "regulated" and "regular" without in any way being the product of obedience to rules, objectively adapted to their goals without presupposing a conscious aiming at ends or an express mastery of the operations necessary to attain them and being all this, collectively orchestrated without being the product of the orchestrating action of a conductor" (Bourdieu 1977, p. 72).

To sum up: the Egyptian mode of thought presents itself in two main variants - a folk model that can be characterized as unconscious or rather subconscious consciousness and a scholarly model that can be characterized as conscious consciousness and these two, for historical, evolutionary reasons, are so strongly affinitive that they are not in contradiction but integrate without discord.

BIBLIOGRAPHY

BAINES, J., 1984. 'Interpretations of religion: logic, discourse, rationality. *Göttinger Miszellen 76.*

- 1985. *Fecundity Figures.* Oxford University Press.

BAINES, J. & EYRE, C.J., 1983. 'Four notes on literacy.' *Göttinger Miszellen*, 61.

BATESON, G., 1972. *Steps to an Ecology of Mind.* Ballantine Books. New York.

- 1979. *Mind and Nature. A necessary unity.* Fontana Press, U.K.

BOURDIEU, P., 1977. *Outline of a Theory of Praxis.* Cambridge Studies in Social Anthropology. Cambridge.

CLARKE, D.L., 1968. *Analytical Archaeology.* London.

DERCHAIN, P.,1965. *Le Papyrus Salt 825 rituel pour la conservation de la vie en Égypte.* Bruxelles.

ELIADE, M., 1978. *A History of Religious Ideas.* Vol. I. Chicago.

ENGLUND, G., 1987. 'Gifts to the gods - a necessity for the preservation of cosmos and life. Theory and praxis'. *Boreas* 15. Acta universitatis Upsaliensis. Uppsala.

HELCK, W., 1954. 'Zu den theophoren Eigennamen des Alten Reiches.' *Zeitschrift für ägyptische Sprache und Altertumskunde.* Band 79. Berlin-Leipzig.

HENRIKSEN, L., 1986. 'Språkets hemlighet'. *Språkvård 4-1986*, pp.22-26.

HORNUNG, E., 1971. *Der Eine und die Vielen.* Darmstadt.

- 1972. *Ägyptische Unterweltsbücher.* Zürich.

- 1982. 'Pharao ludens'. *Eranos Jahrbuch 1982, Vol. 51, Das Spiel der Götter*. Ascona.

- 1987a. 'Eine aenigmatische Wand im Grabe Ramses' IX.' *Form und Mass*. Festschrift für Gerhard Fecht. Ägypten und Altes Testament. Band 12. Wiesbaden.

- 1987b. 'L'Egypte, la philosophy avant les grecs.' *Les Etudes Philosophiques. No. 2-3/1987.*

JACOBSOHN, H., 1939. *Die dogmatische Stellung des Königs in der Theologie der alten Ägypter.* Ägyptologische Forschungen, Heft 8. Glückstadt, Hamburg und New York.

JUNKER, H., 1917. *Die Onurislegende.* Wien.

KAPLONY, P., 1963. *Die Inschriften der ägyptischen Frühzeit I-III.* Ägyptologische Abhandlungen 8. Wiesbaden.

LÄ = HELCK, W. und OTTO, E., 1975. *Lexikon der Ägyptologie.* Wiesbaden.

LEROI-GOURHAN, A., 1964. *Les religions de la préhistoire.* Paris.

LÜDDECKENS, E., 1985. 'Die theophoren Personennamen im pharaonischen, hellenistisch-römischen und christlichen Ägypten.' *Ägypten Dauer und Wandel.* Deutsches Archäologisches Institut Abteilung Kairo. Sonderschrift 18. Mainz am Rhein.

PIANKOFF, A., and RAMBOVA, N., 1955. *The Shrines of Tut-Ankh-Amon.* Bollingen Series XL, 2. New York.

POSENER, G., 1960. *De la divinité du pharaon.* Paris.

RANKE, H., 1935-1976. *Die ägyptischen Personennamen I-III.* Glückstadt

SANDMAN-HOLMBERG, M., 1946. *The God Ptah.* Lund.

SETHE, K., 1929. *Amun und die acht Urgötter von Hermopolis.* Berlin.

TROY, L., 1986. *Patterns of Queenship in ancient Egyptian myth and history.* Boreas 14. Uppsala.

VELDE, H., te, 1967. *Seth, God of Confusion.* Leiden.

VERNUS, P., 1985. 'Traum'. *Lexikon der Ägyptologi* Bd. VI, col. xxx.

WESTENDORF, W., 1974. 'Zweiheit, Dreiheit und Einheit in der altägyptischen Theologie.' *Zeitschrift für ägyptische Sprache und Altertumskunde*, Bd. 100, pp. 136-141.

Ragnhild Bjerre Finnestad
Egyptian Thought About Life as a Problem of Translation

1. Presentation of the topic

The symposium behind this book had its theme: What are the main features of ancient Egyptian thought about life, and how can modern scholars get down to them? By explicitly bringing in the scholar's procedure in reaching his answer, the question of Egyptian thought strikes at the premises of the problem. The end and the way should be considered together; they are reciprocal.

Perhaps nowhere is this fact more challengingly met with than in translation. In my contribution to the discussion I have, therefore, chosen translation as the context for my dealing with Egyptian thought about life.

In the introduction to his history of Egyptian religion, S. Morenz states: "The difficulties encountered in translation are as a rule not of a graphical or grammatical nature, but stem from the fact that the Egyptians had a mode of thinking very different from our own".[1] His translations, however, do not reflect his wrestling with the problem in a particularly definite way, and this is symptomatic of many translations of Egyptian texts and images. They do not integrate the problematic question of Egyptian thought. The latter is most often only referred to sporadically and in a roundabout way.

Also, there has been a tendency to present it as a kind of additional problem to those which stem from language "as such", delegating it to the field of hermeneutics.

This tendency to separate interpretation and translation can even be seen in such a skillful presentation of Egyptian religion as that of E. Hornung in his *Der Eine und die Vielen*. In an excursus he puts forward the opinion that the problem which Egyptian thought entails for modern students can to some extent be defined as a problem of logic. This is an old view in Egyptological debate; it has through generations of Egyptologists been questioned if the Egyptians had some kind of "pre-modern", i.e. non-Aristotelian logic[2], and the discussion received new impetus with Hornung's book. Hornung brings in the question of logic in connection with an especially conspicuous feature of Egyptian thought, namely, the habit of attributing to a given oblect a series of "incompatible" predicates. For instance, heaven can be said to be "vielerlei - Kuh, Baldachin, Wasser, Frau -, er ist die Göttin Nut und ist die Göttin Hathor, und in Synkretismus ist die Gottheit A zugleich eine Andre, Nicht-A".[3] This is a feature which can be taken as a typical example of the kind of problem which Western scholars have found most intriguing and disturbing when dealing with Egyptian sources, as it leaves a paradoxical and self-contradictory impression.[4]

To Hornung, it seems to abrogate the logical yes-no- alternative and to presuppose a non-Aristotelian logic: "Ein gegebenes X kann A und kann Nicht-A sein: tertium datur".[5] Hornung's view in these matters differs from that of evolutionistic theories of "primitive thought" in that he refers to quantum physics as a modern example of a field dealing with paradoxical phenomena which acquires three-valued logic.[6]

The discussion issuing from these reflections seems to have come to an end when U. Berner pointed out that the problem is not actually whether X can be A and be not-A, but whether X can be A and B, and it is not incompatible with Aristotelian logic to say that X can be A and B, but that X cannot be said to be A and B and not be A and B, at the same time.[7]

The question of a particularly Egyptian logic has, then, lost much of its importance. But the point at issue from the perspective of this article, is that it exerted no decisive influence on Hornung's translations - it was added as a supplement to his presentation. The significant hermeneutical premises inherent in this approach to Egyptian thought were of no consequence. The approach presupposes that the paradoxical impression left on European translators by the sources pertaining to Egyptian thought stems from a paradoxical message. But this is not necessarily so. The troublesome question as regards these "incompatible" predicates is: What "are" cow, baldachin, water, woman, Nut, and Hathor in Egyptian systems of meaning? An answer to this question might render the classification of paradox irrelevant, or misleading.

There is another approach to Egyptian documents which has long attracted scholars who try to characterize Egyptian thought about life, through structural analyses. But this approach may also leave the disturbing translation problem concerning meaning untouched.

Studies on Egyptian thought structures have, moreover, shown a habit of developing into a kind of refrain. It has been repeatedly demonstrated that Egyptian thought moves between complementary polarities.[8] The thought about heaven, for instance, moves between the structure of the complementary oppositions of above-below, light-darkness, day-night, life-death, beginning-end, male-female, cosmos-chaos.

It is doubtful whether this particular structure is more prominent in Egyptian religious thought than elsewhere. Structural analyses of religious thought in other cultures have led to similar results[9]. Thus, this feature in itself does not lead us further toward our goal of characterizing Egyptian thought about life.

Only when the structural analysis is used not as a goal in itself but as a tool for the more comprehensive task of uncovering the contents of meaning, will it be of interest as regards our aim. The crucial question concerning our aim is: What are the semantic implications of the complementary thought structures when they refer to the Egyptian outlook on life? In other words, we shall have to correlate the structures with the basic ontological categories in order to bring out their significance for the Egyptian thought about life.

2. Bringing in the ontological context

Taken alone, detached from their textual and functional setting, the statements quoted above about heaven can mean almost anything. On their basis alone, the translator will perform his transferring operation in a vacuum. Only a correlation with material that can give information about the conceptual frame of reference will give us a hint about the contents of meaning. By referring our "incompatible" predicates to the value categories by which the

Egyptians ordered their material, spiritual, and social universe, it can be seen whether they are paradoxical according to Egyptian thought, or only according to Western thought.

Tracing the conceptual frame of reference is an important means of determining what are possible and what are not impossible meanings, so that we have an inkling as to the direction of thought. With regard to our purpose, ontological traditions play a decisive role in making up the conceptual frame of reference. I shall, therefore, adopt the methodological procedure of explaining the incompatible predicates and other disconnected examples of Egyptian thought about life, with reference to the wider ontological ideology by which they are determined and are themselves expressions of. Through this correlating procedure I hope to narrow down their message as regards outlook on life. The theoretical insight underlying this procedure is, then, that the contents of the particular text in a document which is being considered as a source for Egyptian thought, are determined by the ideological context of the document[10]. Therefore a wider range of various types of material which can give information about this factor, has to be brought into the study - they will enable the scholar to take a bearing on the contents of the document.

The ontological "prospect" emerging from this wider range of material is variegated, but it has one particularly prominent feature to which I want to direct attention, namely, its monistic character. There appears to be no essential ontological separation (though there is a conceptual distinction) between the species - human beings, animals, vegetation, cosmic constituents. Or, to put it in another way: The categories applied in Egyptian religious ontology do not accentuate the differences between men and animals, or even between men and vegetative or cosmic phenomena. Rather one sees the opposite interest: to stress the affinities and the connections.

Nor is there any unbridgeable dichotomy between "animate" and "inanimate", or "personal" and "impersonal" objects[11].

Further, there is not any essential cleavage between matter and spirit, body and soul (not even conceptually).[12]

Finally, on the theological level of Egyptian ontology, God's world is not separated from man's world - there is one world: Egypt, and it is this world that Egyptian mythology deals with.

On trying to define more closely the conception of being which determines this lack of unbridgeable demarcation lines between the species, between personal and impersonal objects, between spiritual and material qualities, and between human and divine worlds, we encounter a focussing on **life**. The phenomena of being are categorized in accordance with a theory of life that generates and manifests itself in all phenomena of being, Egyptian ontology revolves around a princlple of life which can be said to be its unifying factor. Egyptian ontological categories are primarily of a biological kind. In this feature lies a clue to Egyptian thought about being.

I shall fill in this character sketch at some points.[13] I said that within the dominant bio-perspective on being, the demarcations which traditional Western ontology draws between particular phenomena of being, fade. The mortological material is an especially rich source of information on this point, which should not come as a surprise when it is taken into account that within this monistic ontology death is a phase of an ongoing renewal of existence.[14] After death, man's life is thought to go on in new generations of human beings; but it can also manifest itself in non-human forms of life, including forms which in our own ontologi are categorized as 'inanimate" objects - like the sun, and the stars, the Egyptian concept of life thus being radically wider than the one implicit in current Western discourse. To Western man Egyptian religious thought about life and death may appear imaginative, fantastic - with its *ba*'s and *ka*'s and *akh*'s, - with its animal, botanical, and cosmic forms of regenerated life. This aspect is, however, less fantastic when it is understood that it is part of a biologically centered ontological framework, which defines a human being as an entity of life belonging to life total, temporarily manifested as a particular body of being, but in essence not separated from other bodies of being. On this biotic level there is a relationship of close connection between man and the world. Man's life can manifest itself anew in other phenomena of being; and from this perspective it can be seen that man's life merges with that of the entire world.[15]

In the abundant source material for this thought, man's **self**, i.e. that which is regarded as man's essential identity, is not defined with reference to his individual person, but with reference to that level of being on which he is inseparably connected with all being, namely, the biotic level. *Ba, ka, akh* are concepts of life.[16] According to this source material, the quality which makes human beings transcend individual death is their life power - which is collectively shared. In life and death, man's ultimate identity is found in the all-comprising biotic whole to which he constitutionally belongs. In this integration into the biotic whole man transcends his given phenomenal and historical limits, but he does not transcend the natural world. His life is expected to go on in this natural world - in new forms. Actually, death has an important function within the process of being, according to Egyptian thought. It is something far more than absence of life: it is a source of new life in the cyclical biogenesis and would be more accurately characterized as a state of latent life capable of manifesting itself anew.

The ancient Egyptians conceived being, then, as an integrated whole of biological affinities - a web undergoing continuous metamorphoses. Into this web human forms enter, along with and inextricably bound to the other life forms, through threads not drawn in the traditional anthropology of popular Western thought. They connect human beings and animals, they connect animate phenomena and inanimate phenomena such as sun, moon, earth, water, plants. The whole world ls seen as one living, changing organism in the religious ontology underlying these literary and artistic statements we are dealing wlth: the biological category is a key category in Egyptian thought about being.

A central mythological-theological concept of this outlook on being is that of the pantheistic creator god. This concept of cosmologically defined god goes with an anthropology in which man is not regarded as separated from the total cosmic reality, but connected with it in his basic identity as a living being, integrated into the world's stream of ongoing life, capable of being reintegrated again into it after death.

An important iconographical reflection of this conception of being can be seen in the composite icon that presents **god** as combining life forms which in Western thought have been carefully held apart.

The inference from these circumstances is that the "incompatible" predicates are not culled from "heterogeneous" species and "opposing" areas of being, according to Egyptian thought. Explanation with reference to the wider conceptual whole does not back this view, and rather indicates that another one might suit better. By focussing on the monistic conception of being documented by the correlated material, the "free" combination of predicates can be seen to be conditioned by the particular conception of being.[17]

Of course, the question "how did the Egyptians reason to conceive of man and the world in their bizarre way?" can be variously answered. One of the determining ideological factors behind this "bizarre" way which comes to light from our angle of explanation is, then, that behind the Egyptians' lack of interest in absolute ontological separations there lies a total conception of being as life - life generating and manifesting itself in a dlversity of forms. The interest of the Egyptians lies with this biological aspect of being. Their ontological categories are of a biological kind - which means that other delineations are drawn than those that can be observed in traditional popular thought in Western religion.

This conclusion is important, especially when we are trying to specify closer the **meanings** of the predicates, including their symbolic meanings, because it limits the choice of meanings and indicates a possible spectrum. By this correlating procedure we have brought into the study a guiding frame of reference.

Nor is it difficult to see its importance with regard to the question of what is the significance of the complementary thought structures for the Egyptian view on life. By referring these structures to this basically biologically oriented monistic ontology, it appears that the Egyptian version of binary oppositions is not expressive of unreconciled ontological powers and qualities surmountable only under a transcendental or an eschatological perspective, as in e.g. Christianity, but is rather expressive of the dynamics of the one and only existing, self-maintaining organism of life. Structural analyses of Egyptian religious thought which are conformable with this fundamental conception of being as processes of self-generating life, can be presumed to come nearer to "Egyptian thought" than such as are not.[18]

3. The translation problem

The features of Egyptian ontological thought discussed above ought to be conveyed in our translations. But here we can see how the culturally conditioned premisses of translation may counteract the good intention, and why also the thought of the translator has to be dealt with, if he wants to communicate that of the Egyptians. Both the thought of the ancient Egyptians and that of the modern translator have to be dealt with, and their relationship of interaction be clarified, when the intention is to identify the main features of Egyptian thought. The latter are easily distorted in the translation process.

The most influential ontology in Western religious thought is very different from that which we have described above. It separates being into an earthly world and a world beyond it. This model comes to expression through a series of dual ontological categories dividing being into areas such as human - divine, profane - sacral, worldly - transworldly, temporal - eternal, material - spiritual. Also, it is to be noted that the phenomenon of man belongs both to "this world" and to "the world beyond", according to this model; while animals, vegetation, and other cosmic phenomena belong to "this world" only, and actually fall outside the focus of interest in religious thought, or are even explicitly excluded, since they are not considered to share in the spiritual, eternal, i.e. the divine world. Man and animals, plants and other cosmic phenomena have widely diverging ontological status. They are not affiliated, when it comes to the heart of the matter. Man can even be looked upon as a lonely stranger in "this world".

Such an ontological partitioning cannot be found in the Egyptian material, as I have tried to point out; and this fact should be borne in mind when Egyptian documents are translated.

What are its implications for translation? Most obvious is its significance as regards the choice of synonyms. The words chosen as synonyms are necessarily expressive of the ontological categories of the culture to which the words belong; a given language is the product of a given culture, being its medium of communication. Thus we can notice that the Western dualistic categories of human - divine, profane - sacral, worldly - transworldly, temporal - eternal, material - spiritual can function in descriptions of ancient Egyptian religious thought almost like axioms, because even when efforts are made to avoid transferring these categories on to the Egyptian material in the translating process, they may indirectly exert their influence through being embedded in the analytical concepts applied, and in the very terminology at the translator's disposal. The contents of his words imply a conception of being very different from that of the ancient Egyptians. Therefore, they will distort the reception and the transference of the message. We can see an example of this effect of Western views in the translations of the basic Egyptian concepts for man's capacity for post-mortem life. From what we have pointed out about Egyptian ontological categories, it follows that the central concepts of *ka* and *ba*, which translations most often equivalate with **soul**, would be more adequately translated through concepts of dynamic life.[19] They are concepts which conceive life as continuative, and as repeatedly renewing itself. The conventional translations of *ka* and *ba* into **soul** can, therefore, be misleading and not bring us nearer the message of the text, unless the word soul is explicitly redefined to designate a concept that can serve as a better equivalent. The quality that makes human beings transcend individual death is, according to Egyptian thought, not their spiritual endowments, but their life powers - which moreover are collectively shared.[20] Conventionally, the definition of soul in Western cultures is not biologically based, and can even be said to go against such a definition; and this is a problem for translation.

To give another example: the conceptual contents of a basic word like *ntr* are so widely different from the contents of the word **god**, its usual synonym, that it might not be an exaggeration to say that they denote different concepts. The usual popular definition of god goes along lines like these drawn by J. Baines: "Almost by definition, the gods are not subject to normal causality and have their being in spheres outside the human and outside this world".[21] This definition holds good only in dualistic ontologies of the kind we are accustomed to in Western religion. The definition also lies behind his further characterization: "Their nature cannot be fully known or described";[22] and on this point Baines' argument implicitly relies on prevailing translations of Egyptian texts which have employed an interpretation determined by a Westernly dualistic ontological frame of reference for the statements about the gods. When Baines on these interpretative premises states that "The true form of a deity is problematic, and no one has encountered a deity face to face in order to report on such a form",[23] this conclusion further involves a particular translation of words like *m3c* ("true") and *ḫprw* ("form") which implies the same interpretation premises.

Actually, the Egyptian deities **were** encountered face to face, in cosmic happenings as well as in temples. They were not invisible, spiritual beings imperfectly revealing themselves in material form. The *ḫprw* of the deity **is** the spiritual and material manifestation of dynamic life. The focus of attention is on the becoming of life which, according to Egyptian ontological thought, is a divine spiritual and material phenomenon.

Along with this goes another example. When Hornung finds that what characterizes Egyptian ontology is that "Sein" and "Nichtsein" coexist,[24] this is not the outcome of a non-Aristotelian kind of logic on the part of the Egyptians, but of a somewhat inadequate rendering of a central ontological dual category belonging within a monistic ontology. The rendering is as good as any; it is difficult to find a synonym for it; but it can be misleading if one takes the terms in their traditional Western meaning (which they will, automatically encourage us to do - though as far as I can see, Hornung resists doing so). On taking a closer look at the source material to which Hornung applies these terms, it will appear that what he designates "Nichtsein" is not absence of being in the Western sense, but rather a level of being which might be more adequately rendered "latent life", "potential life". The Egyptians often characterized it as *jmn* and *št3*, which might in the contexts referred to be translated "hidden".[25] This characteristic should, as I have pointed out above, be understood within the wider ontological frame of reference. The concepts of *jmn* and *št3* belong to a monistic ontology focussing on the dynamics of life; and we cannot make the same deductions from them as from the epithet of the "hidden" God in Christianity: a god that "cannot be understood", or "whose very nature cannot be grasped by man". The tendency in Egyptological research to associate hidden - manifest and incognizable - cognizable is due to one of the tacitly assumed axioms which stems from Western systems of meaning. It is not backed by the Egyptian ones. The question that has so often been asked within Christianity, namely, in which ways can God make himself known and perceptible, being a spiritual and world-transcending God, is not posed by the Egyptians. The ideological explanation of this is to be found in Egyptian ontology. Its consequence is that the epithet "hidden" has different meanings and implications from those given to it in Christian theology-ontology with its spiritual, world-transcending god.

When the ideological context is taken into account, it will appear that the reason why Egyptian god is "hidden", cannot "be seen", is that he has not (yet) come into being (anew) as manifest form of life. We are here in touch with an ontology and a theology which conceives of divine being as alternating between a state of latency and a state of manifestation. Within this scheme theogenesis is a transition from the state of latency.[26]

For the same reason, words like "revelation", "Erscheinungsform" can also be misleading European synonyms in translations (of concepts denoted by words like *ḥcj* and *prj*), if taken to mean "visible, material robe for invisible, spiritual being". "Visible, material robe" and "invisible spirit,' are categories belonging to the kind of dualistic ontology we cannot document in the Egyptian sources for religious thought; and such translations will, therefore, give a distortion of Egyptian thought.

With these examples I have tried to demonstrate how easy it is for the translator to impose himself on Egyptian texts. The great discrepancy between the conceptual contents of the Egyptian words and those imbedded in the language used in translation, presents a fundamental problem.

True, a discrepancy cannot be avoided; and the very concepts of **synonym** and **analogy** make allowance for a discrepancy to a certain degree. In practice the problem we are dealing with is the problem of how to choose the most adequate synonym. The words we select in translation have always contents determined by a non-Egyptian world view, but they have so in a varying degree. Sometimes we will find that in translation phenomena can be equivalated which on closer inspection appear to be plainly incommensurable. The most inveterate of these equivalents concern thought about the nature of man and his world.

The influence which the traditional ontological models can have on translation generally can be seen in the fundamental difficulty Western historians have in explaining religions which interpret the world as "ultimate", i.e, which regard terrestrial world as the reality to which man essentially belongs, alive or dead. He is apt to overlook that this meaning can be given to the world and be mythologically and ritually expressed in religion. Or, he tends to choose an explanation of such cases, when they are noted, which will "explain away" this meaning as figurative: When confronted with a conception which sees the concrete world as the abode of gods, or the body of god, he will explain these mythological expressions by a method of spiritualizing symbolism, on the hermeneutical assumption that the intention of such statements is not to give an evaluation of the concrete material world, but to say something about a spiritual reality transcending the concrete world, According to the implied interpretation behind this method of explanation, **god** is described **as if** he was mundane, which he is not - as god by definition is transmundane; though he can reveal himself through terrestrial phenomena, his existence is independent of these revelations. Within popular religious thought of Western culture it would be almost sacrilegious to suggest that God was existentially inextricably bound to the material world. The two ontologies give divergent estimations of the material world.

4. How to find a better foundation in translation

Translation of Egyptian texts and images involves interpretation and explanation. **Interpretation** tries to bring out the message of the text or the image. This is of course, a very simple way of putting it, and it can be modified in a variety of ways. Also, interpretation can focus both on intended and unintended messages, each requiring its special theory and procedures. So, it is tacitly understood that interpretation deals with a plurality of messages.

The task of translation is to transfer the message to modern readers or beholders, via a modern language. Looking more closely, the transferring task consists in part of finding relevalant synonyms. This involves an understanding of the message as well as finding points of reference in modern conceptual traditions which can enable modern man to grasp the message by analogy.

As regards this search for analogies, it is sometimes said that understanding the message involves a kind of "discovering the I in the Thou". This is a statement which tends to make the historian somewhat uneasy, because all too often interpretation has blatantly proved to be an unreflected projection of the I on the Thou - which I have tried to show.

The common issue of all interpretation is to clarify the act of interpretation on the basis of a theory which takes into account "the total hermeneutical situation". What the historian will want to underline in this connection is that in drawing up the total hermeneutic situation the historical context is central. The aim of the historian is not to make the text or the image meaningful to himself and fellow modern men on the basis of some assumed transcultural psychological inter-subjectivity, or trans-historical truth, as for instance, the kind of interpretation we may encounter in certain examples of homiletic exegesis of religious texts and images. The aim of the historian as interpreter is to understand how a text or an image has been understood, by the writer or the painter, or by those who in a given period read or heard or saw. This is what he sets out to try to convey to modern man, which means that he has to get hold of the historical situation of the people whose understanding he wants to grasp. The kind of interpretation that is offered by the historian is therefore subject to severe restrictions imposed by the obligation to document the historical context. **Explanation** is his tool for this task. It is by explanation that he places his interpretation within a historical context which can be tested and examined.

To **explain** is to relate a phenomenon to other phenomena that can be seen to condition it. An explanation of A refers A to the conditions under which A occurs, or to the whole to which A belongs and functions within. Explanation of our "incompatible" predicates does not in itself pretend to have grasped the meaning attributed to them by the ancient Egyptians themselves. Explanation can be content with the meaning attributed by the scholar. Relating the predicates in a chronological sequence, can explain something to the scholar; or - tracing their functions within society, can explain something to him; or - studying them within the wider ideological context, as we have done, can explain something. The person who sent the message may not necessarily be aware of the explanatory factors behind his message.[27]

Strictly speaking, it is not possible for the historian to verify his interpretation, and especially not when the people whose message he is trying to understand are dead and gone long ago. More correctly, therefore, the aim of the historian as an interpreter is to understand and document how a text or an image **may** have been understood, or, at least, may **not** have been understood. The role of explanation here is not to verify, but to make plausible; explanation has the role of backing interpretation. Even this task is formidable.

It aggravates the difficulties involved that transferring a message into a language understandable to modern man necessarily entails reference to the world views of modern man. Synonyms and analogies imply world views alien to those people who expressed themselves and whose expressions the translator tries to decipher and convey. This cannot be otherwise. It lies in the nature of interpretation and belongs to the heuristic premises underlying all understanding of other people. What deserves greater attention, though, is how the translator can reach a greater awareness of the equivocal nature of such understanding. The interpretation is both a result of perception, analysis, explanation, **and** one of adding something to the material. In all interpretation a supplementing act is involved through which the receiver makes the contents of the message comprehensible to him. The important task is not to prove this, it is plain to see, but to clarify its relationship to the message of the document, and ask the hermeneutical question: in what sense is the interpretation an exegetical "reading into" - and in what sense is it an exegetical "drawing out of" the document.

I shall not delve into what epistemological laws govern our understanding the thought of other people. Some scholars want to stop at explanation, because of the limitations of these laws. What is important here is to underline the point of view that one cannot have a translation without an interpretation. An interpretation is always implied, even when the translator has not explicated it. It lies inherent in his conceptual tools and in his language and in his very perception.[28] It may remain hidden, but from its hidden position it nevertheless powerfully influences the translation. It is precisely when the implied interpretation is hidden that it becomes most problematic. For the implied interpretation is not reflected upon but is taken for granted, and its effect is to camouflage the peculiar and alien features of Egyptian outlook on life. When hidden, it has this influence unchecked; the European outlook on life appears in an Egyptian guise, and the question of historical plausibility is not even raised. No need for explanation is felt. Only when the implied interpretation is made explicit, can it be clarified with respect to the fundamental features of Egyptian outlook.

Finally, I would therefore like to pose the question: How can modern scholars improve their possibilities of registering the distinctive character of Egyptian thought about life?

There are grounds for presuming that scholars belonging to comparative disciplines of culturual history will generally have an advantage, as they are disposed towards registering cultural differences, and also are trained in relating them to each other. But even Western scholars who specialize in Egyptian culture only, can find better points of departure in their own culture than the popular dualistic conception of being. The Western ideological universe is not a homogeneous one. There have always been ontological traditions which are nearer to Egyptian ontological traditions, and which can serve as hermeneutical bridges.[29] In modern times there can be seen a tendency to move away from dualistic and departmentalized outlooks towards monistic and holistic outlooks. In the natural sciences, as well as in the social, and cultural sciences, this tendency to apply holistic models of explanation can be observed, models that are better suited for exposing the connections between the various components of being within a monistic frame of reference. I believe the interest in holistic models in Western thought about nature and man's relationship with nature might be helpful in loosening the historian from his accustomed dualistic frame of reference so incompatible with ancient Egyptian thought. Of particular interest for our purpose are models that regard nature as a biotic organism, and man as a component of this organism - interacting with the other components and on par with them. Such views are held e.g. in ecological research.[30]

To prevent misunderstanding, I want to state explicitly that I do not consider the Egyptian biologically oriented conceptions of the human self and the world as identical with those of modern ecological or other holistically inclined models of explanation that lay emphasis on the biotic connections between everything that exists. What I mean is that the latter may serve as a means for the modern student of Egyptian religious thought to observe aspects of the source material which he otherwise would have overlooked because they fall outside his own perspective on being. The holistic models differ from the traditional ones on significant points as regards our task of explaining Egyptian thought. They do not define man as a unique individual separated from the rest of the species; they do not focus on the distance between man and other living beings. Nor do they split man into a soul and a body, referring them to different and in the last instance, separate areas of being. The effort to find more fruitful approaches in translating Egyptian thought, might benefit from modern holistic models developed in order to observe the interplay between man and natural world, and between "spiritual" and "material" qualities of life, because this was also the centre of attention of the ancient Egyptians. With the aid of such models it might, therefore, be possible to give more sensible presentations of the Egyptians' thoughts concerning life and death, man and god, than those that have been so frequent - and that have a habit of presenting them more like bizarre series of neverending surprises, impossible to anticipate beforehand.

NOTES

1) S. MORENZ, *Egyptian Religion*, transl. Ann E. Keep, London 1973, p.l.

2) The discussion has directly or indirectly been influenced by the general debate on the question of logic in "primitive" societies, instigated by L. LEVY-BRUHL, cf. *Les fonctions mentales dans les societes inferieures*, Paris 1910, and *La mentalite primitive*, Paris 1922.

3) E. HORNUNG, *Der Eine und die Vielen*, Darmstadt 1973, p. 237.

4) Various ways of solving the problem have been adopted, perhaps the most well-known being H. FRANKFORT's "multiplicity of approaches" - demonstrated in his *Ancient Egyptian Religion*, New York 1948.

5) Op,cit. p. 237.

6) Op,cit, p.238.

7) U. BERNER, "Überlegungen zur Übertragbarkeit des Komplementaritätsbegriffes auf ägyptische Gottesvorstellungen", *Göttinger Miszellen* 20 (1976). As regards the question of a special quantum logic, Berner calls attention to the quantum physicist's need to express himself according to Aristotelian logic, op.cit. p. 60.

8) First demonstrated by H. SCHNEIDER, in his *Kultur und Denken der alten Aegypter*, 1907.

9) Cf. C. Lévi-Strauss' research on myths mediating between contradictions in society and regarding the binary structure as a model of the human mind, and other versions of structuralism which imply patterns of binary oppositions seen as representing a basic structure of the human mind.

10) This discussion is also carried on within Egyptian philology and linguistics, under the rubrics context and cotext; see e.g. G. ENGLUND and P.J. FRANDSEN, eds., *Crossroad, Chaos or the Beginning of a New Paradigm, Papers from the Conference on Egyptian Grammar*, Helsingör 1986, (The Carsten Niebuhr Institute Publications I) Copenhagen 1986.

ll) Cf. W. GUGLIELMI, *LÄ* IV 978-987. - The tendency to blur these lines of demarcation cannot be exhaustively explained as mere poeticising; it is so prominent in Egyptian religious ontological thought as to make the scholarly label of "personification" appear both artificial and non-informative, in addition to the rather serious objection that it does not register the significant implications as regards basic world view categories.

12) Cf. L.V. ZABKAR, *A Study of the Ba-conception in Ancient Egyptian Texts*, Chicago 1968; *LÄ* I 588-590.

13) It is a brief delineation of the basic features of my underlying explanation of Egyptian thought about being, details of which can be found, scattered about in my other works on Egyptian religion; see notes 16 and 26.

14) See particularly the royal mortuary literature. There are various expressions of the idea, One of the most cherished ones is that of the dead participating in the creator's repeated journey through the realms of death and life.

15) The royal mortuary literature is our prior source to this train of thought. In my article "Pharaoh - and the 'democratization' of the post-mortem life" I give a more precise explication of the pharaoh category as a category of post-mortem life.

16) I give a fuller presentation of the contents of these concepts in "On transposing soul and body into a monistic conception of being", *Religion* 16 (1986), pp. 359-373.

17) Thus I have explained these connections not along the lines of Lévy-Bruhl, but with reference to a particular biologically defined approach to being.

18) Among recent examples I will mention L. TROY's *Patterns of Queenship in Ancient Egyptian Myth and History*, Uppsala 1986. The procreative contents with which she credits the complementary structures of Egyptian religious thought can be seen to be in agreement wfth the overall biocentric ontology. Thus the system of male-female values drawn up by Troy does not appear arbitrary, but in conformity with a dominant feature of Egyptian ontology.

19) P. KAPLONY, *LÄ* III 275 ff.; L.V. ZABKAR, *LÄ* I 588 ff.

20) This aspect of the transcending capacity is particularly noticeable with the ka-concept, but is also prominent with the ba-concept. Especially the Osiris cult formulates the collective aspect of the afterlife, cf. P. KAPLONY, *LÄ* III 276.

21) "Interpretations of religion: logic, discourse, rationality", *Göttinger Miszellen* 76 (1984) p. 33.

22) Op. cit. p.33.

23) Op.cit. p.33, - His entire discussion can be seen to presuppose this stance.

24) E, HORNUNG, *Der Eine und die Vielen*, p. 174 ff.

25) It is a main concept in Egyptian cosmological-mortological literature like The Amduat and The Book of the Caves from which Hornung draws many of his examples.

26) I have presented a fuller discussion of the ontological premisses of these epithets in *Image of the World and Symbol of the Creator. On the Cosmological and Iconological Values of the Temple of Edfu*, Wiesbaden 1985, p. 104 f.

27) Nevertheless, explanation is no simple and easy task, which can be seen from its scarceness in research. The problem within historical research is usually not lack of data, but of approaches which can make the data explicable, for as U. KING says: "Whether in history or in the hlstory of religions, isolated facts have little value of their own. To collect the necessary data is often not the most challenging problem but to explain or relate them within a wider context is a more difficult task", Contemporary Approaches to the Study of Religion I: The Humanities (= *Religion and Reason* 27), ed. F. Whaling, Berlin, New York, Amsterdam 1983.

28) Knowledge is not knowledge of "mere facts", and "mere facts" do not exist: they are always selected through a particular preparedness, to which belongs a preconceived conceptual frame of reference. What a person perceives and what he does not perceive, is thus culturally conditioned.

29) Cf. for instance, Giordano Bruno's pantheism, Spinoza's *deus sive natura*, or, St. Franciscus' upgrading of nature and of man's communion with all living beings.

30) Ecological perspectives have especially been applied in the study of the relationship with nature instituted in primitive cultures, but have not been explored with regard to their potential for developing the theoretical framework for the explication of nature made cultically relevant.

Jørgen Podemann Sørensen
Ancient Egyptian Religious Thought and the XVIth Hermetic Tractate

The first European accusations against Egyptian religious thought were not that it was pre-logical, but rather that it was pre-spiritual. When Sallustios the Neoplatonic worked out his typology of myths , he had to reserve one type, the 'material' (*hylikos*) kind of myth, especially for Egyptian mythology, for he was informed that the Egyptian gods were believed to be **identical** with various elements of nature, not just connected with or presiding over, but utterly identical with these elements - in flagrant contradistinction to e.g. the Greek gods, who could - by means of an easily applicable allegorical method - be seen to represent important Neoplatonic principles. From the pen of a Neoplatonist, *hylikos* is certainly a strong word, but Sallustios even adds that in spite of particular consideration he is able to see nothing but madness and ignorance in such purely concrete beliefs. He seems to suspect, like many later authors, including some Egyptologists, that the Egyptians were not capable of abstract thinking.

It is a strange irony that this impression of Egyptian religious thought was most probably brought into the Hellenistic world by Chaeremon in the first century A.D. Chaeremon, an Egyptian *hierogrammateus*, certainly did not want to convey this impression of his native religion, as we shall presently see, but he wrote and thought of Egyptian religion in terms of stoic physics. His reinterpretation, however, had no success in convincing the Hellenistic world that Egyptian religion was an ancient wisdom most relevant for modern philosophy. On the contrary, it seems to have left precisely that impression of a religion devoid of abstract thought and spirituality which we found in Sallustios, and which became, in the fourth century, a weapon in the hands of Firmicus Maternus, who delights in telling that Egyptians lamenting Osiris are in fact bewailing nothing but the crops.

Among the preserved fragments of Chaeremon there is, however, a passage about Egyptian priests, which rather tends towards the other extreme:

> "They renounced every employment and human revenues, and devoted their whole life to contemplation and vision of the divine. Through this vision they procured for themselves honour, security, and piety; through contemplation they procured knowledge; and through both a certain esoteric and venerable way of life. For to be always in contact with divine knowledge (*gnosis*) and inspiration keeps them far from all kinds of greediness, represses the passions, and incites them to live a life of understanding....".

This refers, of course, to a time (1st century A.D.) when the Egyptian priesthood was highly emancipated and needs not be applicable to pre-Hellenistic Egypt where priests could hold secular offices. - And, although it is a statement by a man who was himself an Egyptian priest, it expresses Egyptian spirituality in Greek terms and tends to evaluate it by Greek spiritual values. It is a reinterpretation, but even though its continuity with ancient Egyptian tradition is not easy to judge, it is at least a testimony that an Egyptian priest in Hellenistic philosophical circles could feel that he had a spiritual background in his native country.

A more provocative statement, consciously contrasting Egyptian and Greek thought, is found in the XVIth Hermetic tractate. In the introduction to this tractate, its author, allegedly Asclepius (i.e. Imhotep), deals at some length with the character of his writings. Even though readers will find them most plainly and straightforwardly written, they are in fact anything but plain; they guard a secret meaning. Then follows a warning against translation into Greek, which will completely distort the writings. - These considerations are continued in chapter 2, this time with reference to the present tractate:

> "Expressed in the original language, the tractate clearly preserves the sense of the words - for also the very character of the sound and the .... of Egyptian words has in itself the power/meaning (*energeia*) of what is said.
> In as far as it is possible for you, king - and everything is - preserve this tractate untranslated, lest such mysteries get into the hands of the Greeks, and lest the presumptuous and rambling and, one might say, ostentatious idiom of the Greeks dispose of the holiness and the strength and the efficacious (*energetikos*) speech of the words. For the Greeks, O king, have empty arguments fit for proofs, and that is what the philosophy of the Greeks is: a noise of arguments. We, however, use no arguments, but sounds full of efficacy."

The subject of this chapter is much more than just literary problems in translating from one language into another. It is a matter of Egyptian self-esteem. The tractate has come down to us in Greek, and this may very well be its original language. Its author, however, must have been an Egyptian coming to terms with his national heritage and identity by contrasting it with Greek philosophy. Philosophical argument may prove or persuade, but the efficacious words of Egyptian ritual texts work. What he brings out as a national advantage is well known to anyone versed in Egyptian religious literature: almost every heading of magical and funerary texts demonstrates the belief in the ritual efficacy of the formula, the power of words to do things. To a modern observer, ritual and philosophy may seem incommensurable subjects; to our author, they were obviously alternative ways of dealing with reality.

It should be kept in mind, however, that all later interpretations of Egyptian religious thought, including those of Frankfort and Hornung (see introduction), have likewise been based on ritual texts and yet presented to the public in epistemological terms. In pointing out ritual efficacy as the decisive feature, our Hermetic author is, in a way, more faithful to the material basis for generalization than the modern interpreters of ancient Egyptian thought. Yet belief in ritual efficacy does not make a philosophy or a structured religious thought. In order to assess the faithfulness of our Hermetist to his Egyptian heritage, we shall therefore examine, on the basis of a few examples, how this belief could affect the logic and the structure of Egyptian religious literature.

Our first example will be the well known ritual drama of "The Triumph of Horus", richly documented by a series of reliefs and inscriptions from c. 110 B.C. in the great Edfu temple. The Edfu drama of Horus began, if we may trust the series of reliefs representing it , with a scene showing Horus in his boat, harpooning a hippopotamus in the water. On the shore stands the king, likewise thrusting a harpoon into the same hippopotamus. From the very outset the reigning king, Ptolemy IX, is thus parallel with Horus. The accompanying text makes Horus address the king as follows:

> "I cause thy majesty to prevail against him that is rebellious
> toward thee
> On the day of the melée.
> I put valour and strength for thee into thy arms
> And the might of my hands into thy hands"

As we shall see, both text and relief may be taken as an introductory statement on the theme of the drama, the incarnation of the myth of Horus into royal ideology. The text of the introductory scene gradually passes into a delineation of the primeval, mythological situation that is the subject of the next scenes (Fig. 1).

The mythological section proper of the drama consists of five double scenes , each depicting Horus twice, so that a total of 10 harpoons are thrust into the hippopotamus. There are small variations, but the scenes are fairly uniform, and in the texts the only element that clearly indicates progressive action is the numbering of the harpoons from 1 to 10. Although it is conceivable that more than one harpoon is necessary to defeat the hippopotamus, it would not be too rash, I believe, to see in these reliefs and texts a highly redundant sequence. The myth here dramatized, that of the contendings of Horus and Seth, is known in several versions from a great number of allusions to it since the Pyramid texts of the Old Kingdom. As a full narrative it has come down to us in a version from the end of the New Kingdom. In this version a series of contests between Horus and Seth take place; the hippopotamus episode is only one of them and not, as in Edfu, the decisive one. In the Edfu drama the hippopotamus episode alone represents the primeval victory of Horus over Seth, to which the present kingship owes its existence, and thus one stage of a mythical process becomes the recurring theme of a redundant ritual sequence.

With the next scenes (Fig. 2) we enter what Fairman called "Act II" of the drama. The first of them again shows Horus and the king harpooning the same hippopotamus.

Then follows a scene in which Horus is crowned as King of Upper and Lower Egypt. The king is absent from this scene, probably because its reference to kingship is clear enough; but as if the mythological element needed emphasis, Horus is also shown on the shore in the usual harpooning scene.

The dismemberment of Seth and the distribution of the parts of the hippopotamus to the gods occurs twice in "Act III" (Fig. 3), first in a purely mythological scene and then in what looks more like a ritual scene.

The two scenes are interrupted by an interlude very illustrative of the juxtaposition of mythical and non-mythical elements in ritual drama. It is important to notice that the king is here shown harpooning a human enemy, whereas former representations of the king have shown him thrusting a harpoon into the hippopotamus. In the course of the Edfu drama this

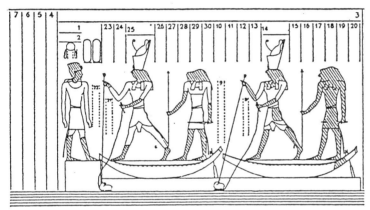

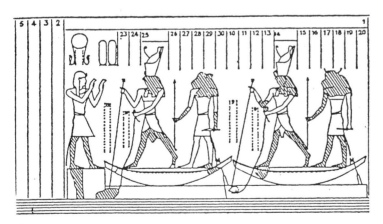

Fig. 1. "Prologue" and "Act I" of the Edfu Drama (cf. Fairman, op.cit. n. 6)

Fig. 1. "Prologue" and "Act I" of the Edfu Drama (cf. Fairman, op.cit. n. 6)

Fig. 2. "Act II" of the Edfu Drama (cf. Fairman, op. cit. n. 6)

shift bears witness to the descent from primeval to present level accomplished in its last section where Ptolemy IX is four times declared victorious over his enemies.

To a very large extent we may account for the myth-ritual relationship in the Edfu drama by saying that what is dramatized is not myth but the incarnation of myth. The Edfu drama is not simply a repetition of the primeval events that established the kind of kingship still adhered to as a source of social and natural order. The renewal of kingship is not simply effected by the reenactment of its mythical cause. But primeval and present are dramatically juxtaposed and made to mirror each other as the stages in a redundant mythological process. Although the drama delineates a descent from primeval to present level, from hippopotamus to human enemy, from Horus to Ptolemy IX, it does not in a historical sense narrate the story of how the present condition came to be. Rather it recasts the present in its mythical form and shows it, idealized in terms of royal ideology, as a variation on a mythical theme. This mythical structure of the drama would thus, to a certain extent, account for the ritual redundancy we have noticed especially in the double scenes in "Act I" (Fig. 1). The structure of the drama is not, however, determined by myth and royal ideology alone; the idea of ritual efficacy is, at the very least, equally important. The drama is designed to accomplish an end: the renewal of kingship through the incarnation of the

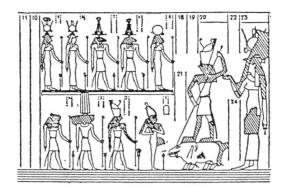

Fig. 3. "Act III" of the Edfu Drama (cf. Fairman, op. cit. n. 6)

mythical, victorious Horus in Ptolemy IX. This is the task carried out by the redundant sequence of scenes, in which the mythical prototype gradually enters the present. The Edfu drama is not "a noise of arguments" in favour of Ptolemy IX as legitimate king of Egypt. It is there to effect his legitimacy through incarnation.

The redundant process of ritual and mythological scenes mirroring or reproducing each other is also found in illustrated funerary literature. This may conveniently be shown in the mythological papyrus of Khonsu-renep, but it will gradually become apparent that our ana-

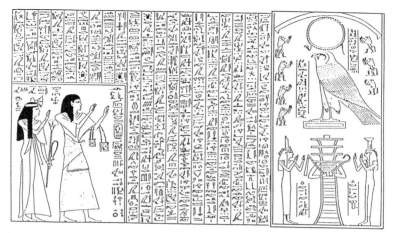

Fig. 4. The first scene of the Book of the Dead of Hunefer (BD Ch. 15) (E. Naville: Das ägyptische Todtenbuch der XVIII. - XX. Dynastie. Berlin 1886)

lysis of the sequence of scenes in this papyrus is also relevant for other mythological papyri and for illustrated versions of the Book of the Dead. Both genres often start with scenes resembling those on votive stelae: the deceased adoring the rising sun and/or Osiris. As it is well known, the famous Book of the Dead of Ani (18th dyn.) starts with a hymn to the rising sun (BD Ch. 15), illustrated by Ani and his wife in a posture of worship and a symbolic representation of sunrise. Parallel introductory scenes are found in other New Kingdom versions of the Book of the Dead; especially instructive is that of Hunefer (19th dyn.) (Fig.4), where the deceased and his wife are represented "worshipping Re as he rises in the eastern horizon of the sky". Like stelophors and possessors of votive stelae, they do so in a hymn written in front of them. The hymn, as it were, materializes into the representation of the rising sun, Re-Harakhti, worshipped by the heavenly baboons. This scene of cosmic regeneration is matched by an Osirian one: Isis and Nephthys worshipping Osiris, who is shown in the form of a djed-pillar. The text "I am your sister Isis" resp. "Nephthys" written in front of each of the goddesses indicates that the scene belongs to the mythical/ritual context of the 'lamentations of Isis and Nephthys', where the two sisters call Osiris back to life. Thus Osirian regeneration, which is also relevant for Osiris Hunefer, reproduces the sunrise shown above - and the worshipping hands of Hunefer and his wife are reflected in the worshipping gesture of both the heavenly baboons and Isis and Nephthys.

The Book of the Dead of Hunefer and, by implication, of many others, may thus be seen as a votive papyrus, in which the deceased is perpetuated worshipping. But whereas votive stelae content themselves with this, the papyri make the votive scene the point of departure of a redundant ritual and mythological process of the kind with which we are already familiar. This process, as well as the relation between the hymn and the subsequent mythological scenes, can be more convincingly shown in the 21st dynasty mythological papyrus of Khonsurenep.

In the votive scene or "etiquette" introducing Khonsu-renep's papyrus, (Fig. 5) Khonsu-renep is shown in a posture of adoration before Osiris who is seated on his throne, an offering table in front of him. Between the offering table and Khonsu-renep, Thoth is shown

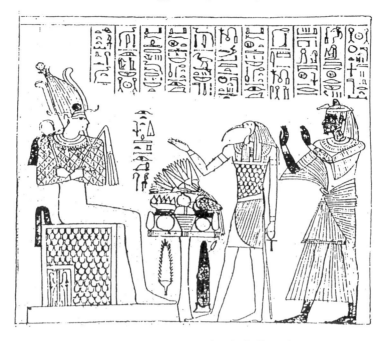

Fig. 5. The Mythological Papyrus of Khonsu-renep. (A. Piankoff, op. cit. n. 15, Papyrus No. 11)

with the gesture of consecration. The ritual title of the whole scene is "doing *ḥtp dj nsw* for Osiris, Lord of the West" - and quite in accordance with the use of the *ḥtp dj nsw* formula on votive stelae, the text above Khonsu-renep expresses the wish that he may ultimately benefit from participating in the cult of Osiris.

The following scene (Fig. 6) again shows Khonsu-renep in a posture of adoration. The text in front of him is a hymn to the rising sun: "O thou shining one in the sky, who illuminates the Two Lands, and whom the *Bas of Pe* and the *Bas of Nekhen* greet with cheers ...". And this is in fact what is seen in the upper left part of Fig. 6: Re-Harakhty in his boat,

Fig. 6. The Mythological Papyrus of Khonsu-renep. (A. Piankoff, op. cit. n. 15, Papyrus No. 11)

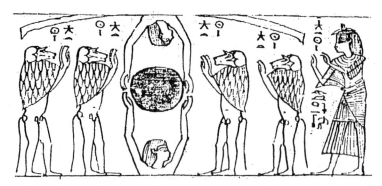

Fig. 7. The Mythological Papyrus of Khonsu-renep. (A. Piankoff, op. cit. n. 15, Papyrus No. 11)

greeted by the Bas of Pe (right, with falcon head) and Nekhen (left, with jackal's head). The scene with the rising sun thus illustrates or reproduces Khonsu-renep's hymn. And, once again, the worship of Khonsu-renep is mirrored in the jubilation of the Bas of Pe and Nekhen. As illustration, it is not there to inform a reader or to help him to conceptualize what it looks like, when the Bas of Pe and Nekhen greet the rising sun - it is part of a ritual process in which Khonsu-renep's worship is made to grow into sky and Netherworld or which makes him participate in cosmic and mythical regeneration. The rising sun is one of the many variations on the theme of regeneration, the representation below is another (Fig. 6, lower left); it shows the mummy of Osiris lying on the ground, flanked by Isis and Nephthys, i.e. the 'lamentations of Isis and Nephtys', in which Osiris is regenerated. To match the eastern and western Bas in the representation above Nekhbet and Uto are also shown. The relation between the two scenes is indicated by this symmetry, but also by the falcon head of the sun hanging down from the sky (exactly below Re-Harakhti) and spreading its rays with stars and suns over the mummy. The regenerating and life-giving power of the sun is well known from the books of the Netherworld, where the passing of the sun-boat awakens the dead and makes everything come to life. In our representation, the sunrays make out a kind of causal link between the solar and the Osirian regeneration shown. Khonsu-renep participates in the mythical regeneration of Osiris not only through the conventional identification with Osiris, but also because this regeneration is a variation on the theme of his worship. A similar parallelism is found later in the same papyrus (Fig. 7). It shows, once again, Khonsu-renep worshipping the sun; the scene is continued into the representation of the heavenly baboons worshipping the rising sun. Next comes the awakening of Osiris by Isis and Nephtys; Osiris is lying in a sphinxlike posture on his bier and Isis and Nephtys have fragments of their songs to the "beloved one" (*mrwtj*) written above their heads. Once again, the idea of regeneration continues the solar and the Osirian, or the cosmic and the mythical representation. Like the introductory sequence (Fig. 6) this (Figs. 7-8) consists of three elements:

    (a) Khonsu-renep worshipping the sun
    (b) heavenly/divine beings worshipping the sun
    (c) Isis and Nephthys awakening Osiris.

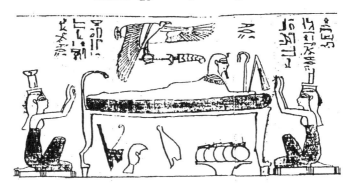

Fig. 8. The Mythological Papyrus of Khonsu-renep. (A. Piankoff, op. cit. n. 15, Papyrus No. 11)

The relation between these motifs is not the temporal or causal one characteristic of our comic strips; they are not episodes in a "natural" sequence of events, but rather reflect each other. In the first sequence (Fig. 6) the representation of the rising sun greeted by the Bas of Pe and Nekhen literally illustrates the hymn of Khonsu-renep. It brings out what we might call the dramatic element of the solar hymn: an Egyptian solar hymn will regularly delineate the rising, the course, and/or the setting of the sun, and - recited during the rising of the sun - it will ritually support this cosmic process. The hymn is instrumental in making the sun rise; in a certain sense we might therefore say that the sunrise shown is produced or caused by the hymn. Through his hymn, Khonsu-renep participates in sunrise; the sunrise shown is one of the forms which his worship takes. In a purely formal sense we may say that (a) generates (b); and (c), the resuscitation of Osiris, is a new variation of the regeneration theme in (b), also continuous with Khonsu-renep's worship. Such a heavenly or mythological extension of human worship is not without parallels: the Bas of Pe and Nekhen and the heavenly baboons are employed in this way in many hymns and ritual texts.

Khonsu-renep participates in cosmic and mythical regeneration as he participates in the offerings of Osiris in Fig. 5 through his worship. The point of departure is the votive scenes of Figs. 5 and 6 where he worships Osiris and Re-Harakhte. His act of worship is mirrored and continued into images of cosmic and mythical regeneration. Exactly the same constellation is found in Fig. 7, but this time Khonsu-renep is more directly related to the cosmic scenery; while Fig. 6 shows the worship of Khonsu-renep and the jubilation of the Bas in two distinct pictures, Fig. 7 has Khonsu-renep standing almost among the heavenly baboons. As we shall presently see, this is part of a sequential progression in the papyrus. Khonsu-renep is shown as more and more integrated into mythical and cosmic sceneries; he can gradually meet the gods and worship them face to face - but still in scenes mirroring the introductory votive representations.

In a later scene (Fig. 9) he again worships the rising sun, but this time as ba, doubly and symmetrically represented. He still has his cone of unguent, his name and title, but he has taken the otherworldly shape of the ba-bird. Above, the solar scene is mirrored in an Osirian representation of Isis worshipping Osiris in a boat. In a still later scene (Fig. 10) the goddess of the West takes Khonsu-renep before Osiris. In front of them, Horus consecrates an offering to Osiris, who is enthroned in his shrine; Isis and Nephthys are with him in the shrine. And as a reflection of Khonsu-renep's worship of Osiris, Isis is shown worshipping Osiris with an offering.

Fig. 9. The Mythological Papyrus of Khonsu-renep. (A. Piankoff, op. cit. n. 15, Papyrus No. 11)

The last scene in the papyrus shows Khonsu-renep worshipping the gods of the underworld. In front of him are prayers for his life in the hereafter. As an extension of his worship, the creative act of Shu lifting Nut from Geb is represented (Fig. 11). In the mythological papyri this scene is not uncommon among the many variations on the theme of regeneration and recreation.

With this scene from the very first beginning Khonsu-renep is in a certain sense taken back to the source of existence. His papyrus is not a wandering in a mythological landscape. First and foremost, it consists in mirrorings and extensions of his worship, and the hereafter represented in it is not a geographically, or cosmologically, defined area. His progressive integration in the "hereafter" is nothing but mythical and cosmological extensions of his worship. His papyrus is a votive papyrus, i.e. a **ritual** aiming at his integration in the regener-

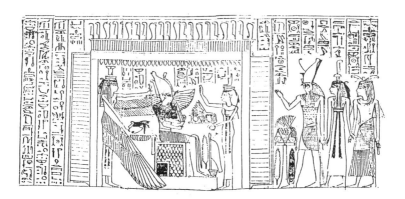

Fig. 10. The Mythological Papyrus of Khonsu-renep. (A. Piankoff, op. cit. n. 15, Papyrus No. 11)

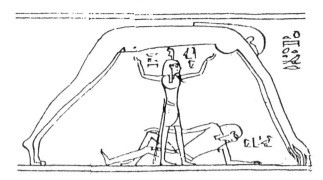

Fig. 11. The Mythological Papyrus of Khonsu-renep. (A. Piankoff, op. cit. n. 15, Papyrus No. 11)

ative process of nature. Its ritual efficacy lies in the cosmic and mythical *exemplars* that it quotes and into which Khonsu-renep is more and more integrated.

Some earlier interpretations of mythological papyri and even of the Book of the Dead have stressed the idea of a "Jenseitsführer", i.e. an informative booklet to which the deceased may have recourse for his orientation in the strange country of the hereafter. Although the idea of a book without readers is alien to the modern European mind one should consider the fact that very large portions of ancient Egyptian religious literature had no readers in the modern sense. To substitute the gods or the dead for such readers is to insist on a preconceived idea in face of evidence to the contrary. Again, our Hermetist has the key to the problem: Khonsu-renep's mythological papyrus is not in need of a reader, for it "has in itself the *energeia* of what is said". It is a ritual designed to effect his regeneration; it does so through a redundant series of variations on the theme of regeneration. Khonsu-renep participates in mythical and cosmic regeneration through his worship and is more and more integrated into a hereafter which remains throughout an extension of his worship.

There is thus a progression in the redundant sequence which is comparable to the one found in the Edfu drama. Khonsu-renep is taken back to the source of existence, whereas the Edfu drama incarnates the primeval in the present. But in both cases the dynamic link between primeval and present is the redundant ritual sequence which gradually, through a process of mirroring, produces the desired result: the renewal of kingship or the regeneration of the deceased. And in both cases the sequence is designed to work, not to prove, persuade, or inform.

If we have thus established that belief in ritual efficacy could, at least in our two examples, affect the logic and structure of Egyptian religious literature, it still remains to be shown that such redundant mirroring processes were what our Hermetist had in mind as an Egyptian alternative of Greek philosophy. The XVIth Hermetic Tractate certainly owes a lot to late Greek philosophy and religious thought. But it is not philosophical in the sense of "a noise of arguments". After the introductory statements the **corpus** of the tractate starts, very much in the style of the classical New Kingdom version of the Book of the Dead, with an invocation of God. This is not necessarily to be taken as a conscious reproduction of that particular literary tradition, but it is certainly continuous with the idea set forth in the introduction: that the aim of the tractate is not philosophical argument, but ritual efficacy.

The invocation of 'God, the ruler and maker and encircler of the universe, he who, being the one, is all, and, being the all, is one' starts a redundant sequence of cosmological images mirroring each other. Six times the creative and ruling divinity is made the point of departure, and six times the various intermediaries through which the divinity acts upon the world and the human condition are described, followed by statements about the nature of the interaction of God and the world.

The first "image" (Chapters 3-5) consists of the above invocation followed by more philosophical considerations on the unity and universality of God, the assertion that sources of water and fire bear witness both to the common root of the elements and to the existence of a kind of treasury of *hylê*, and the idea that the sun links heaven and earth by lifting up *hylê* and sending down *ousía*. The sun is called the *demiourgos*, but no clear distinction is made between God and the sun; in the following sections the sun takes over the role of the divinity.

The second "image" (Chapters 6-11) deals with the acting of the divinity on the world under the aspect of *noêtê ousía*. The 'spirited being' or the 'intelligible substance' is said to be in the sun, which governs the world through the intermediaries of life, soul, spirit (*pneuma*), immortality and generation (*genesis*). In this way the sun creates and nourishes everything with its rays: some go upwards to maintain the immortal parts of the world, while others make the elements below live, move and change.

The third "image" (Chapters 10-11) approaches the human condition. The point of departure is the ceaseless light of the sun and its incessant generation of life. Then the demons are introduced as intermediaries and overseers of the human condition. They receive orders from the gods and interfere with humans, punishing *asebeia* through storms, earthquake, hunger, war etc. For to fear the gods is the only human duty that matters.

The fourth "image" (Chapters 12-15) is a more detailed account of the demons and the human condition. Again the starting point is the sun, which preserves and nourishes everything. The world thus maintained by the sun is always in a process of change, for the sun generates, nourishes, and later, when their time comes, reabsorbs the manifold beings. The relation of the sun to the manifold beings and things is said to be that of the spiritual world (*noêtos kosmos*, *mundus intelligibilis*) to the sensible world (*aisthêtos kosmos*).

But under the sun is the whole **Zwischenreich** of stars and demons. There are good and bad demons, and some are said to be of a mixed nature; the earthly things are in their power, and they are the causes of various kinds of disturbance, both in society and in the individual. They even enter the muscles and veins, the brain and the entrails. As soon as a human being is born, his soul is manipulated by the demons of the constellation at the moment of birth. Only the *logikon meros*, 'reason', remains free to receive God.

The fifth "image" (Chapters 16-17) might be taken as part of the fourth, since it describes another aspect of the same interaction between the sun, the demons, and human souls: For the happy few, a ray of the sun may hit the *logikon meros* and render the demons ineffective. For the rest, however, reason is lead astray, and they are subject to the government of the demons, i.e. the *heimarmene*. Chapter 17 is a summary of the hierarchy and the creative process implicit in this, as well as the preceeding, "images": On God depends the spiritual world, on which, in turn, the sensible world depends. Through both worlds the sun receives its creative power from God, and creation is thus a process of interaction between God, the two worlds, and the sun. The demons are bound to the spheres round the sun, and it is on the demons that men depend. Through this chain of causation and dependence - or this process of creation - all beings depend on God.

Despite the absence of philosophical argument in the Greek sense, we are now approaching a conclusion. The sixth "image" (Chapters 18-19) is a new summary, once again starting with God and the sun and delineating the hierarchy of the intermediaries in order to return, eventually, to the creative process of interaction. It is in dealing, for the sixth time, with the nature of this process (Chapter 19) that the conclusion is reached: With the hierarchy as intermediaries God creates all things. They are all parts of God, and God is all things. Creation is God creating himself, and this process is perpetual and ceaseless as God himself; it has neither beginning nor end.

This is an important conclusion in more than one way: It is remarkable for its contribution to the understanding of Gnostic ideas about creation or emanation as a process, both timeless and eternal, **within** the universal God. It is perhaps even more remarkable if the XVIth Tractate is taken as an **Egyptian** assessment of Hellenistic ideas. For in that case its conclusion plainly states that the Gnostic and Hellenistic themes in the tractate may, in sum, be reduced to traditional Egyptian pantheism! The dynamic continuity of god and world, of creator and creation, and the idea of a ceaseless process of generation and regeneration are important and distinctive features of ancient Egyptian religion.

The XVIth Hermetic Tractate, however, is still a Hellenistic, Gnostic, and dualist tractate; and its conclusion is also a formulation of the Gnostic experience, the *gnosis*, in which the unity of God, the All, and the individual soul is perceived.

This conclusion was reached, not through the syllogisms of Greek philosophy, but in a redundant series of "images", beginning with an invocation and ending in the basic principle at the root of existence, the *principium* which is also the *gnosis*. Each of these "images" may be said to correspond to a certain "avenue of approach", and together they make up a paradigm on the theme of the divinity and the world and the creative process that connects them. There is no reason to believe that our Hermetist was not capable of abstract and logical thinking; but he preferred the Egyptian way, or we might say the ritual way: a redundant, but progressive series of variations on the theme of creation and generation, very similar to the one we have found in Khonsu-renep's papyrus. According to his introduction, the author of the XVIth Hermetic Tractate also believed in its ritual efficacy as something distinct from the persuasive power of Greek philosophy. To account for this, we shall have recourse to the old **Reitzensteinian** concept of the **Lesemysterium**, a text supposed to cause spiritual illumination in its reader - "wie ein wirkliches Mysterium". It was Reitzenstein's idea that no matter whether such texts had an original basis in ritual or not, they were designed to perform very much the same function as the rituals of mystery cults. This rather vague generalization had the disadvantage that the nature of such rituals is also a matter of debate. But there are Gnostic texts that refer to their own purpose in a way which at least resembles Reitzenstein's idea of the "Lesemysterium". In one of the Nag Hammadi texts, **Eugnostos the Blessed**, exposés of Gnostic theories of emanation are called *archênsown* 'beginnings of knowledge'. The epistle ends with the following address to the reader:

> "But all this, which I have told you above, I have told in such a way that you will be able to bear it, until that which cannot be taught is revealed in you - and all this shall it tell you, in joy and in pure knowledge (*sown*)."

The text is thus designed to prepare its reader for spiritual illumination or even to cause such an illumination in him.

Similar ideas about the function of the Gnostic text are found in the concluding words of the IVth Hermetic Tractate: The rather abstract teachings of Hermes in this tractate are somewhat surprisingly characterized as an image of God. The disciple is advised to contemplate it "with the eyes of his heart". The image will show him the way upwards, and the contemplation of it is even said to attract the one who has discovered it and to draw him upwards like a magnet. Such statements may be taken to mean that the Gnostic texts in question are devotional tractates and guides to meditation. It is, however, important to note that the texts, or the teachings they expound, are believed, like the XVIth Hermetic Tractate, to have certain efficacious properties, distinct from the persuasive power of Greek philosophy.

In the XVIth Hermetic Tractate there is express reference to such properties, and they are seen as a ritual efficacy characteristic of Egyptian tradition, a virtue of the national idiom. The redundant, progressive series of variations on the theme of creation and generation we have found in the text shows its connection with this Egyptian ritual tradition. What we can study in this Hermetic text is not only an Egyptian coming to terms with his national heritage, but also the transition from ritual text to devotional and meditative literature, from temple and funerary ritual to *gnosis*. At least in the XVIth Hermetic Tractate, ancient Egyptian religious thought survives through, and exerts a certain influence on, this process of transition.

NOTES

1. SALLUSTIOS: *Des dieux et du monde*. Ed. G. Rochefort, Paris 1961, Chapter 4.

2. CHAEREMON, fragm. 5-7; cf. PIETER WILLEM VAN DER HORST: *Chaeremon, Egyptian priest and Stoic philosopher*. Leiden 1987 (EPRO; 101).

3. FIRMICUS MATERNUS, *De errore profanarum religionum*, cap. 2; cf. MIGNE, *Patrologiae cursus completus, Series Latina*, T. 12, Paris 1845, col. 986 sqq.

4. CHAEREMON, fragm. 10; cf. note 2 above.

5. *C.H.* XVI, 2.

6. *Edfu* VI, pp. 60-90 (text); X, Pl. 146-148 (line drawings); Pl. 494-514 (Photographs). Translation and commentary in A.M. BLACKMAN & H.W. FAIRMAN: The Myth of Horus II: The triumph of Horus over his enemies: a Sacred Drama. *JEA* 28 (1942), pp. 32-38; 29 (1943), pp. 2-36; 30 (1944), pp. 5-22. - A handy translation in H.W. FAIRMAN: *The Triumph of Horus,* London 1974.

7. The reliefs here reproduced in Fig. 1-3 (From FAIRMAN 1974) are of course no photographic account of the ritual. It is, however, safe to assume that they represent the structure and the content of the ritual fairly well. As it is well known, versions of e.g. the Daily Temple Liturgy on temple reliefs have been found to correspond rather closely to those versions on papyri, which were actually used by the priests.

8. *Edfu* VI, pp. 63, 1 sqq. Quoted from FAIRMAN 1974, p. 80.

9. *Edfu* VI, pp. 63-78 (text); XIII, Pl. 497-506 (photos); FAIRMAN 1974, p. 84-100.

10. Cf. J. GWYN GRIFFITHS: *The Conflict of Horus and Seth*. Liverpool 1960.

11. A.H. GARDINER: *Late Egyptian Stories*. Brussels 1932 Bibliotheca Aegyptiaca 1) pp. 37-60.

12. *Edfu* VI, pp. 78-84 (text); XIII, Pl. 507-510 (photos); FAIRMAN 1974 pp. 101-108.

13. *Edfu* VI, pp. 84-90 (text); XIII, Pl. 511-514 (photos); FAIRMAN 1974 pp. 109-118.

14. *Edfu* VI, p. 90; FAIRMAN 1974 pp. 119-120.

15. ALEXANDRE PLANKOFF: *Mythological Papyri*. Princeton 1957. Papyrus no. 11.

16. Cf. R.O. FAULKNER: *The Papyrus Bremner-Rhind*. Brussels 1933 (Bibliotheca Aegyptiaca 3) pp. 1-31; transl. in *JEA* 22 (1936), p. 121 sqq.; P. Berlin 3008, ed. Faulkner in *Melanges Maspero* I, Cairo 1935-38, p. 340 sqq.

17. Cf. ERIK HORNUNG: *Ägyptische Unterweltsbücher*. Zürich 1972, p. 39 sq.

18. Cf. J. ASSMANN: *Liturgische Lieder an den Sonnengott*, Berlin 1969 (Münchner ägyptologische Studien; 19) p. 208 sqq. and p. 322 sq.

19. Cf. RAGNHILD BJERRE FINNESTAD: *Image of the World and Symbol of the Creator*. Wiesbaden 1985 (Studies in Oriental Religions; 10), notably p. 93 and p. 147.

20. Cf. JØRGEN PODEMANN SØRENSEN: Gnosis and Mysticism as illustrated by Eugnostos the Blessed in Nils G. Holm: *Religious Ecstasy*. Uppsala 1982 (Scripta Instituti Donneriani Aboensis; 11), pp. 211-217.

21. R. REITZENSTEIN: *Die Hellenistischen Mysterienreligionen*. 3. Aufl. Leipzig 1927, p. 52 sqq. - The whole idea of "Lesemysterien" is rejected as "insensitive" by Garth Fowden: *The Egyptian Hermes*. Cambridge 1986, p. 149. Fowden is certainly right in his idea that Hermetism was no desk or armchair religion, and his excellent book is ample proof of a communal religious life of Hermetists. This is, however, no obstacle to the assumption that some Hermetic texts were designed to initiate or illuminate the reader.

22. NHC III, 74, 20; 76, 12. Cf. op. cit. note 20.

23. NHC III, 90, 4 sq. I follow Krause's translation in *Die Gnosis*. Bd. 2. Zürich 1971, p. 37 sqq. In *The Nag Hammadi Library in English*, Leiden 1977, p. 225, Parrot translates: "until the one who does not need to be taught is revealed among you".

24. CH IV, 11.

Lana Troy
The Ennead: The Collective as Goddess
A Commentary on Textual Personification

The way in which the ancient Egyptians describe the divine world is full of incongruities for the modern observer. In particular, the imagery associated with their many deities is difficult to penetrate and often quite simply contradictory. Given these circumstances there are essentially two attitudes which can be taken. The incongruities can be accepted as the result of the interweaving of a number of related theologies - a view familiar to all - or an attempt can be made to perceive patterns which explicate these incongruities. Once a pattern is perceived, then means can be formulated for analysing the significance of this diversity.

One attempt at working in this direction was presented in the dissertation of the present author which utilized the concept of the feminine prototype as a tool of analysis (Troy 1986). In the following presentation the results of that study are applied to an examination of two seemingly contradictory presentations of one figure in Egyptian thought, that of the Ennead, found in the early text collections as both divine collective and as goddess.

The term Ennead, *Psḏt*, is primarily associated with a group of gods. The Egyptians often organized their gods into groups. These groups consist of pairs or triads, as well as larger groups of four or more deities. The significance of these groupings has been considered from different perspectives (cf. Säve-Söderbergh 1977). There seems however to be a general consensus that the association of different gods in complexes is a way of expressing the diversity of the components of cosmic order.

This interpretation holds particularly true when applied to the Ennead. The term *Psḏt*, "the nine", is used in reference to a large group of gods. The nine gods of the Heliopolitan Ennead provides our most immediate reference point but the term is also applied to other groups with differing numbers of gods, such as the Theban "Ennead" with its various numbers of gods such as twelve or fifteen (Barta 1973, pp. 59-60 and cf. Naville 1896, Pl. 46). The number nine, it has been repeatedly argued, stands for the ultimate expression of plurality (cf. e.g. Griffiths 1958, p. 37; Barta 1973, pp. 23-26; Hornung 1971, pp. 217-219: Goedicke 1986, col. 128; all with references). It is the sum of the plurality of three times itself. It is the last number before the beginning of a new cycle, represented by the number ten (Graefe 1986; Englund 1989, p. 15). The number nine is also the combination of eight plus one, the eight of chaos and the one of creation (Troy 1986, pp. 146-147). It is thus the perfect representative for the total diversity of the cosmos.

This diversity is however not static. The members of the Heliopolitan Ennead, the descendents of the creator god Atum, are described with characteristics which can be related to the gradual differentiation of the cosmos and thus to the dynamic of creation. Each generation represents a more complex distribution of the elementary cosmic components, beginning with the birth of Shu and Tefnut and the introduction of gender and continuing to the four children of Geb and Nut and their complex role interaction (te Velde 1984; Troy 1986, pp. 146-147; Englund 1989, pp. 13-15).

The Heliopolitan Ennead is also characterized by the manner in which it refers both to the structure of the physical world and to the organization of the human family. Its completion with the birth of Horus supplies the kingship with a genealogy (Barta 1973, pp. 41 ff.) and proclaims the coming into being of history (Morenz 1973, p. 164) as the world of the gods is linked into the society of man.

The Heliopolitan Ennead is the ideal *Psḏt*, analyzed, described and incorporated into the mythology of the Egyptians. It functions as an explication of the nature of the divine collective. Thus the Ennead, represented by the nine from Heliopolis, the fifteen of Thebes or presented as an undefined collective term, consists of the plurality of the gods. Hornung's (1971, p. 217-218 with references) observation that the term *Psḏt* may have been preceded by the term *ḥt*, "body" passes well in the this view. This collective is placed in relationship to the image of the sole god-king, represented by e.g. Re or Amun. The god and his Ennead provides a divine model for the king and his court.

The function of the Ennead, as a divine collective, comes through quite clearly in the texts. It appears as the court and counsil of the god-king. It is the body which constitutes the highest judicial authority of the divine world. The Ennead are members of the counsil, the *ḏ3ḏ3t* (cf. Griffiths 1958, p. 51; Barta 1973, p. 32 citing e.g. PT 1174c-d, CT II 52g, VII 18c; for a discussion of the *ḏ3ḏ3t* in the judgement of the dead see Grieshammer 1970, pp. 93 ff.). In the Pyramid Texts, the Ennead, here specifically the gods of Heliopolis, appears as the court of Geb, overseeing the deliberation of the conflict between Horus and Seth in the *ḥwt-sr* "Mansion of the Prince" (cf. Barta 1973, p. 31 with references). This is a role more explicitly described in the text known as the Memphite Theology (l. 7; cf. Griffiths 1960, p. 65; Lichtheim 1973, pp. 51-52, with references). The New Kingdom story The Tale of the Two Brothers, retains the imagery of the official status of the Ennead as it describes the hero meeting the Ennead as it "attends to the business of the entire land" (*irt sḥrw n p3y.st t3 ḏr.f* = Gardiner 1932, p. 19: 9,3).

The position of the Ennead as the members of the highest judiciary, although documented as early as the Pyramid Texts, is obviously still a current tradition in the New Kingdom. It is during this period that the Ennead is found in the role of jury in the scenes assoicated with the judgement of the dead by Osiris (cf. Barta 1973, p. 33; CT IV 87d-e; BD Chapter 41 = Hornung 1979, p. 112, l. 4, Chapter 81B = Hornung 1979, p. 168, l. 11; discussion of the pictorial motif in Seeber 1976, p. 133 ff.).

The Ennead, in its role as the obediant subjects of the god, as the divine officials who serve the god and function as his administration, is, in general terms, the *entourage* of the god-king (Barta 1973, pp. 38-41). This analysis of the role of the Ennead functions well as long as plurality remains its major characteristic. The concept *Psḏt*, "the nine" can, however, also be used in a personified form. The Ennead can be treated as if it was, not a group of many deities, but the name of a single deity which then can appear alone or in groups of two or more Enneads (cf. Gugliemi 1982 and Baines 1984, pp. 7 ff. for discussion of personification).

It is common when discussing personification to refer to the use of a pictorial image of a deity to represent an abstract quality or non-living substance. Looking for examples of pictorial personification of the Ennead only one example has been found (cf. below and Fig. 1). There are, however, several examples of textual personification (cf. discussion in

Baines 1985, esp. pp. 22-23) of the Ennead. These are found primarily in the Pyramid Texts, Coffin Texts and, in survivals from the earlier text collections, in the Book of the Dead. These passages may be identified as examples of personification both in terms of content and by comparing texts of similar content in which the role played by the Ennead in one example is related to other individual deities in another.

All of the examples of textual personification of the Ennead discussed here relate to one idea complex. In these passages the term *Psḏt* is used as if it was the name of one or more goddesses. This aspect of the role of the Ennead was observed by Barta (1973, p. 35) who spoke of the "belebende" function of the Ennead and its status as a "Muttergottheit". It is best to state at the outset that this aspect of the Ennead is most clearly expressed in the Pyramid Texts. It is somewhat developed in the Coffin Texts, but it is evident that by the time of the New Kingdom the idea of the Ennead as the *entourage* of the gods essentially dominates its presentation in the texts. References to the Ennead as goddess in New Kingdom sources are only evident in a few examples known to this author, all of which are clearly survivals from the earlier text collections.

The term *Psḏt* "the nine", grammatically feminine, is treated as a feminine deity. In discussing the concept of personification, it has been noted that the form taken by the personification tends to reflect the grammatical gender of the thing personified (Baines 1985, p. 9 citing e.g. Kees 1941, p. 163, cf. Baines' comments and references) and this is indeed the case here. The total way in which the Ennead is integrated into its feminine identity is however best illustrated by relating it to the concept of the feminine prototype (cf. Troy 1986, pp. 43-50).

The term prototype refers here to a collection of attributes which are shared by all deities or mythological figures placed in one and the same role. There is not a necessary correlation between a prototype and a specific deity although one or more deities may represent an outstanding representative of the prototype (cf. Troy 1986, p. 53 ff. for discussion of Hathor in relationship to the feminine prototype). The various representatives of a prototype have a homologous relationship to one another and may also have a hierarchal relationship which provides structural relationships useful in the expression of the idea of microcosm. For example the states of chaos contra creation, found at the highest hierarchal level, have homologues, such as night and day within the created world. Thus the concept of prototype can be used to help analyze the function of categorization in the expression of Egyptian thought.

The elements of the feminine prototype are easily summarized. It consists of the status of consort and mother, sister and daughter and employs the rich symbolism associated with these roles emanating from the numerous mythic complexes. There is tendency to present the feminine role as a duality. This aspect is well represented by the status given Isis and Nephthys. The duality of feminine elements can function both on the level of equivalency, such as in the relationship of two sisters or in the complementary roles of mother and daughter. Ideally every pair has both characteristics of an equivalent and a complementary relationship. Two symbolic complexes relate to the complementary roles of mother and daughter. These are most simply outlined in terms of the mother role with reference to the night sky which its associated cow imagery and the daughter solar eye with associations with the uraeus and also with the raging lioness of the myth of the solar eye (cf. Troy 1986, p. 30).

Beyond the creation of dualities, Egyptian myth also sets up other groupings such as that of four (cf. the canopic goddesses) and seven (the seven Hathors). Each group again expressing a conceptual unity, often in combination with a single male figure (cf. Troy 1986, p. 49).

The personification of the Ennead, as found in the Pyramid Texts and Coffin Texts, falls clearly into the category of the female prototype. This may be illustrated by examples from the texts.

The Ennead is projected into the role of "consort", as the god-king, or the figure given that status, is called "bull of the Ennead".

> "I am the bull of the Ennead, who goes forth from the horizon, the owner of the five portions in Heliopolis, three in the sky and two on earth." (CT III 169 a-c cf. PT 511a, 1238c, 2248d; CT VI 310n, BD Chapter 15B2 = Allen 1974, p. 21, l. S1.)

The term "bull" *k3*, beside denoting domination (cf. Brunner's interpretation of *k3* as meaning "lord" 1982 col. 476) has sexual connotations, such as in the term *k3 mwt.f* "bull of his mother" referring to the self generation of the male principle (cf. Barta 1973, p. 36 and Troy 1986, pp. 23-24 for discussion of the bull as god of fertility). This expression are among those which survives in the references to the Ennead from the Book of the Dead (cf. ref. to Chapter 15B2 above).

The role of the Ennead as mother of the god-king appears to be associated with that of Nut, as the Ennead is paired with Geb.

> Hail to you , O Wise One (*si3*)! Geb has created (*km3*) you, the Ennead has borne (*ms*) you. (PT 258b W, cf. CT IV 382 a-b, where three variants read Nut and one the Two Enneads, BD Chapter 174 = Hornung 1979, p. 363 l. 5-6.)

Interesting enough, in the text from a stela of Horemheb (Univerity College 14391: Stewart 1976, p. 5-6, Pl. 1.2) the Ennead takes Geb's role rather than Nut's, providing an apt illustration of the change in the perception of the status of the Ennead during the New Kingdom.

The association of the Ennead with Nut as the mother of the young Re in the texts under discussion is further underlined in the description of the Ennead as giving birth.

> Unis is a great one: Unis has come forth from between the thighs of the Ennead; Unis has been conceived by Sakhmet, Unis has been given birth by Shezemetet. (PT 262a W cf. Allen 1984, p. 272, 406B for the use of the emphatic in this passage, and parallels PT 1087b-c, 2206a-e.)

In the citation above, the Ennead gives birth in one line, but in the following lines the functions of conception and birth are divided between two goddesses. This too is a typical characteristic of the pattern of the feminine prototype. (cf. Troy 1986, 26-27 with references). And indeed the Ennead, particularly as it appears in the Pyramid Texts, is repeatedly identified as a duality (cf. e.g. PT 121d, 127a, 304e, 371b, 458b, 483b, 536a, 538b, 730d, 819b, 902a, 906c, 956c, 1032a-b, 1044b, 1063b, 1087c, 1093a, 1100a, 1116d-7b, 1127a,c, 1196a-b, 1203d, 1259c, 1262a, 1312a, 1343c, 1373b, 1405d, 1449c, 1489b, 1562a, 1573c, 1651f, 1696a,

1707c, 1710c, 1714a, 1719d, 1750b, 1982b, 1993a, 2020b, 2094b, 2105a, 2246e, 2248d and cf. CT II 164b, III 186a, IV 36e, IV 90p, VI 95b, VI 310n, VII 159j).

In a number of the citations where the Ennead is referred to as a duality, the contexts in which they are found are often analogous to those associated with Isis and Nephthys. The Two Enneads are, for example, paralleled with the night and day barks (cf. PT 210a-b, for reference to Isis and Nephthys as the barks.)

> Your white crown is that of Thoth, your forehead (wpt) is that of Wepawet, your eyebrows are those of the Two Enneads, your eyes are those of the Night-bark and Day-bark, your tresses(*šwty* ?) are those of Isis and Nephthys. (CT VI 123i-124d, with alternative readings "your tresses (*inḥ*) are those of the Enneads".)

The association of the Two Enneads with the role of the two sisters is made even more clear as they address Osiris as brother.

> The Two Enneads are indeed joyous, O my father at meeting you, O my father Osiris the king, and they say: "Our brother comes to us, say the Two Enneads about Osiris the king, my father Osiris. (PT 1696a-d.)

Compare this citation with Isis and Nephthys in the same role:

> How lovely to see says she, namely Isis! How pleasing to behold, says she, namely Nephthys, to my father, to Osiris, this King. (PT 939a-c, cf. 1362a-b.)

The use of the image of the Two Enneads as a feminine duality is even more evident when it is found in association with the symbols of the crown, the uraei.

> O King at the head of the Two Enneads as the two serpent- goddesses (*wtty*) who are on your brow, that they may raise you up. (PT 902a-c, cf. CT IV 202/203c-d, 204/205 d-206/207a; BD Chapter 17, with the allusions to the two uraei vis à vis Isis and Nephthys, Hornung 1979, p. 62 f. = 1. 9-10, and discussion in Troy 1986, p. 127.)

In these examples the duality of the Ennead has been related primarily to that of the two sisters Isis and Nephthys. But it does have another aspect. The duality of the Ennead appears however in two forms, that of equivalency, in which two synonyms '*3t* and *wrt*, "Great" are used to describe the pair, and complementary where the terms are '*3t/wrt* and *ndst* "Great" and "Lesser". Griffiths (1958, p. 44-45) suggested that the *Psḏty*, the two Enneads actually refer to this combination of the *Psḏt '3t* and the *Psḏt wrt*, great and the mighty Enneads. Griffiths identifies the *Psḏt wrt* as the Ennead of Upper Egypt and thus suggests that the two Enneads represent the duality of Egypt.

Barta (1973, p. 29, 50-53) also takes up this discussion. He refers to the relationship between the Enneads and the two shrines (*itrty*) of Egypt (cf. PT 1262a-b, 1251c-d, and CT IV 90p). He also cites the presence of the Enneads at Karnak (Legrain 1929, p. 223, Abb. 131;cf. Nelson 1981, Pl. 53) represented as the falcon- and jackel-headed figures, normally known as the "Souls of Pe and Nekhen" who are called here the Great ('*3t*) Ennead in Pe and the Lesser Ennead in Nekhen.

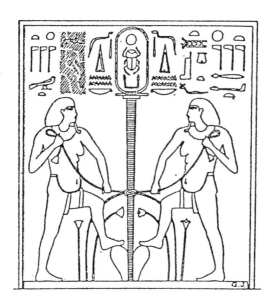

Fig. 1. The Great and Lesser Ennead as "fecundity figures". (Taken from Kuhlmann 1977, p. 54, Abb. 30)

Although there is only one reference to the lesser Ennead in the Pyramid Texts (PT 177a, *ndst* is read by Griffiths as a scribal error for *wrt* cf. 1958, pp. 42-44), the combination of the greater (*wrt/'3t*) and lesser (*ndst*) Ennead becomes a familiar one (Barta 1973, p. 52 with references). It is the combination of the Greater and Lesser Ennead which appears in the only example of the pictorial personification of the Ennead cited by Baines (1985, p. 134) in his extensive study. This is found on the side of the throne of one of the Lisht statues of Sesostris I (Kulhmann 1977, p. 54 Abb. 30: here Fig. 1). Here the Great (*'3t*) and Lesser Enneads are depicted as Nile gods, or as Baines (1985, pp. 112 ff.) prefers, "fecundity figures" (for discussion of this example see discussion in Baines 1985, pp. 134-136).

The Two Enneads are seen participating in the *sm3 t3wy*, the Uniting of the Two Lands, symbolized by the knotting of the plants of Upper and Lower Egypt. The transposition of the Two Enneads into the figures of the Nile gods relates to many of the assertions made concerning the significance of this duality. There is an obvious reference to the Two Lands as the Two Enneads participate in this rite. This recalls the association between the Two Enneads and the *itrty*, the two shrines of Egypt. Barta (1973, p. 35) is correct is seeing a re-lationship between the "belebende" function of the Ennead and this projection into the role of the Nile gods. The Nile gods, and the *sm3 t3wy* motif, have however, as a general rule, reference to male participants (cf. Baines 1985, p. 136 on the exclusion of female deities). The most common being Horus and Seth (cf. Kuhlmann 1977, pp. 55-56 with figures). The presentation of the Enneads as essentially male figures in this context both supports the im-pression given by the distribution of the texts that the projection of the Ennead as a god-dess is primarily confined to the periods associated with the Pyramid and Coffins Texts. It should however be noted that the generative function of the Ennead is not impaired by the representation of the duality as masculine. The combination of two complementary elements are, in themselves, generative, irrespective of formal gender (cf. discussion of Horus and Seth as a generative duality in Troy 1986, pp. 40-41, 147).

Other than the use of the duality in the presentation of the personified Ennead, many other plural references are found, a few of which can be related to other groups of female deities. In one instance for example, the duality of the Ennead in the Coffin Texts seem to reflect the role played by the four Canopic goddesses in the Pyramid Texts.

> Horus swells up around his eye, but his Two Enneads are about his throne and they will give rid of the severe pain which he suffers. (CT VII 395a-c.)

> Fetch me to your side, so that I may kindle a light for you and that I may protect you, even as Nun protected these four goddesses on the day when they protected the throne. (PT 605b-606c.)

The Enneads also appear as a group of seven.

> I am a *naw*-snake, a bull-snake who leads, who swallowed his seven uraei, and his seven neck vertebrae came into being who gave orders to his seven Enneads. (CT V 36g-37b, variations read "four Enneads", and simply "Enneads" in plural.)

The most significant aspect of the feminine identity of the Ennead has been left to last. It is also the most evident. It is that element which can perhaps be motivated as a word play on the term *Psḏt*. This is the association between the Ennead and that complex of ideas which includes the solar eye and the daughter of the god. This association has a very concrete basis in the word play between *Psḏt* "the nine" and the verb *psḏ* "to shine" (WB I, 556-557). This is exploited in the Pyramid Texts in the ocassional choice of a disk from which rays extend as the determinative (cf. PT 717a; Gardiner Sign List: N8; see Barta 1973, pp. 19-20 for discussion). This play on the words "Ennead" and "shine" is of course also used thematically in the Pyramid Texts.

> The King washes himself when Re appears, the Great Ennead shines forth and He of Ombos is high at the head of the *itrt*-shrine. (PT 370a-b.)

This association is further developed in the Coffin Texts in the interest that text collection devotes to the brother-sister pair Shu and Tefnut.

> He spat me out as Shu together with Tefnut, who came forth after me as the Great Ennead, the daughter of Atum who shines on the gods. (CT II 18 e-f.)

Another reference to the Ennead as a "sister" is found in a fragmentary Coffin Text Spell 144 (CT II 178 f-g, note the use of the pregnant woman (?) , Gardiner Sign List: B2 as determinative here).

The Ennead, as Tefnut, the sister of Shu, the daughter of Atum is thus also the solar daughter, the eye of the god.

> He judges them-so says she, the Great Eye of Horus, the Great Ennead. (CT II 175e.)

To round out this complex of association one may add a reference to the Ennead as bark. Boat imagery belongs to the same sphere as that of the solar eye (cf. Troy 1986, p. 23).

The King goes aboard, for he is pure; he receives the oar, [the King takes his seat in the Ennead], the King rows in the Ennead, the King plies his oar in the Ennead. (PT 2125a-d cf. PT 1981c-1982a for the equation of eyes and barks.)

It should also be noted however that Tefnut, the divine daughter, and the "Sole Eye" is, in the same text collection seen as the mother and mistress of the Enneads.

O you bowmen of Shu, regard me, for I am eternity, the father of the Chaos-gods; my sister is Tefenet, the daughter of Atum, who bore the Ennead....I am he who fashioned the Chaos gods who Atum repeated and this my sister is eternity. (CT II 21f-22b, 23a-c.)

This N has nurtured millions and has brought up millions by means of the Sole Eye, the Mistress of the Enneads, the Mistress of all. (CT IV 86v-w.)

Thus the Ennead is placed in a feminine role in these texts: as consort, mother, sister and daughter of the god. The question remains as to what this emphasis on the role of Ennead as a manifestation of the generative force of the feminine represents. The Ennead is treated as a homologue to deities such as Nut and Isis and Nephthys. And this suggests that the there is a thematic coherence between the status of the Ennead, even as a divine collective, and that of these goddesses.

The role of the pun is of course important in the application of feminine characteristics to this group of gods. The term *Psḏt* has a feminine form. The motivation for this is unclear although given that the feminine element is strongest in the Pyramid Texts it may reflect the influence of the early conceptional status of this group found in these texts.

The relationship between *psḏ* "nine" and *psḏ* "shine" is also evident. It is acknowledged both in the use of the sun determinative, found in the Pyramid Texts and in the obvious pun in the citations above. Read as "she who shines", *Psḏt* has a direct reference to the role of the feminine deity as the solar disc. The step between *Psḏt* "she who shines" and *Nbw* "the golden one", epithet of Hathor (cf. e.g. Troy 1986, 22 with references) is not far. With this juxtaposition, incorporation of the *Psḏt* into the complex of goddesses associated with role of solar daughter and bearer of the young god is almost given.

Beyond however the question of the pun on the verb "to shine", there are aspects of the role of the Ennead as a collective which help to explicate its presentation as a female deity. First of all it can be of value to look once again at the Heliopolitan Ennead as judiciary and note that it appears repeatedly in this role. It is here that one may find a relationship between the Ennead as collective and the feminine prototype. In order to delineate this relationship it is necessary to introduce another deity into the discussion, the goddess Maat.

Maat is a personification of a central concept in Egyptian thought. Maat, the principle of "justice", "truth", "order" is fundamental to the dynamic of the cosmic order. It is the responsibility of the ruler to maintain Maat by his actions and for each individual to act according to Maat. When personified Maat becomes the daughter of Re, his companion (cf. Helck 1981). The imagery associated with Maat is that of the solar daughter, the eye, the uraeus (e.g. Altenmüller 1975 pp. 67 ff.). Maat, like the Ennead, is described using the imagery of the feminine prototype, such as the barks of the sun (CT II, 210o) and the groups of seven (CT II 148b). Maat also functions, as does the eye, as the offering *par excellence* (cf. Englund 1987, p. 57-60).

Maat, like the Ennead, the *Psḏt*, is a solar daughter. The Two Enneads like the Two Maats, provide the context for judgement (cf. Grieshammer 1970, pp. 89-90; Altenmüller 1975, pp. 71-72).

> When he finds the Two Enneads, they will give their hand to the King and he will sit between them to give judgement. (PT 1093 a-d.)

> The Two Maats have judged, though a witness was lacking. The Two Maats have comanded that the thrones of Geb shall revert to me, so that I may raise myself to what I desired. (PT 317a-c.)

> The sky is strong and Nut jubilates when she sees what Atum has done, whilst he sat among the Two Enneads and gave the authority which is on his mouth to Horus, the son of Isis. (CT IV 86p-t.)

The concept of "justice" and "truth", is thus, like the members of the court which oversee the dispensation of justice, associated with female imagery. Additionally one may observe that this association extends to the earthly office of judge, as the image of Bat, an early Hathoric form, and later Maat, is used as the emblem of that office (Grdseloff 1940).

The question remains, however, as to the motivation for the association of the feminine prototype with the judicial process. The answer to this can be approached from several different perspectives, all of which provide a similar answer. Once again the familiar pattern emerges, the combination of complementary elements provides a context for renewal. In this instance the complementary elements consist of the god-king in role of "judge" and the feminine element, represented by the principle of justice, the solar daughter Maat, and/or the Ennead, the *Psḏt*, a figure which, in its feminine personification, is expressed as a homologue of Maat, and which, as a collective, complements the god-king with its plurality.

What is more interesting in this context, however, is the observation that for the Egyptians, the deliberations of the courtroom, the pronouncement of judgement, appear to have been understood as yet another occasion on which the process of renewal took place. And thus the presence of representatives of the feminine prototype is appropriate. And this appears to be true not only of the court of Osiris but also of the court of the Egyptian community where the judge bears the symbol of Bat and later Maat. The process whereby acts are judged as "right" or "wrong" is equated with regeneration. The interaction between the primary judicial official and Maat and/or the Ennead provides the context for the ethical renewal of the one being judged. But then this conclusion need hardly surprise anyone, as the Egyptians themselves placed the judgement of the dead as the initial step in the regeneration of the dead. All of the pieces of the puzzle fit neatly together.

The role of the Ennead as a collective, as the court of the god is thus almost self-evidently analogous to that numerous female deities. In applying the imagery of the feminine prototype to the Ennead, the status of this collective in its relationship to the god is explicated and, invertly, in differentiating the components of the *Psḏt* as goddess into a divine collective the deity is provided with another kind of complement, that of the plurality of his *entourage*.

The personification of the Ennead as a goddess provides an example of the systematic associative logic of the Egyptians. What to us may appear contradictory is, when examined in a larger context, the expression of a congruent line of reasoning based on a well developed system of categorization. The examination of this system and its application to our various objects of study is one approach toward achieving a holistic view of ancient Egyptian thought.

BIBLIOGRAPHY

ALLEN, J.P., 1984. *The Inflection of the Verb in the Pyramid Texts.* Bibliotheca Aegyptiaca, Vol. Two. Udena Publications. Malibu.

ALLEN, T.G., 1974. *The Book of the Dead.* Studies in Ancient Oriental Civilization. No. 37. University of Chicago Press. Chicago.

ALTENMÜLLER, B., 1975. *Synkretismus in den Sargtexten.* Göttinger Orientforschungen. IV. Reihe: Ägypten. Otto Harrassowitz. Wiesbaden.

BAINES, J., 1984. *Fecundity Figures.* Aris & Phillips. Warminster.

BARTA, W., 1973. *Untersuchungen zu Götterkreis der Neunheit.* Münchner Ägypologische Studien, Band 28. Munich.

BRUNNER, H., 1982. "Neunheit." *Lexikon der Ägyptologie*, Band IV, col. 473-480.

ENGLUND, G., 1987. "Gifts to the Gods - a necessity for the preservation of the cosmos and life. Theory and practice." *Gifts to the Gods. Proceedings of the Uppsala Symposium 1985.* Boreas 15. Uppsala. pp. 57-66.

- 1989. "Gods as a Frame of Reference." In the present volume pp. 7-28.

GARDINER, A.H., 1932. *Late Egyptian Stories.* Bibliotheca Aegyptiaca, Vol. 1. Bruxelles.

GOEDICKE, H., 1986. "Symbolische Zahlen." *Lexikon der Ägyptologie*, Band VI, col. 128-129.

GRAEFE, E., 1986. "Horus der zehnte Gott der "Neunheit"." *Hommages à François Daumas*, Vol. II, pp. 345-349. Publication de la recherche. Université de Montpellier. Montpellier.

GRDSELOFF, B., 1940. "L'insigne du grand juge égyptien." *Annales du Service des Antiquités de l'Egypte*, Vol. 40:1, pp. 185-202.

GRIESHAMMER, R., 1970. *Das Jenseitsgericht in den Sargtexten.* Ägyptologische Abhandlungen, Band 20. Otto Harrassowitz. Wiesbaden.

GRIFFITHS, J., 1959. "Some Remarks on the Enneads of the Gods." *Orientalia*, Vol. 28, pp. 34-56.

- 1960. *The Conflict of Horus & Seth.* Liverpool University Press. Liverpool.

GUGLIELMI, W., 1982. "Personifikation". *Lexikon der Ägyptologie*, Band IV, col. 978-987.

HELCK, W., 1981. "Maat". *Lexikon der Ägyptologie*, Band III, col. 1110-1119.

HORNUNG, E., 1971. *Der Eine und die Vielen.* Wissenschaftliche Buchgesellschaft. Darmstadt.

- 1979. *Das Totenbuch der Ägypter.* Bibliotek der alten Welt. Artemis Verlag. Zürich and Munich.

KEES, H., 1941. *Der Götterglaube im alten Aegypten*. Mitteilungen der Vorderasiatisch-Aegyptischen Gesellschaft. 45. Band. Leipzig.

KUHLMANN, K., 1977. *Der Thron im alten Ägypten*. Tübingen.

LEGRAIN, G., 1929. *Les Temples de Karnak*. Brussels.

LICHTHEIM, M. 1973. *Ancient Egyptian Literature. Vol. I: The Old and Middle Kingdoms*. University of California Press. Berkeley, Los Angeles and London.

MORENZ, S., 1973. *Egyptian Religion*. Methuen & Co. Ltd. London.

NAVILLE, E., 1896. *The Temple of Deir el-Bahari. The Ebony Shrine. Northern Half of the Middle Platform*. Part II. Plates XXV-LV. Egypt Exploration Fund. Fourteenth Memoir. London.

NELSON, H., 1981. *The Great Hypostyle Hall at Karnak* Vol. I, Part 1. University of Chicago Oriental Institute Publications. Volume 106. University of Chicago Press. Chicago.

SÄVE-SÖDERBERGH, T., 1977. "Götterkreise." *Lexikon der Ägyptologie*, Band II, col. 686-695.

SEEBER, C., 1976. *Untersuchungen zur Darstellung des Totengerichts im Alten Ägypten*. Münchner Ägyptologische Studien, Band 35. Munich.

STEWART, H.M., 1976. *Egyptian Stelae, Reliefs and Painting from the Petrie Collection*, Part One: The New Kingdom. Aris & Phillips. Warminster.

TROY, L. 1986. *Patterns of Queenship in Ancient Egyptian Myth and History*. Boreas 14. Uppsala.

- 1989. Have a Nice Day! In this volume Part two.

te VELDE, H., 1984. Relations and Conflicts between Egyptian Gods, particularly in the Divine Ennead of Heliopolis. *Struggles of Gods. Papers of the Groningen Work Group for the Study of the History of Religions*. Mouton Publishers. Berlin-New York-Amsterdam. pp. 239-257.

PART TWO

Bergen 1988

Ragnhild Bjerre Finnestad
Religion as a Cultural Phenomenon:
Introduction to the Symposium in Bergen May 26 - 27 1988

The participants of the symposium held in Bergen May 1988 were requested to apply a perspective on religion which sees religion as a phenomenon integrated in culture. By way of introduction I want to make a comment on this approach and its place within the discipline of the History of Religion.

The discipline offers a wide choice of approaches to religion, entailing various definitions of religion, different aims for the study, different problems to solve, and different material bases for the study. Since the 1950s, however, a certain line of development, as regards approaches, can be discerned. There is a tendency towards an ever growing preference for a type of approach that includes a broader cultural base for the investigation of religion. [1]

Earlier research on religion aimed on the whole at describing religion as it appears "as such", and prescribed an approach that studied it more or less abstracted from its cultural environment. The specifically religious phenomena such as myth, cult, sacred institutions, were not explained with reference to their wider socio-cultural functional and ideological contexts.

Moreover, the kind of sources frequently resorted to for information was textual, and primarily written. There were many reasons for this, some of which were of a practical kind, while others were due to the particular implied view of religion. In any case, the outcome of this choice was that it was primarily the values and customs of the religious scholars and literates that were studied and implicitly (or explicitly) deemed as most "legitimate" or "authentic" expressions of religion. But religious scholars are as a rule relatively few, and though their influence on religion is greater than their number would suggest, it is not sufficient to justify disregarding the religious values and customs of the major part of society in our discussion of the ancient religion. Also, there are generally frequent discrepancies between textual discourse and practical behaviour - irrespective of social identity; texts and praxis can give diverging and even contradictory information. So, concentrating on the texts alone will lead to a distorting simplification and a curtailed image of religion. Religion will appear no larger and no more complicated than the source material permits.

There is considerably more to be seen when religion is defined as a phenomenon belonging to the whole of culture, integrated into it on all social levels, and differentiated according to these. Thus regarded, religion is expressed in an abundance of forms. This broader perspective of religion has entered the study from the disciplines of Cultural - and Social Anthropology, and testifies to a fruitful cross-disciplinary influence.

The image of a given religion which emerges from this perspective presents religion as a highly heterogeneous phenomenon, socially and culturally differentiated into a complex, multi-valued, inconsistent, even internally contradictory entity. This image is in striking contrast to the one based upon the homogeneous, coherent systems clarified by the religious scholars, who leave, outside the picture, an unruly ocean of "popular misconceptions" and "superstitions" (entrusted to the care of other scholarly disciplines, such as folkloristic studies).

There is another characteristic feature of research which ought to be mentioned. Western culture, to which the majority of the Historians of Religion have belonged, has developed an institutional dicotomy - running parallel to a conceptional distinction - between **religion** and **culture**. This dichotomy is reflected in language, and thus influences all discussion of religion. **Religion** is referred to more or less as an autonomous domain alongside with, and independent of, **culture**. Grantedly, when Historians of Religions became acquainted with non-Western cultures, it was discovered that these do not necessarily make such distinctions. Thus it has been pointed out that most of them, including the ancient Egyptian religion, do not have a word denoting this concept of religion. Notwithstanding this acknowledgement, there was, for a long time, an established research procedure that dealt with religion independently of culture, on the basis of a theory of religion (as a rule tacitly presupposed) that understood religion as a phenomenon existing independently of culture and developing according to its own laws.

The tendency of research in the later decades has, then, moved towards an increasing interest in defining and handling religion as a phenomenon belonging to culture, living its life and developing in a reciprocally conditioned relationship with the culture in its totality. Accordingly, the source material on religion when defined thus, has been expanded to include sources pertaining to this cultural context as well. It is not enough to study the documents for myths, rites, sacred institutions, in cultural and social isolation. The student who studies the particular item of source material, say a myth, isolated from material related to its cultural context, has cut himself off from material that can inform about, or explicate, its message. The message is conditioned by the conceptual universe documented by the total Egyptian culture.

Precisely how the relationship between religion and culture is to be explained theoretically, is a topic of never-ending discussion and disagreement. Without having to delve into the various arguments and conclusions, it will suffice here to point out that the consensus of general opinion is that the relationship is a close one. Whether religion is regarded as a dimension of meaning, or as a sector of activity co-operating with the other sectors, or - regarded according to other models of explanation, is another question.

This close connection is reflected in different ways. Changes in religion can be seen to be correlated with cultural changes. And, in the same manner that culture as a whole is socially differentiated according to economical status, political power, sex, age, etc., so is religion as well. As part of culture it is not exempted from the differentiations of the whole of culture. Thus regarded, religion varies with social variations, - in this perspective, the distinction between **proper**, **authentic** religious expressions and their popular **distortions** appears irrelevant - even though a distinction between **normative** and **popular** religion can be maintained and applied to significant socio-cultural features of religion.[2]

This perspective on religion will uncover many **world views** in a given religion, some of which are mutually exclusive, while others are parallel. The question of what decides the choice of the one or the other, is not a simple one. To a certain extent, it can be answered by a reference to social differentiation. But even each individual person holds contradictory world views to which he adheres without being excessively bothered by the lack of logical consistency involved in this, as they are connected with varying existential situations. Through introspection this will appear to be the case with anyone, so perhaps we ought not make too heavy demands on the logical consistency of the ancient Egyptians.

Finally, I would like to refute an objection that has been raised by some historians of religions against the approach to religion which I have sketched, namely, that it is "reductionistic", in the sense that it "reduces" religion to mere culture. The objection abuses the word. It would only be reductionism if culture and society were regarded as the only frames of reference for a definition of religion. There are other frames as well, for instance, psychological ones. It would, however, also be reductionism if one denies religion, culturally defined, cultural distinctiveness, even if it may be difficult to define this cultural distinctiveness more precisely. But unless we attribute to the cultural phenomena we label "religious", characteristic features, the label is not justified. By analogy, art is equally difficult to characterize as a cultural phenomenon in its own right. But all definitions of art are implicitly or explicitly based on the presumption that art can actually be regarded as a distinct cultural phenomenon. This part of the discussion ties up with the concern of earlier generations of historians of religions who wanted to describe religion "as such"; but from the wider cultural perspective on religion, it has to do with the need for differentiating culture.

There are grounds for describing religion as a cultural phenomenon, possessing its own distinctive character and meaning. These grounds exist for the cultural- and social anthropologist as well. The anthropologists have often been concerned with structure and function, and to a lesser degree, with contents of meaning - a point of issue to which the historians of religions have paid greater attention.[3] To the anthropologists the historians of religions sometimes seem to over-dramatize religion when they present their analyses of religious meaning; and to a certain extent the criticism might be taken to heart - after all religion belongs to everyday life. But even everyday life has dimensions of meaning other than the pragmatical and material ones. Nor will clarifying the structural and functional relations give sufficient information as regards questions that should be of importance to the anthropologist, such as the question of **why** do religious traditions have the function and the structural position that they do? Religious values can wield a stupendous power, even in secular societies. They can explain and motivate the social order, with greater conviction than other explanations and motivations. They can endow legitimacy or illegitimacy through an authority that outbids other authorities. By definition, its explanations, motivations, legitimations, and rejections, are regarded as fundamental and ultimate. If we want to account for the power which religious beliefs and rites notoriously exert, when they are adhered to, we shall have to study their contents of meaning as well. Many anthropologists have, of course, realized this; I would like to quote R. M. Keesing: we have looked at religious beliefs and rites "often, as expressions of 'something else': as modes of adapting human behaviour to the demands of an ecosystem or pressures of demography, as 'celestializations' that maintain the power of a ruling class or disguise the subordination of women. Such questions need not be left behind. But we need now look at religious systems in their own right: to ask why humans have populated their universe with unseen beings and powers, spun out mythic accounts of ancient and wondrous happenings, created elaborate rituals that must be performed correctly if human life is to prosper. What gives religion its emotional power, its central place in human experience? Religions may serve the purposes of adaptation and earthly politics; but they seem to meet deep needs in relating the lives of individuals and the ways of communities to ultimate concerns, a world beyond that of immediate experience".[4]

I shall not discuss his definition of religion. But his words can be taken as an underlining of the main inducement to our symposia, namely the need for cross-disciplinary exchange of points of departure. and procedures of study. It is a need shared by all who study this complicated phenomenon that we call human culture.

NOTES

1) For a survey, see F. WHALING, ed., *Contemporary Approaches to the Study of Religions*. I: The Humanities; II: The Social Sciences (Religion and Reason 27, 28), Berlin, New York, Amsterdam 1984, 1985.

2) An impression of this discussion is given by P.H. VRIJHOF and J. WAARDENBURG, eds., *Official and Popular Religion* (Religion and Society 19), Haag, Paris, New York 1979.

3) Although interpretive theory has naturally been an important issue in anthropology. For a discussion with reference to both earlier and contemporary theory, see e.g. R.C. ULIN, *Understanding Cultures*. Perspectives in Anthropology and Social Theory, Austin 1984.

4) *Cultural Anthropology*. A Contemporary Perspective, New York 1981.

Gertie Englund
The Treatment of Opposites
in Temple Thinking and Wisdom Literature

Pondering on the Egyptian religion, on similarities and differences between theoretical, theological teaching and popular applications, I was struck by a dissimilarity in the treatment of opposites in the temple material and the wisdom literature. The problem of opposites has been treated before from a psychological point of view (Jacobsohn, 1955) but will be approached here from a different angle.

The temple material represents the thinking of the Egyptian scholars and is presented in texts and iconography originating in the cultural centres of the temples and found in temples and tombs. Even though this material is not cast in a theoretical, analytical mould, it is the most abstract and theoretical expression of Egyptian thinking at our disposal. The world view which lies implicit in this material can be characterized as empirical and intuitive and yet at the same time highly speculative. It is a kind of implicit philosophy as it represents a search for knowledge in order to structure human experiences. The thinking of the temple was all-encompassing and was the synthesis of religion, psychology, and natural science. It also included political science, as it comprised the ideology of kingship. The wisdom literature on the other hand emanates from the temple thinking. In it the knowledge of the temple is transposed onto another social context. The wisdom literature is a practical application of the more abstract theoretical ideas of the temple. Common to both is the great principle pervading all things Egyptian - i.e. **Maat**.

1. The temple material

The temple material works very much with opposites. It constantly opposes concepts like **chaos** and **cosmos, night** and **day, death** and **life, Osiris** and **Re, female** and **male.** In this binary thinking the two opposed concepts are considered to be complementary and each pair of concepts forms a unit. The binary concepts exemplified above were expressed in antithetical pairs of words but binary concepts can also be expressed by means of dualities for example 'the two lands'. Whichever way of expression chosen, it is the relation and interaction between the two poles and the integration of them (*coincidentia oppositorum*) that constitutes the unity, a living, creative, and life-giving unit.

Let us take a few examples to illustrate it. Let us take some of the images of the Egyptians for they who were wont to express their thinking in images have of course created symbols for it. Let us start with *sm3-t3wy* 'the union of the two lands' (Fig. 1). What we see is

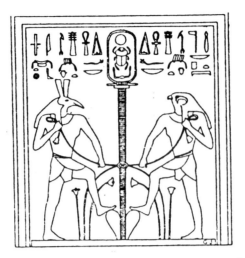

Fig. 1. The union of the Two Lands. (Kuhlmann, K.P., 1977. Der Thron im alten Ägypten. Glückstadt. p. 56)

- an image of the respiratory organ with its **single** windpipe and its **two** lungs; this organ has **one** function, the respiration, that consists of **two** movements, the breathing in and the breathing out; it thus is a symbol for unity and duality both in form and function.

- **two** figures, antithetically placed on either side of this symbol: Horus and Seth representing the good and the evil, the positive and the negative, or the constructive and the destructive.

- further **two** plants, also placed antithetically; they are the emblems of the two parts of the kingdom, Upper and Lower Egypt that together form the **one**, united kingdom of Egypt.

- the two figures making a knot with the plants they are holding around the windpipe in the center; the knot is an image of the integration of the opposites into a solid unit.

The whole group constitutes the emblem of the united kingdom and was placed as a decoration on the base of the throne. The symbol can be given a political interpretation but

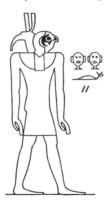

Fig. 2. 'He with the two faces.' (te Velde, H., 1967. Seth, God of Confusion. Leiden. p. 69)

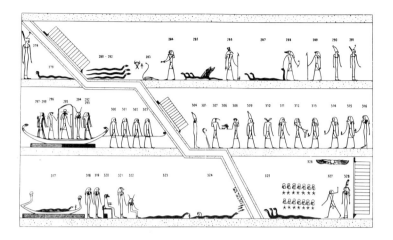

Fig. 3. The Sokar land. (Hornung, E., 1963. Das Amduat I. Wiesbaden. Vierte Stunde)

it is also valid in other fields, psychologically for instance. If the kingdom is to function, the two parts of it must cooperate, if the executive power of kingship is to work properly, the two opposite forces must be harmonized, if man is to be complete, he must know the two sides of his nature.

Another good representation of binary unity is *Ḥrwy.fy*, 'He with the two faces' (Fig. 2). This image represents one body with two faces, one Horus face and one Seth face, i.e. a figure where two opposite forces are integrated, the good and the evil, the light and the dark, the intellectual side and the instinctive one. *Ḥrwy.fy* is an image of the union of the forces of both Horus and Seth (Kees 1923, p. 44).

Horus and Seth are two separate gods in mythology but they are worshipped as one in local cults (Kees 1923, p. 14). Despite their lasting conflict Barta (1973, p. 175) does not consider them as really opposed ennemies but gods associated in symbiosis. When they appear as two separate units, they represent the two principles that, according to the Egyptian concept of life, make up reality. They divide the world between them in two parts (*psšty*), each being the lord of one part of Egypt, Seth, the lord of *t3 šmˀ* and *dšrt*, Horus, the lord of *t3 mḥw* and *Kmt*. Further divisions occur as the mounds belonging to each of them, *i3wt Ḥr* and *i3wt Stš*. Also the primaeval flood that surrounds the world is divided into two, *ḳbḥw Ḥr* and *ḳbḥw Stš*. (For these portions and divisions see te Velde 1967, pp. 60-61 with references.)

In *Ḥrwy.fy*, the opposites are integrated in a higher unit. This figure occurring in Amduat (2nd hour, upper register, no. 138) and in the Book of Gates (10th hour, upper register; 11th hour, middle register) seems to represent the mystery of totality of the other world (cf. te Velde 1967, p. 70).

These two images show the integration of opposites into a living unit. Now everything within the created world functions as a part of the totality and is a separate unit within plurality. Everything contains its opposite in conformity with the original unit that in itself comprised two potential opposite poles whose interaction was to give rise to creation.

Let us take a few examples of this and start with the Sokar land (Fig. 3). The Sokar land (Amduat, 4th and 5th hours) is situated in the very depth of the Duat on the border of chaos. It is the darkest area of the Duat, its darkness is so dense that the light of Re cannot dissipate it as in the other parts of the Duat. Thus the entities who inhabit this Sokar land cannot see each other nor perceive the sun god on his passage except by his voice. The entities of this region are further immobile and fixed in their places. There is, however, a potential sprouting capacity contained in this darkness and this passivity. There is an image with stars and sun disks above a serpent with three heads over which there hovers a winged sun disk (Amduat, 4th hour, 3rd reg.). The accompanying text says: "It is the secret image of *Imhet*. There is light in it daily until the birth of Chepri who comes out of the faces of (the serpent) 'He who moves'. Then Chepri moves away." Dynamic forces and light are thus contained in the fixedness and the impenetrable darkness as the liberating and generating factor that will give rise to the new life.

The gods are often the units of integrated opposites. Let us start with Horus. Among all the Horus forms attached to different localities Horus of Letopolis is particularly interesting in this context. Horus of Letopolis comprises two opposites, two aspects of himself (Junker 1942). There is Horus who has not his two eyes, *Horus-mkhenty-n-irty*, i.e. the sources of light, the sun and the moon, and this Horus form must represent the unity of the godhead before creation, before the coming into existence of duality. There is also Horus who has his two eyes, *Horus-mkhenty-irty*, which represents the godhead after the differentiation process has started, and duality, the first step on the way to plurality, has come into existence and transformed the unity of the godhead into the creator god who manifests himself in the light. These Horus forms correspond to Atum as sole god and Atum as triune god together with Shu and Tefnut.

Re is also an integrated unit of opposites. The strong sun god becomes weak. After spending his life-giving force all day from his birth in the east he is worn out by the end of the day and passes the western horizon leaning on his stick like an old man. He must find new strength and this is obtained in meeting and joining this other side of him, his passive,

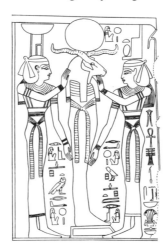

Fig. 4. Re-Osiris. (Piankoff, A. & Rambova, N., 1954. The Tomb of Ramses VI. Bollingen Series XL p. 34)

inactive, immobile side, which the texts call his corpse, i.e. Osiris. It is in the integrated figure Re-Osiris (Fig. 4) that the sun god is regenerated and finds his new life force that will enable him to carry on his task of maintaining creation. This union of Re and Osiris in one is the synthesis of the speculations of the New Kingdom about the unity in the godhead, about the integration of aspects that are apparently each other's opposites, Re, the light day with its dynamism, and Osiris, the night side, the lethargy, all that is bound and immobile. They are, however, not opposed to each other but function as the two complementary sides of a totality, both aspects of which are necessary for the whole to subsist. The union of the two sides is the condition for the regeneration of energy necessary for the maintenance of creation.

Hathor also integrates opposites, Hathor the splendid, golden goddess, life-spending, mother and companion of the sun, the lady of music and dance, who can transform herself into the terrible, destructive force of Sekhmet.

These are just a few of the numerous examples of this phenomenon in the material emanating from the temples. They can all be brought back to the chaos-cosmos problem of which they represent different aspects.

2. The wisdom literature

Let us now leave the temple material proper and go over to the wisdom literature. The wisdom literature was related to the temple. The instructions were written by educated people belonging to the class of scribes formed by the temple and this literature was used to form future scribes during their stay at the temple schools. Also the instructions work with the problem of opposites and here as well it is a question of chaos versus cosmos but transposed onto the level of the praxis of life. The idea of Maat, structure, order, harmony, balance, is transformed into rules of morality and ethics.

2.1 The opposition of the Silent One and the Hothead

In the wisdom literature the two opposites are presented in terms of different types of human beings, called the the Silent One and the Hothead. The types can also be called the Cool One and the Hot One, and in the last of the instructions, Pap. Insinger, there are two new denominations, the Wise One and the Fool or the Man of God and the Fool. Whatever the types are called, the description is always the same at all periods. The ideal man is always during almost 3000 years characterized as: silent, moderate, sensible, completely adapted to a way of life approved by society. His opposite is characterized by being guided by his emotions and instincts which leads to a behaviour disapproved by society. It would be too long to go into detailed descriptions of the two types here. In short the Wise One is characterized by self-control, moderation, modesty, kindness, generosity, discretion, truthfulness, and serenity and the Fool by the lack of these virtues which shows itself in gluttony, greed, arrogance, bad temper, and vindictiveness as M. Lichtheim puts it in her analysis of the two types in Pap. Insinger (1979, p.291). This definition holds good for the Silent One and the Hothead at all different periods. Typical of the Hothead is thus his egoism and his aggressivity and the fact that he follows his emotions and instincts without resistance whereas the Silent One is disciplined and altruistic.

I consider it to be completely unthinkable that an Egyptian would ever have got the idea to unite the Silent One and the Hothead in one single figure as was the case with Horus and Seth in the temple iconography despite the fact that the Hothead and the Silent One actually correspond to the Horus-type and the Seth-type respectively. That this is so is seen in the so-called Dream Book (Chester Beatty III recto 1-11) that presents two categories of human beings referred to as the Horus and the Seth types corresponding exactly to the two types that are described in the instructions.

Only at the very end of the Egyptian civilization do we find the notion that the wise man is not an absolutely perfect human being but that his virtues may fail him under certain conditions, so that he becomes a fool (Pap. Insinger 34/12, Lichtheim 1979, p. 292). This does not of course necessarily mean that the Wise one unites and integrates the two sides of himself in a living unit but only that he alternates between the poles within himself. The relation between the poles is, however also indicated in this papyrus: "Before the god the strong and the weak are a joke" (Pap. Insinger 11/20).

In the earlier instructions the two types are not only opposed to each other but they are irreconcilable opposites. One had to keep away from the Hothead, if one belonged to the category of the Silent Ones sanctioned by society. This comes through very clearly, if we look at the advice given in the instructions as to how the Silent One should behave, when he comes across the Hothead. The Silent One must stay away from the Hothead on the physical level: "Keep your distance from him", "Withdraw from him, leave him alone", "Don't leap to join such a one" says Amenemope (XVIII 6-7, V 16, XIII 8). Ani is of the same opinion and gives the advice: "Do not enter into a crowd, if you find it in an uproar and about to come to blows. Don't pass anywhere near by. Keep away from their tumult" (8.15). Ptahhotep recommends against having him for a neighbour (Pt.480) and Ani (5.10) says: "The wise lives off the house of the fool".

If, however, in the course of life one happens to come close to the Hothead, one must not mix with him, not force oneself to greet him for that might injure one's own heart, one must not speak falsely to him for the god abhors it and the heart and the tongue must be in complete accord (Amenemope XIII 11-18). One must not converse with a heated man so as to befriend a hostile man (Amenemope XV 13-14), nor speak rudely to him but only hold oneself back (Ani 6.15).

This pattern of how to react is, however, not the only possible one when the Silent One encounters the Hothead. There are cases when the wise teacher recommends a different behaviour. Ptahhotep envisages a case where the Silent One wants to probe the character of a friend in order to find out what a kind of person he actually is. But then "If he does a thing that annoys you, be yet friendly with him, don't attack; be restrained, don't let fly, don't answer with hostility, neither part from him nor attack him; his time does not fail to come, one does not escape what is fated" (Pt. Maxim 33). So the recommendation is not always just to turn away. The advice is not to judge but to leave the judgement to the lords of fate. There is also a humourously pragmatic advice for those who are faced with an ill-tempered master: "Do not talk back to an angry superior, let him have his way; speak sweetly when he speaks sourly. It's the remedy that calms the heart" (Ani 9.8).

There is only one instruction that differs in this respect and that is the Instruction addressed to King Merikare. In it we reach up to the sphere of royal affairs and to that of the kingship ideology that were dominated and dictated directly by the temple. The king admonishes his son to fight the evil and the revolts that he comes across in accordance with the fact that the first and foremost task of the king is to maintain the Maat order in the world and that he should, for that reason, clear away all chaotic powers that threaten to disturb the established order. "The hothead is an inciter of citizens, he creates factions among the young; if you find that citizens adhere to him, denounce him before the councillors, suppress him, he is a rebel, the talker is a troublemaker for the city. Curb the multitude, suppress its heat" (Merikare 24-27). The instruction for Merikare also contains many recommendations, however, not to exaggerate conflict and aggressivity. "If you are skilled in speech, you will win, the tongue is a king's sword; speaking is stronger than all fighting" (Merikare 32). "Do not kill, it does not serve you" (Merikare 48) and "Don't be evil, kindness is good, make your memorial last through love of you" (Merikare 36-37).

As a comparison it might be interesting to consider how the Horus and Seth motif is treated in three literary works from the Ramesside period, 'The Two Brothers', 'Truth and Falsehood', and 'The Adventures of Horus and Seth'. All three are in accord with the instructions through the fact that the evil, Sethian side is allowed to coexist with the good (cf. Lesko 1986, p.101). They differ, however, from the way the wisdom literature tackles the problem of opposites in that the representatives of the good do not avoid the conflict but fight against the evil.

In the tale of 'The Two Brothers' Inpu takes up the Seth role through lack of perspicacity in the conflict with his brother Bata. However, he rapidly realizes his mistake, takes vengeance on the culprit and then becomes the collaborator of good. That is why he can in the end be rewarded with the highest office in the country and become king of Egypt.

In 'Truth and Falsehood' and in 'The Adventures of Horus and Seth' the tale follows the mythological prototype as presented by the temple more closely. In both, good takes up the fight with evil. In 'Truth and Falsehood' evil is punished, Falsehood is bereft of his eyes and has to take over the disdained task as doorkeeper that Truth had occupied. In 'The Adventures of Horus and Seth' good is given its rightful heritage whereas evil is not punished but raised up to be the protector of Re as part of the divine order, as a necessary counterpart of good (Lichtheim 1983, p. 124).

There is thus a different message contained in the instructions and in the literary works. The message of the instructions seems to have been: keep away from those with a hot character, don't mix with them, that is the best way of supporting Maat in the world, whereas that of the literary works seems to have been: if you come across injustice in life, do something about it, don't use violent methods though, but go about it with cunning so that the antagonist traps himself and pronounces his own judgement.

2.2 The one-sidedness of the wisdom literature

The kingship ideology thus gives a subtle interpretation of how to react in different circumstances, taking into account all sides of the problem, making room for the necessity to intervene with strength and even violence, if the circumstances demand it. The practical philosophy of life as we meet it in the wisdom literature on the other hand opts for the ideal of the Silent One, for the good, for positive and constructive emotions and behaviours. The instructions dissociate markedly from everything that is typical of the Hothead. This is obviously necessary when giving general rules for good behaviour addressed to the people as a whole. Onesidedness, however, generally leads to fanaticism that in its turn provokes oppression and persecution. This does not seem to be the case in Egypt. It seems that the onesidedness meant a dissociation and no more. Those belonging to the influential circles were probably always guided by the idea that one must keep one's balance. The idea is well expressed in Pap. Insinger (4.19): "If a wise man is not balanced, his wisdom does not avail".

The fact that balance was such an important idea is connected with the importance of the Maat concept that completely dominated Egyptian thinking during all periods. According to the Maat concept the world from the cosmic to the human level is structured and ordered for the best. To live in accordance with this order established by the gods was to do right and to disturb this order was to do wrong. If, in one's one-sided attitude in favour of good, one started to pursue the Hotheads, that would lead to violence and disturbances that would upset the order so highly esteemed.

Another question also comes to mind and that is how the pupils of these teachers reacted when they were confronted with all the virtues and the decency demanded of them and all the pieces of good advice that inundated them. Pushing hard provokes resistance in the opponent. There were probably young people and even adults who could not stand pressure also in a hierarchic and authoritative society like Egypt, even if the individual by necessity was wont to keep his place in line and follow orders there in a way quite different from here.

We actually have a description of such a conflict in one of the instructions, in the epilogue of Ani (c. 9.10-10.10), where the son and pupil does not at all want to accept the wise words and admonitions of his father and master. The passage presents the conflict between emotionality and reason very well and the difficulties that the master meets with when trying to transmit his knowledge and make a recalcitrant individual accept his ideas. Every human being is lead by his inborn nature, says the son. If the good words of advice correspond to the son's own ideas about life, he can accept them. The virtues presented to him are, however, too numerous and the fact that the pieces of good advice are written on his tongue does not mean that he is going to adhere to them, he says with a certain perspicacity. From the point of view of the father, the problem looks different. In his opinion nature can be tamed and he presents this thought in a long row of splendid similes describing how animals can be made to cast off their natural behaviour and comport themselves as man wants them to according to a pattern set up by man:

> "The savage lion abandons his wrath,
> and comes to resemble the timid donkey.
> The horse slips into its harness,
> obedient it goes outdoors.
> The dog obeys the word,
> and walks behind his master." (Ani c. 10.1-10.5)

Not only animals, however, can adapt themselves to a certain cultural pattern, also human beings from other cultures can be imbued with new patterns:

> "One teaches the Nubian to speak Egyptian
> the Syrian and other strangers too." (Ani c. 10.5-10.10)

From the point of view of the master it is thus nonsense to come and say that everybody is lead by his own nature.

"Say: 'I shall do like all the beasts'
Listen and learn what they do." (Ani c. 10.5-10.10)

The son does not give in but points out once more that the number of virtues demanded of him in order to follow the teaching is too great, it is an impossible enterprise and anyway how can one "alone possess a mind, if the multitudes are foolish" (Ani c. 10.5-10.10).

The father, the wise master, nonetheless persists in his unwavering belief in the importance of culture and its possibilities to influence and transform even the most recalcitrant person:

"The crooked stick left on the ground,
with sun and shade attacking it,
if the carpenter takes it, he straightens it,
makes of it a noble's staff." (Ani c. 10.5-10.10)

This is the first and only time in the Egyptian wisdom literature that the pupil's opinion comes to the fore and that we get a glimpse of the viewpoint of the subject of this indoctrination and his reaction to being pressured to follow the path of wisdom and decency. Accepting the part of the advice of the elders that suits oneself and seems appropriate for the moment, rather than to live as one was taught, as the son Khonsuhotep puts it, not to follow the advice written on one's tongue, is of course a common and pragmatic way of dealing with the wisdom of the elders. This easy-going attitude is probably the best for the majority and it avoids the moral conflicts, the pangs of conscience, that can otherwise be the result for the one who disregards the rules he has learnt to consider as sacred.

Thus even if there were teachers of wisdom who were conscious of the problem that their teaching might cause resistance (cf. Lichtheim 1983, p.63), none of the instructions with one single exception, as far as I can see, has paid any attention to the reaction that is bound to come up as the result of strong pressure. This is what I call the one-sidedness in the instructions. The exception is once again the Instruction addressed to King Merikare, i.e. other standpoints may be expressed in a text related to the kingship ideology dictated by the temple.

"Beware of it! A blow is repaid by its like,
to every action there is a response." (Merikare 122-125)

and

"So no river allows itself to be concealed,
it breaks the channel in which it was hidden." (Merikare 126-127, idem. 75)

2.3 The river that does not allow itself to be hidden Resistance and their possible outlets
The ideal of a good well-adapted citizen as presented in the instructions was not acceptable in all its details by everyone as we saw in the passage from Ani. There must have existed many different degrees of acceptance and rejection of the ideal of virtue of the instructions. Even if the majority of the people accepted and rejected the teaching as it suited them and

thus managed to avoid moral problems, a demanding pattern contributes to the formation of a strong *persona* in the individuals constituting an obstacle on the way to self-knowledge and an integrated personality. The demands imposed on the individual lead to a repression of all that does not correspond to the ideal. Now it is, however, exactly as the intruction for Merikare says: "No river allows itself to be concealed". Repressed emotions and reactions generally emerge from the subconscious and make trouble sooner or later, not with everyone but with certain indiviuals. I believe that the great upheaval during the First Intermediate Period beside the political and climatic causes and the related economic causes also had a psychological background of this kind. The literary sources are evidence of this.

If the instructions were onesided, the thinking of the temple was not, and those in leading positions must have been aware of the problem with the "river that does not allow itself to be concealed", if not from the very beginning, at least from the Middle Kingdom and onwards. In some way or other they are most likely to have tried to build in some safety-valves into the system in order to prevent explosions. Are there any to be discerned? Are mock battles in the form of dances and boat fights enough to let out the aggressivity that was normally repressed? Are the drunkenness and overwhelming excitement during the public manifestations of the temple festivals enough to counterbalance the strong rules of decorum that governed everyday life?

Besides the group for whom decorum is a means to check overpowering emotions and instincts there will probably also have existed a group of people who had other aspirations than to live a well-adapted life according to the rules, only doing their imposed duties, i.e. the type of people who want to go beyond the frame of the established system, those with a searching mind who want to go further and reach other goals.

I suppose ways were open for the latter category. J. Assmann (1983 passim) is of the opinion that there was an intense discourse going on during the New Kingdom and I can see no reason why this can not have been the case even earlier although there is no surviving evidence. According to Assmann there are two trends in the hymns of the New Kingdom tombs, the reproductive type i.e. the type that uses old traditional material, and the productive type, i.e. the type that is innovative, presenting new ideas and new expressions. This would indicate, according to Assmann, that the tomb owner had been in contact with or belonged to a the stratum where the discourse took place. This stratum had access to the knowledge assembled in the *House of Life* belonging to the higher priesthood. It is the acquired knowledge of the tomb owners and their personal understanding that breathes in their hymns.

3. System and subsystems - the importance of the complementary pattern

The point of departure for these reflexions was the difference in the treatment of the problem of opposites in the instructions and in temple learning. It is of course not at all surprising that the texts destined for the majority of the population show onesidedness and advice keeping aloof from the hot, egoistic, aggressive type of man. It is not possible to go out to an unprepared mind that first of all needs to be tamed and formed into an adapted and mature civilized being and say that everything is fundamentally one and the same. It is impossible to tell him: "You are both Horus and Seth". No cultural system gives such a double message in its more popular forms.

The temple that seeks to penetrate the principles of life and whose knowledge is reserved for a minority of well prepared individuals can represent quite a different view. That is why the temple can have recourse to and recommend emotions and behaviour that must be kept in check, if society is to function properly. What must be prohibited for people in general can be useful for other aims than those of everyday life, as for instance, to confront aggression which is the foremost duty of the king but strongly denounced in the rest of society. Another example is wine drinking even to the point of drunkenness that occurred in connexion with rites intended to go beyond the limits of ordinary consciousness and reach other levels of the mind as in the temples festivals e.g. the feast of drunkenness in Denderah and the beautiful feast of the valley in Thebes. The learned in the temples had apparently reached the insight that the great forces in themselves are neutral and that it is the way they are used that makes them bad or good. Thoughts of this kind are to be found in the texts as e.g. in the Book of Gates (3rd hour, upper register), where the water of the fire lake is a horrible experience to certain entities and makes them flee, whereas it is experienced as inoffensive by the just.

Cosmos would not exist if chaos had not generated cosmos. When the force of chaos passes the *3ht*-border into cosmos, it becomes positive, structuring, and good, whereas the same force, personified in the Apophis serpent, is destructive and a continual threat for the created world.

I would now like to apply the principles that emanates from the temple material and to continue reasoning according to the antithetic pattern of complementary parts integrated into units. I would like to consider the complex consisting of the Hothead and the Silent One i.e. the wisdom literature and its onesidedness as a subsystem applicable to the practical level of everyday life and the thinking of the temple as a complementary subsystem applicable to greater contexts and say that the two together form one system. In this larger system emotions, common sense, and theoretical speculation are all taken into consideration and put in a well balanced relation to each other interacting so as to create and maintain order.

The thinking of the temple is centered around the idea of Maat and it is its main concern to bring about and to preserve Maat. The subsystem that the wisdom literature represents is also on this level and inspite of its onesidedness supporting the concept of Maat. Aggressivity and disturbing behaviour are rebuffed. However, no system no matter how well designed will be able to check the real rascals like Pa-neb in Deir el-Medina.

It is a kind of pragmatic thinking that we meet. Age-old experience had led to the insight that the human community functions better the more there are who live according to the ideal of the instructions. It is simple common sense that made them put the Silent One forward as the ideal for man to follow.

As long as the system with the temple thinking and the thinking of the wisdom literature functioned together, all went well in the country. However, the system got out of balance a few times. These are the so-called intermediary periods. During these periods, especially during the first, the Hothead prevailed and the great upheaval broke out, when all standards were cast aside and everything was turned upside down.

Once the system was intentionally overthrown. And that time it was the king himself who brought about the upheaval, a king who had probably not realized what he inherited. It was doomed to be only a short paranthesis in the long history of Egypt. What Achnaton did was to eliminate one pole from existence. Under his reign the temple thinking paid no attention to the regenerating capacity of the night and to the importance of the integration of opposites. And this onesidedness brought with it a dogmatic and fanatic attitude leading to accusation and persecution.

In the postulated great system the subsystem represented by the wisdom literature dominates society as a whole. It is this system that people knew of and lived with. The temple system on the other hand was the hidden system, unknown by the people. And yet the temple teaching had an important position in the totality as a complementary subsystem.

It is astounding how thin the stratum must have been that was concerned with the temple teaching. It can only have been a reality for a small fraction of the literate elite. The wisdom literature with its different message was intended for the majority of the scribes and through them for the people as a whole. For the majority of the population the onesided standards known from the instructions were valid. The importance of the integration of opposites can only have been known by a handful of higher priests who participated in the discourse on theological matters and in the creation of the texts that have hitherto dominated our comprehension of Egyptian thinking.

BIBLIOGRAPHY

Amduat, see HORNUNG

ASSMANN, J., 1983. *Re und Amun. Die Krise des polytheistischen Weltbilds im Ägypten der 18.-20. Dynastie*. Orbis Biblicus et Orientalis, Band 51. Freiburg, Göttingen.

BARTA, W., 1973. *Untersuchungen zum Götterkreis der Neunheit*. Münchner Ägyptologische Studien 28.

Book of Gates, see HORNUNG

HORNUNG, E., 1963. *Das Amduat. Die Schrift des verborgenen Raumes*. Ägyptologische Abhandlungen, Band 7. Wiesbaden.

- 1979-1980. *Das Buch von den Pforten des Jenseits*. Teil I, II. Aegyptiaca Helvetica 7-8. Genève.

KEES, H., 1923. *Horus und Seth als Götterpaar*. Leipzig.

JACOBSOHN, H., 1955. 'Das Gegensatzproblem im altägyptischen Mythos'. *Studien zur analytischen Psychologie C.G.Jungs*, II. Festschrift zum 80. Geburtstag von C.G.Jung. Zürich.

JUNKER, H., 1942. *Der sehende und der blinde Gott*. München.

KEES, H., 1923. *Horus und Seth als Götterpaar*.

LESKO, L., 1986. 'Three Late Egyptian Stories Reconsidered'. *Egyptian Studies in Honor of Richard A. Parker*. Ed. Leonard H.Lesko. Brown University Press. 1986.

LICHTHEIM, M., 1979. 'Observations on Papyrus Insinger'. *Studien zu altägyptischen Lebenslehren*. Orbis Biblicus et Orientalis 28. Freiburg, Göttingen.

- 1983. *Late Egyptian Wisdom Literature in the International Context. A Study of Demotic Instructions*. Orbis Biblicus et Orientalis 52. Freiburg, Göttingen.

Ragnhild Bjerre Finnestad
The Pharaoh and the "Democratization" of Post-mortem Life

This paper is an expanded comment given in response to the paper delivered by Jørgen Podemann Sørensen, *Divine Access: The So-called Democratization of Egyptian Funerary Literature as a Socio-Cultural Process*. The comment concerns a contiguous problem of inquiry to his, namely, the problem of how to establish the social identity of the *pharaoh* as a category of post-mortem life. This is a task that can be attacked in different ways; mine being one of referring to Egyptian concepts of social **self**. My paper thus concentrates on one specific line of reasoning and has, moreover, the simplified and pointed form of an argument.

To resume life in the cosmos after death was, according to Egyptian thought, a divine capacity, and the king was the only mortal who possessed it, who was *ntrj* and, like the gods, could transform himself into new cosmic forms and continue to live in the Egyptian world.

This ideology is found in the Pyramid Texts, which belonged to royal tombs and were designed for the pharaoh. But it was included in the later Coffin Texts of the noblemen and higher civil servants, and in the still later Book of the Dead, which could be found in the tomb of every one who could afford it.

Thus this particular source material pertaining to pharaonic post-mortem life can be seen to have had an ever widening social distribution. "Democratization" is a label often applied by Western research to this widening social distribution of mortological literature which gives the pharaoh access to post-mortem cosmic life.

This development has attracted much attention in research. It obviously signifies more than a mere increase of source material, as this particular literature makes its owner like the gods, in the sense that he has access to the divine cosmic life after death as presented in the texts and illustrations. The gradual spread of this literature has therefore been interpreted as a sign that even "private" man (to use a Western concept) was granted this royal privilege of attaining the divine cosmic life which renews itself after death.

There are other kinds of continuity of life after death, according to Egyptian thought, which are not "royal", such as that of existing in the social remembrance - being kept alive through posthumous recollection,[1] or, that of living in the children to come.[2] But partaking of the life of the world and its overall capacity for renewing itself, demonstrated in its biogenetic cycles, is a "royal prerogative". The kind of life after death that is attributed to the king *qua* king comprises the cosmic dimension of the entire Egyptian world.

This cosmic feature of the "royal" life after death must be stressed; it is important for our explanation of the "democratization" process and should be focussed on in our discussion of the latter. Lack of differentiation between the various notions of post-mortem life will veil the issue. The discussion is not about the preconditions for access to **any** kind of "eternal life", but to the all-comprising, cyclically regenerating life of the Egyptian world. The discussion is about the capacity to merge with the divine power of life inherent in all being and which enables the pharaoh to transform himself into other cosmic forms of life after death. Expressed in the mythological language of the Pyramid Texts it is about the state of having "eaten" the gods of the Egyptian world.[3] Expressions like "royal monopoly of eternal life" will only hit the target when this identification of "eternal life" has been made.

In research, the wider social distribution of the royal mortuary ideology witnessed in literature and imagery has, then, been understood in accordance with a central concept in Western social ideology, namely, as a **democratization**; and because of the special functions of this literature and imagery it is a democratization not only as regards possession of this literature but even as regards possession of the post-mortem life connected with the king. The argument goes as follows: Originally, only the pharaoh had access to the cosmic life after death; gradually, however, access was widened to include ordinary Egyptians as well. They acquired royal status. This is the implication of the transference of royal literature to "private" persons.

An acquisition of royal status has also been seen reflected in the decorations of tombs belonging to persons existing more or less in the proximity to the pharaoh.[4] Also architectonic features of royal tombs can be seen to be transferred to "private" tombs, such as the pyramid form, a form associated with the symbolism of cosmic renewal.[5]

My own point of view on the "democratization" process takes as its point of departure the question: what is the social identity of **the pharaoh** as a category of post-mortem life, applied to "private" man? **Royal status** obviously lends more than social glamour - as it is connected with participation in divine life, i.e. the life which is expressed as the whole world. It remains to define more precisely the concept of social identity involved in this category when it is associated with the bestowal of divine post-mortem life.

However, this question cannot be answered by the mortuary literature alone - its language is mythological. We have to consult other material, material that can explicate the mythology. I will, therefore, look at royal status from the greater, integrated whole of pharaonic ideology. From this it appears that the basic socio-ideological identity of the pharaoh is that of **the Egyptian people functioning as a community**. When it is stated that the task of the pharaoh is to recreate and maintain the life of the world of the Egyptians, it is not this individual, private person that is thought of; it is the Egyptian people as a community that creates and maintains its cosmic and social world. In Western research this identity of the pharaoh is paraphrased through the concept of **delegation of authority**: The king delegates this job to others, since he cannot do it all alone. It may be discussed how apt this paraphrasing is, as it posits an ideological separation between **pharaoh** and **community**. The whole pyramidal social system is, on the ideological level, an expression of the kingship. The king's **divinity** lies embedded in this social reality; it is manifested in the activities of the Egyptian community when it aims at creating and maintaining the life of the Egyptian world. According to the ancient Egyptian mythological world view, the Egyptian cosmos had to be maintained actively and continually by the Egyptian community, conceptualized as king, and the gods in cooperation. The mortological traditions we are discussing should be understood against the background of this social identity. It explains the pharaonic "Unsterblichkeit".

There are two social units which stand out prominently in the material on Egyptian religion. The one is the community of the Egyptian people; the other is the community of the family. Any Egyptian, alive as well as dead, belonged to both of them. The community of the people, then, is what **pharaoh** is according to the socio-religious status documented by the total, variegated source material for Egyptian culture. The family is represented by the **father**. These two identities are also reflected in the mortuary source material; it centres on the life of the pharaoh and the life of the father.

The thesis at which I arrive, from this socio-religious definition of pharaonic status, is that the category of pharaoh in our mortuary sources represents one of these two central identities of Egyptian man. Alive and dead he partakes in the Egyptian community through these identities. When the category of pharaoh, or the role of pharaoh, or the person of pharaoh, is applied to the dead Egyptian "private" man, this implies that his death, or rather, his life after death, is not regarded as a merely private matter, or as a matter for his family only, but as something that is conditioned by, and belonging to, the entire Egyptian people. It is through this evaluation that "private" man has access to the cosmic life described in the royal mortuary literature. The community of the Egyptian people disposes of a collectively shared life, manifesting itself in the cosmos of the Egyptian world.

This idea has its primary cultic expression in the royal temple cult, which aims at communicating with the life forces of the Egyptian world - and thus is of prime importance for the maintenance of this world. The "private" mortuary cult primarily focusses on the jointly shared life of the family,[6] although the two types of cult co-operate[7] as these aspects of Egyptian life are not separated - which is shown through the application of the category of pharaoh on "private" man.

We have, then, brought into our analysis socially defined Egyptian concepts of collective **self**. Of course, ancient Egyptians were not without individual consciousness. But when they defined what they were, essentially and fundamentally, when they related their existence to life and death, the social community was their preferred reference point.[8] In the sources with which we are dealing, the community is specified as that of the family and that of the people.

It is this collectively defined self that lives the communal life of the Egyptians which is the object of the Osirian mummification ritual. The ritual aims at bestowing the fate of Osiris on the dead man. The Osirian **person** incorporates both the pharaoh and the father and belongs to all those who carry the name of this god.

The influence of the concepts of collective **self** can be seen in all kinds of cultural products of ancient Egypt. This is important for our interpretation of our select items of cultural products. The socially defined identities can be documented through a correlation with the wider source material for Egyptian culture. Their influence on Egyptian art can be taken as an example. They play a decisive role in the depiction of persons. I would like to quote K. Weeks: "...even when one of these figures is accompanied by a personal name, that name is generally preceded by one or more titles, as if to reinforce the notion that the carving is of a person (in a sense a named person rather than an individual) filllng a certain role. What seems to have been of primary importance was not so much the indication of **who** (the individual) but of **what** (the person) was represented.[9]

The categories of **status, role, person**, are apt aids in our analysis, because they focus on social identity rather than individual identity. The social identity of the pharaoh comprises the whole people.[10] Such are the contents of royal status, role, person. Through the application of this particular status to the individual dead man, his life after death is regarded as integrated into that of the people, and contributes to and partakes in the on-going life of the whole people. To the ancient Egyptians life is necessarily shared in a joint ownership. The life of the individual Egyptian belongs to the all embracing life community of all Egyptians. R. Schlichtings stresses these characteristics of the Egyptian concept of life in this way: "...Lebendigkeit heisst für den Ägypter eingebettet sein in eine menschliche Umgebung von Familie oder Dorfgemeinschaft, in eine bürokratisch geordnete Umwelt".[11] Or, as J. Assmann puts it: "Als Einzelwesen ist der Mensch nicht lebensfähig, er lebt in der und durch die Gemeinschaft".[12] The social criteria of the Egyptian concept of life should be given proper attention in the study of the Egyptian concept of life after death.

From this approach to the pharaoh as a category of post-mortem life it appears that the on-going life of the "private" man's **person** is perceived to be tied to the community of the Egyptian people. It is through the latter identity that this life is transformed into the forms of cosmic life on which our mythological material centres. The ontological premise underlying this kind of post-mortem life is the interdependent relationship between the Egyptian community and its cosmos. We are here in touch with an ontology according to which **life** is perceived in all phenomena of the cosmos and there are no no constitutional barriers between the diverging manifestations of life.

For this conclusion the term "democratization" appears to be somewhat misleading, as it concentrates too heavily on the individual person - democracy being a concept that stresses the equal rights and privileges for all individuals, while it is rather the collective dimension of a person which is brought into focus by the category of pharaoh. The acquisition of Pharaonic attributes must be understood with reference to this social identity and the kind of life connected with it. It is not so much an acquisition of royal privileges by everyone as a statement that **when** everyone is seen to partake in the social identity of the Egyptian community, they all gain access to that cosmic, repetetive life of which the Egyptian people are in charge as a community.

Finally, I would like to add a methodological comment. We cannot conclude from our source material pertaining to royal status that a change in mortology took place. The only thing we can ascertain is an increase in these expressions of royal status - these particular statements of the preconditions for everyone's cosmic life after death, due to a widening of cultic context for these expressions.

The widening of cultic context might be taken as an indication that the royal mortuary cult became an unsatisfactory context for these expressions. But the preconditions for cosmic life after death can perfectly well have been the same throughout the whole "democratization" process.

NOTES

1. C. ALDRED, Grabdekoration, *LÄ* II 855; J. ASSMANN, Totenkult, Totenglauben, *LÄ* VI 659 f.

2. P. KAPLONY, *LÄ* III 276 f.

3. Pyr. 397,

4. Cf. JØRGEN PODEMANN SØRENSEN, Divine Access, part two of this volume.

5. H. BONNET, *RÄRG* p. 620.

6. The shared family life is central in many cultic situations. Addresses to the dead family members request from them health, prosperity, children, the continuity of the house. Living and dead members of the family jointly partake of and maintain the ka-life of the family. It is transmitted in the form of new generations.

7. S. SCHOTT, *Das schöne Fest vom Wüstentale. Festbräuche einer Totenstadt*, AMAW 11 (1953); U. VERHOEVEN, Totenfeste, *LÄ* VI 645 f.; J. ASSMANN, Totenkult, Totenglauben, *LÄ* VI 662 f.

8. Thus the interest of the autobiographical texts lies with the social status and career of the deceased.

9. *Egyptology and the Social Sciences*, ed. K. WEEKS, Cairo 1979, p. 71.

10. Consequently, there are no autobiographical texts in the royal tombs - the king's "biography" is constituted by all the individual biographies. I explain thus the absence of biographical texts in the royal tombs with reference to the social ideology, unlike J. Assmann (*LÄ* VI 660) who on this point unwarraantedly leaves the social aspect in his description of post-mortem life: "Ihm (*i.e.* the king) fehlt der soziale Aspekt, seine Unsterblichkeit ist nicht soziogen, beruht nicht auf 'soziale Fortdauer' "; and "Seine Unsterblichkeit ist nicht abhängig von sozialen Masstäben, sie hat - in scharfem Gegensatz zu personaler Fortdauer - sie hat - in scharfem Gegensatz zu personaler Fortdauer - mit diesseitiger gesellschaftlicher Eingebundenheit nichts zu tun. Sie beruht auf eigener Kraft, auf göttlicher Natur".

The analytical categories of **social** and **physical** "Fortdauer" are incommensurate and not interchangeable. And, even the pharaonic post-mortem life is "soziogen", but Egyptian thought about the social "Fortdauer" of the pharaoh involves a socially defined concept of person.

Also, it seems a bit inconsequent to refer to the mythological form of expression only when characterizing the pharaoh's post-mortem life.

11. *LÄ* III 951.

12. *LÄ* IV 974.

94

Paul John Frandsen
Trade and Cult

Above the entrance to Abu Simbel, the famous rock temple of Ramesses II, there is a scene whose content has not yet been fully explained. It not only holds the key, so to speak, to the proper understanding of the purpose of the temple, but also provides evidence for one of the fundamentals of life, that of the acts of giving and receiving, which will form the main subject of this paper.[1]

The scene is divided into three parts (Fig. 1). In the middle we see an *en face* representation of a hawkheaded human figure wearing the **nemes** headcloth, the sun disk and an uraeus. The hands 'hold' two signs, *wsr* in the right and *m3't* in the left hand. To the left and right of this image of Re-Harakhte the King of Upper and Lower Egypt, Weser-maat-re, Ramesses, is seeing offering a small maat-like figure to the god. The texts that fill out the remaining space explain what is happening. The ritual text accompanying the king's presentation runs: 'Presenting maat to the possessor of maat', to which Re-Harahkte replies: 'I have given you the lifetime of Re and the years of Atum.'

The god, then, is the sun-god; and at the same time, moreover, a representation which may be read as the throne name of Ramesses II, *Wsr-m3't-r'*. The figure is therefore not

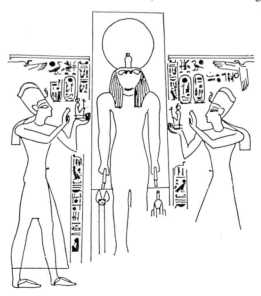

Fig. 1 After L. Habachi, Features of the Deification of Ramesses II (ADAIK, Ägyptologische Reihe, Bd. 5, Glückstadt 1969.

only a manifestation of the sun-god Re-Harahkte, but also one of the god Weser-maat-re, a divine form of Ramesses II.[2] We are thus faced with a case of the **king** Ramesses offering to a **god** Ramesses and to his father, the sun-god. But even, however, if it is somewhat unusual to find a 'double' representation like the present one, we shall not go into a discussion of this phenomenon. What is of interest is the offering gift itself, and in order to grasp its full significance we must widen the perspective and go beyond the scene in Abu Simbel. In the following I shall sketch the broad outline of an argument. There are, admittedly, several loose ends and many problems to be worked out, and it is intended that a more thorough examination of the subject will be presented elsewhere.

In a well-known paper, 'Elementi "irrazionali" nel commercio armaniano', published in 1972,[3] Mario Liverani gives a fascinating account of some of the seemingly irrational phenomena in the trade practices of the Amarna period which he, following the path of M. Mauss and others,[4] wanted to interpret 'by means of an analysis which takes into account the configuration of the Amarna trade as a global social phenomenon in which the criterion of action is dictated concurrently by economic and non-economic factors'.[5] In order to show what this actually implies I can do no better than cite from and paraphrase his own analysis of the relevant material:

> In a letter to the **rabisu** of Egypt, the **rabisu** of Alasia (Cyprus) recalls having already sent certain products, including two elephant tusks, and announces the shipment (as a gift for the addressee of the letter) of other objects amongst which was yet another elephant tusk. In soliciting the habitual countergift, the **rabisu** of Alasia explicitly asks for a shipment of ivory. One has, therefore, ivory travelling from Cyprus to Egypt in exchange for ivory travelling from Egypt to Cyprus. From a purely economic point of view, this exchange is irrational to the limit: transportation costs, involving as they do a trip by sea of a messenger-merchant entrusted with delivering the gifts and receiving the counter-gifts, are considerable when viewed in the context of the technology of the period and lead simply to a financial loss in the case of the exchange of ivory against ivory. One more aspect of irrationality, secondary and ancillary, has also often been brought to light namely, the anti-economical nature of exporting ivory from Cyprus, which does not produce it, to Egypt, which by virtue of having access to the vast African reserves is the privileged exporter of the material in the whole area of the Near East.[6]

The transaction is carried out between two persons, two colleagues, but on closer examination they will be seen to be more than just two individuals. The letter, *EA* 40, was probably appended to *EA* 39[7] in which the king of Alasia sends his greetings to his 'brother', the king of Egypt, and requests that his agents be exempt from dues and that they be allowed to return to Alasia as soon as possible. The same requests are repeated in the letter from the **rabisu** who has also been charged with the task of dealing with the 'details'. The Alasia-**rabisu** participates in the transaction with 17 talents of copper, 2 logs and the said small quantity of ivory. The shipment from Egypt consists only of ivory. The volume involved and the fact that the Alasia-**rabisu** sends products typical for his country, whereas ivory, characteristic of Egypt, is shipped to Alasia, which does not produce it, clearly show that the exchange is of the kind that we usually call trade. The two persons are acting on behalf of groups, in this case states, they are middle-men or intermediaries.[8]

The principal function of the gift is to create social contact. It carries with it an obligation to repay, and thus it creates bonds of relationship that may benefit this and future transactions. This may already be deduced from the request that the ship and its merchant be allowed to return without delay and without his having paid customs.

To sum up, 'It is clear therefore, that the three tusks of ivory sent "counter-current" did not have an economic significance (economically they are cancelled by the restitution of as many tusks), but functioned as catalysts in the establishment of good relations between the two **rabisu**. At this point it becomes clear why this "error", this "irrationality" was in the explicit intentions of the Cypriot **rabisu**; clearly, he had sent ivory, not in spite of it being a disadvantageous shipment, but precisely because the shipment was disadvantageous, not in spite of his needing these goods, but precisely because he had need of this merchandise. It is prestigeous to be able to send a particularly rare and precious commodity, and a sort of stimulus, of provocation to obtain the same commodity in exchange; if the **rabisu** of Alasia has foregone, in favour of his "colleague", his "brother", the possibility of detaining the ivory which for him is so precious, his colleague will not hold back from sending in exchange still more ivory (as it is explicitly requested) and even in a larger measure, corresponding to the lesser scarcity of the product in Egypt. The behaviour of the Cypriot **rabisu** at this point seems clear and "rational" to me: he exchanges copper and timber for ivory, thereby stimulating the mechanism of the exchange by means of the shipment of the very material of which he has greater need, and at the same time firming up the friendly relations which are necessary for a correct follow-up of the exchange (actual shipment of the counter-gift which begins to be late; a faster rhytm of the trip; customs exemptions)'.[9]

This pattern is not unique, and it is not the only one that we should consider. Let us take a brief look at those cases where the 'counter-current' gifts in fact are gifts. 'The gift in these instances is not a mechanism for carrying out the exportation of an object from the country in which it is produced and is abundant toward the country which lacks it; the gift is an end in itself. The object acquires worth inasmuch as it is given, not inasmuch as it is acquired; one can perhaps say that it had the function of being given and not that of being acquired, if it is the same object passing from one court to the other, returning sometimes to its point of departure'.[10]

A possible example of this latter pattern of exchange has been discovered in the material from the Amarna period and if Liverani's interpretation of the data be correct, we would have an excellent example of the type of ceremonial exchange known to anthropologists under the name of 'Kula'.[11] Be this as it may, the exchange that we are looking at here is similar to the one discussed above in that in both cases one gives away that of which one is in need. 'Thus, *EA* 13, a list of gifts sent from Babylon to Egypt, frequently includes gold and one time ebony, two products which characterize the flow in the opposite direction. Also the materials sent from Mitanni to Egypt frequently include gold and sometimes also ebony; (...). In quite a similar way, even if in the opposite direction, the list of gifts sent from Egypt to Babylonia includes objects of silver and copper, metals certainly more rare in Egypt, obtained prevalently as imports from Asia, and even an object of lapis lazuli material which travels typically from Mesopotamia (Babylonia, Mitanni) to Egypt'.[12]

It falls outside the scope of this paper to take up the question of to the 'nature' of possible differences between the two patterns of exchange with which we have dealt thus far. The emphasis of the discussion will be on establishing the connection between the two themes that we have introduced: those of offer-giving and of gift-giving.

The act of offering is at the center of the cult. In the Egyptian temples shorter or longer versions of the daily temple ritual were performed every day culminating in the presentation of an offering to the god. The offering was made up of a variety of objects, not least food, which is of course closely related to the notions of life, vitality and abundance.[13] But whatever is offered in each specific case, the offering will always be said to be (denoted) the Eye of Horus, or Maat, both being the epitome[14] of an offering. The literature on offergiving in Egypt is very comprehensive, but here we shall take up only some of the more recent discussions.

In Assmann's opinion an explanation of this 'merkwürdige Verfahren'[15] - the 'Ausdeutung' of food and other offerings as the Eye of Horus must be sought in the origin of the cult- offering, i.e., in a situation of the kind for which he has coined the term 'Konstellation', by which is meant certain basic patterns or circumstances of life prototypes, as it were.[16] In this case the prototype is the 'Opfergabe' from the son to the dead father which serves to help the latter bridge death so that he may be transposed from one form of existence into another. At the level of myth[17] to which the prototype (constellation) is transposed through the process of 'sakramentale Ausdeutung', the 'corresponding 'götterweltliche Konstellation', the 'Ikon'[18], is Horus who gave his eye to his father. The dead and Osiris are both in a state of want and deprivation. Their vitality must be restored and restitution is made when they receive the Eye of Horus. Thus, the cult of the dead not only provides a model for man's transition between life and death, but also for communication between man and god, i.e. between two spheres of existence.[19] 'Das besondere man könnte auch sagen: die Funktion oder Leistung dieser Konstellation liegt darin, dass sie Diesseits und Jenseits umgreift. Daher wird sie zum Grund-modell des Kultes überhaupt'.[20] In the cult the king or the priest officiating on his behalf enters into such a 'constellation' in which he is the son while the god is the father. His gifts of offering are 'raised' to the level of divinity through the above-mentioned process during which the identification between the offering and the Eye of Horus takes place. This conception of the offering, which moreover implies that the act itself takes on the form of an exchange or interaction between gods,[21] is not wholly convincing. However, since this is not the place to take issue with Assmann's assertion about 'der Totenkult als die Vorschule der Theologie'[22], let it suffice to point out that it is not very obvious how the offering of Maat fits into this interpretation, and also, that it takes no account of other 'forms' of offering.

The account of the offering that follows next has been worked out by Lana Troy in her stimulating book *Patterns of Queenship in Ancient Egyptian Myth and History*.[23] The scope of this work and the frame of reference within which it is inscribed differ considerably from Assmann's conceptual framework and it is therefore rather pointless to search for dissimilarities in the two discussions. But Troy's discovery is interesting because it makes us understand why the offering could also be identified with Maat. Here are some quotes from her very succinct discussion of the Eye of Horus: 'In the culmination of the conflict [between Osiris, Horus and Seth] the eye is regained by Horus and then given to Osiris as an offering. Possession of the eye transforms the god into the ruler of the Netherworld, the "Foremost of the West". It is in the role played by the eye in the resurrection of Osiris that the analogy between this myth and the solar complex is seen most clearly. (...). The eye belongs to Horus, but it is, as we learn from PT 188b - 192 (...) the daughter of Osiris, just as the solar eye is the daughter of Re. And just as the eye of Re mediates in the renewal of the father, the eye of Horus provides the means by which Osiris is resurrected. (...). It is the offering meal given the god (...). Osiris consumes the eye, his daughter, and his belly grows round. (...). As possessor of the daughter mother eye Osiris takes on the qualities of the self-generating god. (...). The eyes of Horus and Re play analogous roles in the resurrection of Osiris and the renewal of Re'.[24]

This account of the offering highlights the creative aspect of the cult: making an offering means active participation in the cyclical re-creation of the 'world'.[25] But it may also serve to illustrate another important property of the offering, viz., its affinity to the recipient. The nature of this relationship was discussed by Derchain in his well-known chapter *'Physique et théologie'* in which he wrote:

'Le mécanisme de l'offrande apparaît du reste très clairement dans les textes tardifs. L'un d'eux par exemple, explique que le roi apporte le bijou représentant les millions d'années "à celle qui a créé les millions", et qu'il "élève vers elle le bouquet de la vie". La déesse Hathor, installée dans la barque solaire, appelée "barque des millions d'années" lui répond qu'elle "prolonge la vie, qu'elle fait respirer celui qui est sur son eau, (c'est-à-dire celui qui lui obéit)". Le principe qui est ici mis en lumière c'est que le roi offre **au dieu justement le symbole de ce qu'il attend de lui**. Il trouve son application dans toutes les offrandes, en particulier dans la plus importante de toutes, dans l'offrande de l'ordre (*m3't*) (My emphasis).[26]

In this otherwise fine account of the offering 'mechanism', the term 'symbol' seems somewhat ill chosen, and the subsequent remarks on the maat-offering do not clarify the matter: 'C'est une application du même principe que j'ai montré dans le rituel d'offrande de l'éternité: l'offrande revient a son créateur'.[27] As a description of the interaction it may be adequate, but it does not bring out the all important point about the nature of the offering: its consubstantiality with the recipient. The eyes/daughters are not (merely) symbols, they are flesh and blood of the creator, and by implication, moreover, all offerings must share in the essence of the recipient.

Altenmüller has considered the question of the 'mechanism' in terms that come close to this kind of formulation: 'Bei den Übergabeszenen der Tempel fällt auf, dass der das Opfer entgegennehmende Gott häufig als Herr dessen, was dargebrachtwird, bezeichnet wird. Die Opfersubstanz stärkt also Kräfte, die zum Wesen der Gottheit gehören und die in der einen oder anderen Form von der Gottheit an den Opfernden wieder zurückgegeben werden'.[28] At the beginning of his paper Altenmüller tries to establish what the various forms of offerings have in common, what an offering (Opfergabe) in fact is as opposed to an ordinary gift. He thus takes it for granted that they are essentially distinct, although he does not consider whether the difference applies only to the thing presented or whether it would also embrace the forms of presentation (procedures of exchange) and the status of the partners. The offering is seen as 'einer mit Macht und Kraft ausgestatteten Substanz' which has acquired this property 'durch einen Ritus (...). Dies liefert ein willkommenes Unterscheidungsmerkmal zur einfachen Gabe. Denn erst durch die rituelle Übergabe an den Kultempfänger gewinnt die einfache Gabe die Qualität eines Opfers. Die für den Götterkult in Magazinen gelagerten Gaben oder die für den Toten im Grab gehorteten Gegenstände der Grabausrüstung sind zwar potentielle Opfergaben dürfen aber wegen der fehlenden Weihung durch das Ritual nicht unmittelbar als Opfergaben angesprochen werden'.[29]

Altenmüller has thus carried Derchain's analysis one step further in that he recognizes the existence of shared properties between the offering and the recipient, and it is against this background that he wishes to connect the offering with the idea of reciprocity: 'Die

Vorstellung, dass durch das Opfer dem Opferempfänger eine von diesem begehrte mach-
terfüllte Substanz zugeführt wird, lässt den Opfernden auf der Basis des Grundsatzes des
"do-ut-des" auf eine Gegenleistung hoffen. Der Gott wird durch die Opfergabe zufrieden-
gestellt (*sḥtp*); in Gegenzug erwartet der Opfernde einen Lohn für sein Opfer'.[30]

We are now in a position to see that the scene in Abu Simbel is in perfect harmony with
this pattern of 'exchange'. The recipient, the Lord/possessor of maat is presented with maat
in the shape of a small figure, and in return the king is granted 'the lifespan of Re and the
years of Atum', in other words: participation in the work of creation. But even so the scene
has not yet been fully elucidated.

The above-mentioned accounts of the offering (and all the writings on the subject as
well) have one thing in common, that they view the offering as an offering. I shall presently approach the problem of what 'really happens' in the offering situation by looking at the
offering as being essentially a gift. The starting-point for our discussion will be the fundamental book by M. Mauss, *Essai sur le don, forme archaïque de l'échange* (cf. above n. 4).

In Mauss' opinion the system of exchange that we find in 'archaic societies' (which also
includes ancient Egypt) is one of 'total prestations'. It is characterized by three features:

(1) Exchange takes place between groups, and not individuals. Chiefs act as intermediaries.

(2) They exchange not only real 'things', but feasts, rituals, gods, etc.

(3) Gifts must be given, be received and repaid.[31]

The last feature is absolutely crucial and this is also reflected in the title of the first of
the four chapters of the book: **Gifts and the Obligation to Return Gifts**. The heart of the
chapter and the corner-stone of the whole book and subsequently, for example, of Lévi-
Strauss' concept of **échange généralisé** is that a thing given is a part of the giver, and that
persons and groups 'behave in some measure as if they were things'.[32] Thus, **'One gives
away what is in reality a part of one's nature and substance, while to receive something is
to receive a part of someone's spiritual essence'.** Or in a different wording: '... **to give something is to give a part of oneself'.** (My emphases).[33]

Mauss arrived at this conclusion by analysing a set of data from the Pacific, and in his
discussion he tried to understand the phenomena in terms of the Polynesian concept of
mana. There is no doubt that Mauss' interpretation is basically correct, and it is therefore
most interesting that we can provide 'proof' of this with material from ancient Egypt without having recourse to **mana**, a notion that should not be used outside its own proper context.

We have already mentioned the well-known fact that the offering of maat is the epitome of an offering.[34] In some respects maat and life may be synonymous, one may live on
maat, etc. Maat is the daughter of the creator, and when offered to her father, he is in fact
receiving his own flesh and blood, his own substance. But what about the giver ? If Mauss
is right this must mean that the king himself is 'of' maat, that maat is his flesh and blood.
The accent is no longer resting exclusively on the recipient of the gift, but has been transferred to the giver. It is equally well-known, of course, that the king must be a giver. As a
matter of fact it is his principal duty to give, whether it be gifts (rewards, donations, etc.) of
all kinds to his subjects in response to their gifts (services) or gifts (offerings) to the gods
and the blessed dead;[35] but the crucial thing about the scene in Abu Simbel is that in the
maat-offering the king gives himself to the god. Let us take a closer look at the scene again.

The ritual text states that the king is presenting maat to the possessor of maat, but if we look at the object that is being given, we see that Ramesses is offering up his name: the maat-figure may be read *wsr-m3't-r'*. In accordance with the Egyptian ontology the **name** is a completely inseparable part of the 'identity' of a person or a thing: 'Die ägyptische Theorie des Namens basiert auf dem Grundsatz, dass zwischen dem Namen und seinem Träger eine Wesensbeziehung besteht. Der Name ist eine Wesensaussage und eine Devise, wie wir am Beispiel der Thronnamen gesehen haben, die sich die Könige bei ihrer Thronbesteigung zulegten. Die Beziehung zwischen "Name" und "Wesen" gilt in beiden Richtungen: alles, was man aus einem Namen herauslesen kann, sagt etwas über das Wesen des Benannten aus und alles, was man über das Wesen einer Person aussagen kann, lässt sich ihm als Name beilegen. Der ägyptische Begriff des Namens umfasst also auch das was wir unter einem "Prädikat" verstehen'[36] Thus, when Ramesses offers his name as maat, it 'proves' that maat is part of his essence. By giving his name he gives maat and thereby himself to the god.

At this juncture three points may be made. First of all, this 'form' of the maat-offering is by no means restricted to the scene in Abu Simbel. It is well attested throughout the Ramesside period even though much of the material is unpublished. The following list of name-offerings is based on the entries given in *PM* II, p. 548.[37] A perusal of some of the more recent publications of tempel scenes and other material has yielded only a few additional examples:

SETHOS I: *LD*, III, 139b; *PM*, II, 410 (23-26), 412 (52-53), 414 (70), 419 (111), all from Gurna and unpublished.

RAMESSES II: *The Great Hypostyle Hall at Karnak*, I (= OIP 106), Pls. 75 and 136; *Karnak VI*, p. 36, cf. Barguet, *Le temple d'Amon-Re*, p. 255; *PM* II, 211 (30-31) (Karnak, unpublished); II, 307 (27) (Luxor, unpublished); Osing, *Der Tempel Sethos' I in Gurna*, Pls. 3 (= p. 16, 1.6), 11 (= p. 20, 2.2) and 16 (= p.23, 2.13); Gauthier, *Ouadi es-Seboua*, II, Pls. LXII (= I, p. 219) and LXV (= I, p. 242).

RAMESSES III: *Reliefs and Inscriptions at Karnak*, II (= OIP 35), Pl. 97 F; *Med. Habu*, VII, Pl. 499; *Med. Habu*, VIII, Pls. 603 and 617 B and C.

RAMESSES IV: Champollion, *Monuments*, Pl. CCLXXXVIII, 1; Christophe, *CHE*, Ser. III, 1950, p. 61; Nelson, *Key Plans*, Pl. XVII, Fig. 17, nos. 367 (= Jéquier, *L'architecture et la décoration dans l'ancienne Egypt. Les temples ramesside et saites de la XIXe dynastie*, Paris 1922, Pl. 71,4), 365, 370, 371 and Fig. 18 no. 402 (all unpublished);[38] *PM* II, 237 (47), 238 (64) and 239 (73), all unpublished; Steindorff, *Aniba*, II, Pl. 11 no. 38 (= p. 24 no. 41) (= *KRI*, VI, 63).

RAMESSES V: *LD*, III, 223b (= *KRI*, VI, 224).

RAMESSES XI: *The Temple of Khonsu*, II, (OIP 103), Pls. 157 A, (?)161 C, 177 A and 189.

Secondly, in some of these scenes the act of offering is not accompanied by any ritual text, and we may therefore ask whether this is accidental or not. For reasons that will presented in the following discussion I would be inclined not to attach too much importance to the presence or absence of the text: most of the scenes do in fact have a phrase such as *ḥnq m (ḥnq) m3't n*, and there seems to be no perceptible difference between e.g. Osing, *Der Tempel Sethos I ...*, Pl. 3 (no ritual text)[39] and Pls. 11 and 16. Likewise, the 'designer' of the offering scenes in Wadi es-Seboua seems to have had a general preference for purely 'visual presentations' of the offerings. On the other hand, some of the scenes showing Ramesses IV offering his name in the Khonsu Temple are explicitly said to be presentations of his name. Thus, in Nelson, *Key Plans*, Pl. 17, 367 the ritual text runs: *ḥnq rn šps* and in Fig. 18, 402 we find: *ḥnq.i n.k rn wr*; in order to throw more light on this problem we must therefore bring forward some additional material.

The first pieces of evidence to be mentioned consist of some statuettes representing a crawling king 'pushing before him his name written in sculptured hieroglyphs'.[40] These statuettes have been studied quite extensively[41] and it has been suggested that they formed part of the offerings presented during the coronation rites.[42] The idea of a coronation context is not entirely free of problems, but regardless of their specific function it can hardly be doubted, also on the analogy with the evidence to be discussed next, that they were used as offerings of a kind. Several two-dimensional representations of offerings in the form of small figures are known. In a sense all of the above-mentioned instances of name/maat-offerings may be said to fall into this category[43] in that maat is always rendered as a figure and not just as e.g. a feather. But in the scene published by Jéquier the king is presenting Amaunet with a figure of a sphinx in front of whom there is a squatting prince. He has a finger in his mouth, a feather and a disk on his head, and is therefore to be 'read' as *ḥq3-m3't-R'*.[44]

The latter representation calls to mind two famous scenes from Amarna in which the royal couple are offering some small figures/statuettes and cartouches of the Aten to the Aten.[45] There has been some discussion as to the possible 'identity' of the figures in both representations, with Aldred and Rössler-Köhler[46] taking the view that the figure lifted up by the queen is in both cases a representation of Nefertiti herself, possibly 'in der Rolle bzw. anstelle der Maat, der Re-Tochter und Schu-Schwester nämlich, eine Rolle, die auch an anderer Stelle für Nofretete nachweisbar ist'.[47] This entails that the figure offered by Akhenaten is likely to be Schu as Maat[48], and 'eine solche Opfergabe (i.e. those of both the king and the queen) füllt damit exakt den Platz des Maat-Opferfigürchens aus, das ja in Amarna nicht mehr auftritt, obgleich dort der Maat-Begriff und das Maat-Opfer eine wichtige Rolle spielen'.[49]

This material seems to be matched by a type of three-dimensional objects that some scholars have thought to be 'cult objects'.[50] The best known example is a plaque from Berlin on which a neeling figure of Akhenaten is lifting up the two cartouches of the Aten.[51] This representation is paralleled on a scarab in London;[52] and several objects of a similar type are known.[53] But we may go further back, possibly even to the time of Amenophis III if he be the king who offers an object obviously belonging to the same class of material on a block about which nothing seems to be known[54] (Fig. 2).

Summing up the evidence, we may distinguish four types of two-dimensional representations:

(1) Scene: maat/name, text : presenting maat.
(2) Scene: maat/name as part of a statuette group, text : presenting my/the name.
(3) Scene: statuette group with figure of giver as maat (maat/Schu or maat/Tefnut).
(4) Scene: name as an element of a composite object.

It seems likely, moreover, that we possess actual specimens of the objects represented in (1)[55] and (4). From a structural, contextual, point of view all of these representations may be said to enter into a paradigmatic relationship with each other, and we must therefore infer, I think, that there is no substantial difference between the various forms of offerings: the giver is, in all cases, giving himself. This conclusion is borne out by the observation that only 'ramesidische Könige, deren *nsw-bjt*-Name den Begriff *m3't* enthält, erscheinen auf

Fig. 2 After E. Prisse d'Avennes, Monuments Égyptiens, Paris 1847, Pl. XI, 5.

Tempel-wänden in Darstellungen des Maat-Opfers oft mit diesen ihren Namen anstelle der hockenden Maat-figur in der darreichende Hand'.[56] As a matter of fact, with the block showing the representation of the throne-name of Amenophis III it appears that this observation could be extended to cover the material from the major part of the New Kingdom. True enough, no instances have been noted from the reigns of Ramesses VI, VII, VIII and X, but then virtually none of their monuments are extant. And this in turn enables us to see that there is nothing unique or special about these offerings in the sense that only here may the giver be presumed to give himself. On the contrary, the kings whose names include the element maat 'utilized' the possibility of making also the essence of the ritual act visible, and it is this very manifestation that reveals the principle underlying all other offerings: one gives what one values the most, what one covets the most, i.e. oneself.

The third point to be made is that offer-giving is compulsory - contrary to Hornung's opinion in his chapter on mankind's response to the gods:

> Eine Antwort des Menschen auf ihr Dasein und ihr Wirken ist den ägyptischen Göttern erwünscht. Sie verlangen keinen Kult und sind auf keine materielle Darbringung angewiesen, aber sie freuen sich des Echos, das ihr Schöpferwort findet, und gern nehmen sie die materiellen wie ideellen Gaben des Menschen an. Entscheidend ist der Dialog, der darin sichtbar wird. Das "Hintreten" vor die Gottheit bedeutet "die Aufnahme des direkten Kontaktes", und der Mensch, repräsentativ der König, will nicht mit leeren Händen vor einen Gott treten. Die Gabe, die er bringt, bedeutet keinen geforderten Tribut und keinen Zwang zur Gegenleistung, sondern ist Geschenk, enthält etwas von der Freiheit, welche die Götter mit ihrem Schöpferatem dem Menschen spenden.

> Wir haben unsere Deutung des Götterkultes bewusst in einer Richtung zugespitzt, die weit von der gängigen Formel des"do ut des", mit der man jeglichen Kult erklären will, fortführt. Denn diese Formel scheint auch im ägyptischen Kult gelegentlich zu

passen, erklärt aber wenig und darf vor allen Dingen keine ausschliessliche Geltung beanspruchen. Ehe der Mensch etwas gibt, haben die Götter schon alles gegeben.'[57]

As stated above, making an offering means active participation in the cyclical re-creation of the 'world'. Without the exchange between the king and the god(s) cosmos would revert to its chaos- state, and man must therefore do his utmost to contribute to upholding the ordered universe. Considered in this light, the offering becomes a question of life and death and, in the last analysis, man must give himself.[58] Maat's role in the creation - being the essence of an ordered cosmos and at the same time the means by which its creation comes about - is well documented, from CT Spell 80, the daily temple ritual, chapter 42, etc., but I cannot help calling attention to a late source, published very recently, in which the 'total' character of the exchange-situation has been made abundantly clear. I am referring to the so-called Khonsu Cosmogony.[59] Here the king offers maat to two different triads and they respond by creating the world and returning maat to him. Or in the wording of the editors: 'These two texts were certainly intended to involve the Theban gods with the Memphite and Hermopolitan cosmogonies, and also to represent a Theban or Khonsu cosmogony, but the form of the texts is the typical presentation of maat by the king. The king has very little to say and the gods have rather short statements following their lengthy, exaggerated epithets, which are in fact the principal means used to convey most of the intended information.'[60]

Having come this far the reader will have sensed, I hope, what I have been driving at, i.e., the fundamental identity of the transactions of exchange in trade and cult, two acts that have not, hitherto, been connected with one anther. I am aware of the shortcomings of my presentation of the evidence and realize that I cannot expect to be 'believed' until all 'aspects' of the problem have been fully worked out the status of the partners (especially the god(s)), the procedures of exchange (transfer, gifts, trade, offering), a typology of things exchanged (including sacrifices, burnt offerings, etc.), but by way of conclusion I wish, nevertheless, to outline the argument in the hope, that this will make the whole idea seem less 'strange'.

The exchange that we have been discussing falls within the category which is sometimes labelled 'aristocratic'. The partners act as intermediaries (king < — > king or king < — > god) for the entities they represent and the primary aim of the action is to achieve social contact in the widest possible sense of the word. This must not be taken to mean that what is exchanged has no utilitarian value. On the contrary, it is eminently useful both for its own inherent (economic) properties and for its ideological/religious and social implications. The point is, however, that these qualities cannot be separated! In the exchange of the kula-type[61] the transaction would sometimes appear to be 'reduced' to a purely ceremonial exchange. And it is precisely this double nature of the transaction that modern people find so hard to understand. But the evidence from the Amarna-letters (and much other material) is clear in this respect. Something similar holds in the case of maat. Maat is both real material and at the same time a symbolic expression of the social and cosmological necessity of the 'cult-exchange'. The things exchanged bear out the assertion. The kings exchange objects, of course, but also 'life and health'[62], gods[63] and medical assistance.[64] The king and the gods exchange 'things', but also maat in the form of maat in return for maat or maat in return for the 'lifetime of Re and the years of Atum', in short, reciprocal creation. And at the foundation of all of this is something which should no longer be looked upon as irrational: the basic fact that one gives away what one values the most, in the last analysis, one-self.

NOTES

1. I am grateful to Dr. Lana Troy for revising my English text.

2. See HABACHI, *Features of the Deification of Ramesses II*, Glückstadt 1969, p. 10. Cf. also WILDUNG, 'Göttlichkeitsstufen des Pharao', *OLZ* 68 (1973), cols. 549-565; id., 'Ramses, die grosse Sonne Ägyptens', *ZÄS* 99 (1973), pp. 33-41; CHRISTOPH, 'La salle V du temple de Sethi Ier à Gournah', *BIFAO*, XLIX (1950), pp. 117-180.

3. *OA* 11 (1972), pp. 297-317, with an English translation published in *MANE* 1/5 (1979), pp. 93-105 to which the following citations refer.

4. MAUSS, *Essai sur le don, forme archaïque de l'échange*, originally published in *Année Sociologique*, II serie, I (1923-24), pp. 30-186; with an English translation in 1954, with corrections in 1969, London RKP; the following citations refer to this edition. Cf. also LIVERANI, op.cit., pp. 93-94.

5. op.cit., p. 94.

6. op.cit. pp. 94-95.

7. See MORAN et al., *Les lettres d'el-Amarna*, Paris 1987. p. 209 n. 1.

8. It is possible that the 'trade' was balanced in the sense that the parties exchanged goods of equal 'exchange-value', as LIVERANI thinks. There is, however, no evidence for this, and I am not convinced that the gift from one side would in the long run be offset by the countergifts from the other. The position of Egypt and Alasia was not one of complete equality - even though the kings address each other as 'brothers'. This may also be inferred from the fact that Alasia had to make two shipments of which the second was a 'reminder' which, at the same time, increased the volume of the transaction. In the first shipment 2 tusks plus 9 talents of copper, etc. were sent, while the second one contained an additional 8 talents, 1 tusk and more of the other commodities. Thus, in the protocol the rank of the two **rabisu** was probably the same, but this did not hold good for the 'social groups' they represented. Within the very limited scope of this short paper it is not possible to enter into a further discussion of this and related problems, but I intend to deal with the question at greater length in a separate publication.

9. LIVERANI, op.cit., pp. 95-96.

10. op.cit., p. 97.

11. ibid., with n. 24.

12. op.cit. p. 96.

13. I am echoing ASSMANN's definition of Maat, for which see his *Ägypten, Theologie and Frömmigkeit einer frühen Hochkultur*, 1984, p. 11 ff.

14. I use this term for want of a short, adequate denotation. The eye is often said to be a symbol - 'ein extrem vieldeutiges' one, of course (ASSMANN, op.cit., p. 61) and this may hold good in some contexts. But not so in connection with the offering-situation where it is - at best - a misnomer.

15. For what follows see ASSMANN, *Ägypten...*, pp. 60-62 and 118 ff.; id., 'Politik zwischen Ritual und Dogma', *Saeculum* 35 (1984), pp. 97-114, esp. p. 104; id., in Tellenbach

(ed.), *Das Vaterbild in Mythos und Geschichte*, Stuttgart 1976, p. 30; id., *Liturgische Lieder...*, p. 339 ff.

15. If we are to use terms with astral connotations, **configuration** might even be better.

16. In the sense defined by ASSMANN, *Ägypten...*, p. 118 ff.

17. op.cit., p. 135.

18. See op.cit., p. 62: 'Der Totenkult liefert das Modell dieser Überbrückung zweier Seinssphären: zwischen Lebenden und Toten im Grab, zwischen Mensch und Gott im Tempel. Auch dem Gott wird das Horusauge dargebracht, auch der Gott wird dadurch mit Lebenskraft gestärkt und von seiner Bedürftigkeit geheilt'.

20. op.cit., p. 118.

21. Cf. in an earlier discussion e.g., DERCHAIN, *Le Papyrus Salt 825*, p. 15: ' Il était d'ailleurs théoriquement impossible qu'il [i.e. le public] y fût associé, car sa présence aurait introduit un élément de réalité matérielle qui ne pouvait que contrarier l'action idéale des prêtres délégués du roi, lui-même représentant tout le peuple et qui, étant dieu, était seul assez "idéal" pour se trouver sur un plan d'équivalence avec le dieux.' Cf., however, DERCHAIN-URTEL, 'Gott oder Mensch?', *SAK* 3 (1975), pp. 25-41, esp. pp. 37-39 and 31-32: 'Die im gleichen Zusammenhang, eben mit dem Priesterdienst an anderer Stelle vorgenommene Einschränkung, der König stehe nicht ausserhalb des menschlichen Bereiches, sondern besetze innerhalb dessen nur einen priviligierten Platz, scheint mir dem wahren Sachverhalt sehr viel näher zu kommen und findet gerade in dem hier behandelten Text aus Esna seine Bestätigung. So nahe der König auch an die Gottheit rückt, die unüberwindliche Schranke des "Bildes" hindert ihn, den letzten Schritt zur vollen göttlichen Identität zu tun.'

22. ASSMANN, op.cit., p. 62.

23. Uppsala 1986.

24. op.cit., pp. 41-43.

25. For the priest as a theogon see FINNESTAD, *Image of the World and Symbol of the Creator*, Wiesbaden 1985, p. 150.

26. DERCHAIN, op.cit., p. 13.

27. op.cit., p. 14; Cf. MORET, *Rituel du culte divin en Égypte*, p. 148: 'Quelle signification doit-on attacher à la présentation de Mâit? On s'accorde à reconnaître une intention symbolique dans ce fait qu'on substitue aux offrandes matérielles, *mâïtou* (justa), l'oblation d'un symbole abstrait, la déesse Mâit. Mais l'interprétation de ce symbole a entrainé beaucoup d'égyptologues à des considérations métaphysiques. Un des sens du mot Mâit est celui de "chose vraie, **vérité**"; on en a conclu qu'offrir Mâit aux dieux c'est leur présenter "le Vrai, le Bien, le Beau". Le culte grossier des premiers âges, le repas matériel, se transformerait ainsi en une manifestation intellectuelle, en une offrande morale. Sans nier que le mot Mâit ne signifie souvent **vérité**, ni que la déesse Mâit ne puisse personnifier cette abstraction, je crois, cependant, que, dans les cultes divin et funéraire, l'offrande de Mâit n'avait pas, le plus souvent, cette signification symbolique. (...) A mon sens, Mâit, symbolise non la force morale, mais la force matérielle: c'est la vie qu'elle donne au dieu, et non l'intelligence ou la raison.' (...) and p. 152: 'Offrir Mâit au dieu, c'est donc lui donner tout ce que vit réellement; c'est le mettre en possession non d'une **Vérité** morale, mais de toute la Réalité matérielle que lui-même a créée.'

28. *LdÄ*, IV,581; cf. also *RÄRG*, p. 431: 'Der Gott ist (...) ganz von Maat erfüllt. Wenn man ihm Maat bringt, stärkt man also die ihm innewohnende Maat-Kraft'.

29. op.cit., col. 579.

30. op.cit., col. 581.

31. MAUSS, *The Gift*, p. 3: 'In the systems of the past we do not find simple exchange of goods, wealth and produce through markets established among individuals. For it is groups, and not individuals, which carry on exchange, make contracts, and are bound by obligations; the persons represented in the contracts are moral persons-clans, tribes, and families; the groups, or the chiefs as intermediaries for the groups, confront and oppose each other. Further, what they exchange is not exclusively goods and wealth, real and personal property, and things of economic value. They exchange rather courtesies, entertainments, ritual, military assistance, women, children, dances, and feasts; and fairs in which the market is but one element and the circulation of wealth but one part of a wide and enduring contract. Finally, although the prestations and counter-prestations take place under a voluntary guise they are in essence strictly obligatory, and their sanction is private or open warfare. We propose to call this the system of **total prestations**.

32. op.cit., p. 11.

33. op.cit., p. 10.

34. See nr. 14 above.

35. Cf. ASSMANN, *Ägypten...*, p. 11 ff.

36. op.cit., p. 103.

37. It is impossible to gauge the number of scenes in the Theban area on the basis of the information given by *PM*, because many scenes classified as maat-offerings will 'also' turn out to be name-offerings. See also OSING, *LdÄ*, IV,337. 38. I thank professor J. Osing for having put his material on these scenes at my disposal.

39. Other scenes without ritual texts: GAUTHIER, *Ouadi es-Seboua*, II, pls. LXII and LXV; *Med. Habu*, VIII, 603.

40. CGC nos. 42142, 42143, 42144 and MATTHIEW, 'A Note on the Coronation Rites in Ancient Egypt', *JEA*, 16 (1930), pp. 31-32.

41. Cf. *Ramsès le Grand*, Galeries Nationales du Grand
Palais, Paris 1976, pp. 232-237; HABACHI, *Features of the Deification of Ramesses II*, p. 38 ff.

42. Cf. above n. 40.

43. This applies also to *Med.Habu*, VIII Pl. 617 where the king is offering both his throne-name and his birth-name.

44. JEQUIER, loc.cit. As already mentioned the ritual text accompanying this scene runs: *ḥnq rn šps n mwt.f* ... .

45. Brooklyn Museum 41.82 (= ALDRED, *Akhenaten and Nefertiti* no. 18 = pp. 104-105) and DAVIES, *The Rock Tombs of El Amarna*, IV, pls. XXXI and XLIV (= ALDRED, op.cit., p. 78, fig. 47)

46. 'Der König als Kind, Königsname und Maat-Opfer', in *Fs Westendorf*, pp. 929-945.

47. op.cit., p. 941.

48. Cf. BD, Ch. 130, and for the iconographical problems see VAN DER WALLE, 'Survivances mythologiques dans les coiffures royales de l'époque atonienne', *CdE*, 55 (1980), pp. 23-36.

49. RÖSSLER-KÖHLER, loc.cit.

50. REDFORD, *JARCE* XIII (1976), p. 61 n. 144.

51. Berlin, inv. no. 2045 = ALDRED, op.cit., no. 47, p. 126 and *Nofretete. Echnaton, Katalog*, Berlin 1976, no. 76.

52. UC 2233 = SAMSON, *Amarna*, p. 98-99.

53. Cf. SA'AD and TRAUNECKER, *Kemi*, 20 (1970), pp. 124, 169-170 and Pl. XX.

54. PRISSE D'AVENNES, *Monuments Égyptiens*, Pl. XI,5.

55. Cf. the small bronze figure published by RÖSSLER-KÖHLER, op.cit., Pl. 1; and also ROEDER, *Ägyptische Bronzefiguren*, 258. Cf. also GAYET, *Le temple de Louxor*, (= MMAF XV, 1), Pl. XX.

56. OSING, *LdÄ*, IV, 337.

57. *Der Eine und die Vielen*, 1971, p. 198-199.

58. Curiously enough, HORNUNG cites Rilke for a passage in which this under-standing of the offering is brought out in a clear-cut way: 'Wieder ist es der Dichter, der mit feinerem Organ spürt, was sich im Opfer wirklich vollzieht, dessen Ahnung von unseren primären Quellen bestätigt wird. Angesichts der unzäh- ligen Opferszenen, welche die Wände des Karnaktempels und der anderen Tempel Ägyptens überziehen, spürt Rilke, wie das Unermessliche in der Beziehung zwischen Gott und Mensch hier in ein klares "Mass der Opferung" kommt, das dem letztlich immer sich darbringenden Menschen ermöglicht, "immerzu ... der Geber" sein.' op.cit., p. 199.

59. PARKER and LESKO, in *Pyramid Studies and Other Essays Presented to I.E.S. Edwards*, London 1988, pp. 168-175.

60. op.cit., p. 174.

61. See above.

62. Wenamun.

63. Cf. EDEL, *Ägyptische Ärzte und ägyptische Medizin am hethitischen Königshof*, 1976, p. 62.

64. op.cit., pp. 49 ff.

Jørgen Podemann Sørensen
Divine Access:
The So-called Democratization of Egyptian
Funerary Literature as a Socio-cultural Process.

If we are to believe Herodotus, the ancient Egyptians were the most pious of all peoples. If also Breasted can be trusted they had only gradually become so; just as the moral sentiment awakened in them during the First Intermediate Period, personal piety seems to have reached a culmination in the Ramesside Period, the 'Age of Personal Piety'. What follows, according to Breasted, is essentially an inert sacerdotalism preoccupied with the institutional maintenance of a glorious past. The achievements of this glorious past, to which Breasted's survey[1] is almost entirely devoted, are described as a religious progress: "We have seen the Egyptian slowly gaining his honest god. We gained ours by the same process..."[2] There is an air of optimistic evolutionism and liberal theology in Breasted's historiography which may not fit today's taste, but the fact remains, that in Egyptian religious texts and representations from the Old Kingdom to the Late Period the ancient Egyptians - and more and more of them - were apparently getting nearer and nearer to their god.

What is, however, the nature of the process that can be studied in our Egyptian religious texts? To Breasted it was the successive dawn of consciousness, something that happened to, or took place in, the human mind, not without its historical and social causes, but still a kind of psychological development, in which the human potential gradually unfolded itself. This approach is, however, only possible if our sources for each period of Egyptian history reflect the way people felt and thought in a direct and straightforward manner. This is, however, not the case; not only does the number of extant sources differ greatly from period to period - so that virtually everything may be seen to culminate in the Ramesside period - but the social conditions of each period set their own rules as to what is put in writing and determine the context and the meaning of our sources. As it is well known, Egyptian religious texts are traditional texts, and within each period the use of a tradition may be socially limited. Thus the Pyramid Texts are, in the Old Kingdom, an exclusively royal literature; in the New Kingdom the Books of the Netherworld constitute a similar marking of royal status. In the course of time these texts become used outside the royal context and their style and content are adapted to their new tasks; but we are still facing a tradition which undergoes change according to changing conditions. The use of certain texts or certain motifs at a given time - or the fact that a certain motif occurs more often in one period than in another - should therefore not only be seen as an intellectual discovery, but rather be treated as part of a broader socio-cultural process.

What I shall try to show in this brief presentation is that the so-called democratization of religious literature, a process which goes on throughout ancient Egyptian history, may, when seen in this broader socio-cultural context, serve as backbone of an account of the development of religion and thought in ancient Egypt. The literary process must, however, be studied in a quite formal way. If we believe to be able, as it were, to feel the pulse of a period's religiosity in its religious texts, we shall end up with an autonomous mental process, a sort of historical **Bildungsroman**. To study the life of the tradition within shifting social fields of meaning, we need an exclusively formal thematization. The title of this paper, "divine access" has been coined to fill this need.

The religious texts which are our sources - funerary texts, representations on stelae and in tombs - are essentially **ritual** texts. 'Divine access' is an aspect of ritual; a ritual person (a king, a priest, a tomb or stela owner) may have access to the divine in at least three ways:

    (a) by officiating in temple ritual,

    (b) by imitating mythical roles or by identification with a god,

    (c) by religious knowledge.

In our sources, we shall thus consider a person represented as worshipping a god face to face with no intermediary as having divine access of type (a). As it is well known, only the king and the priests could actually officiate in temple ritual. Before the late New Kingdom, however, only the king could be represented as worshipping the gods face to face; not even the *ḥm nṯr* or the *wʿb ʾ3* who actually saw the god every morning, could be represented performing the sacred service. In the Ramesside period - "the Age of Personal Piety" - even persons who hardly ever had access to the interior parts of a temple were free to have themselves represented on stelae face to face with one or more gods.

In funerary texts and representations, we shall likewise consider a deceased person, who is identified with a god or represented as acting in a mythical role, as having divine access of type (b). The 'religious knowledge' of type (c) is very much of the same character and distribution as the identification with a god and the mythical imitation: the deceased is said to know the god, his name, or some mythological feature of the god.

'Divine access' will thus also refer to a principle of **decorum**. There are social restrictions to divine access, and these restrictions, i.e. the literary limits between royal and non-royal status, are subject to change in the course of Egyptian history. The following sketch of the socio-cultural process which can be traced by observing these changes deals almost exclusively with well known facts; it should, however, be worth while to outline, in face of the basic material, the consequences of the perspective here proposed.

Old Kingdom funerary monuments

The outstanding mark of royal status in the Old Kingdom is, of course, the pyramid. In the fourth dynasty virtually no significant comparison can be made between the tomb of the king and those of his officials. Towards the end of the Old Kingdom, however, when the pyramids tend towards more moderate proportions, other distinctive features appear. The royal funerary ritual is inscribed on the walls of the pyramid chambers, and in these **Pyramid Texts** the king is identified with gods, assimilated into mythological roles, and said to ascend to the sky to take his place among the gods. There is no need to elaborate this point, since it is well known, and the evidence can be found on almost every page of the Pyramid Texts. It is important to note, however, that the king is also said to have religious knowledge. This knowledge is sometimes a mere consequence of the king's mythological status. One text makes the king say:

"I have trodden in the path of Horus, and what I do not know, he does not know."[3]

Whatever the meaning of the Horus-role of the king in this particular context, the knowledge in question seems to be derived from it. But above all knowledge denotes the king's access to the hereafter and to the gods: One text describes in a very dramatic manner the king's arrival in heaven; one of the gods says about him:

"He split open the earth by means of what he knew
on the day he wished to come thence."[4]

Another spell addresses the primeval gods:

"You shall not hinder the King when he crosses to him
(i.e. the father of the primeval gods) at the horizon,
for the King knows him and knows his name ..."[5]

The knowledge that helps the king to split open the earth and protects him on his journey in the hereafter is not a personal, subjective knowledge; it is a 'magic' knowledge, or better: a ritual competence. The king knows his spell (i.e. his Pyramid Text), and through his spell he has access to the gods. Thus, in another Pyramid Text, at the end of a hymn to the sun-god, we read:

"Whoever really knows it, this utterance of Re,
and recites them, these spells of Harakhti,
he shall be the familiar of Re,
he shall be the companion of Harakhti.
The King knows it, this utterance of Re,
the King recites them, these spells of Harakhti,
and the King will be the familiar of Re,
the King will be the companion of Harakhti..."[6]

To know the spell is already to participate in the divine. It is important to note that these very explicit statements about ritual, knowledge and divine access are found at the end of a hymn to the sungod. This takes us - after considering divine access of types (b) and (c) - back to type (a), the divine access that is obtained by officiating in temple ritual. For the Old Kingdom, clear evidence of temple ritual or **culte divin** is scarce and scattered, but it seems safe to assume, that the king was already at this period the *nb jrt jht*, the lord of rites, as he was from the Middle Kingdom onwards.[7] In principle he would thus be the only person with a ritual competence, whereas in actual fact he had to delegate the enormous task of worshipping the gods of Egypt to the priests.

The idea of the king as the sole worshipper of the gods lies behind the *htp dj nsw* formula, and another consequence of it was that all representations of the temple ritual would show the king as the officiating person. This is known also from the rich documentation of temple ritual of the New Kingdom. Not even a priest, who actually carried out the temple ritual on behalf of the king, could have himself represented worshipping a god.

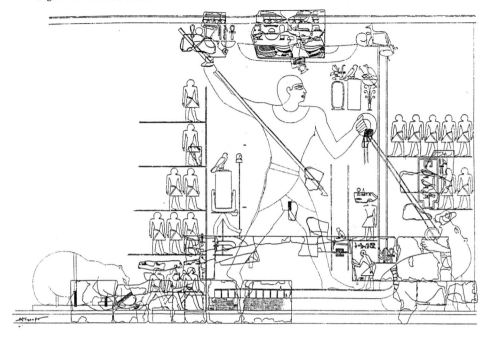

Fig. 1. King Pepi II harpooning the hippopotamus. (G. Jéquier: Le Monument Funéraire de Pepi II. Le Caire 1936. Vol. 3, Pl. 32)

Among the few representations of temple ritual from the Old Kingdom, we shall concentrate on one: Blocks from the funerary monument of Pepi II permit a reconstruction of a scene, in which the king stands in a papyrus boat, harpooning a hippopotamus (Fig. 1). He is surrounded by courtiers, and there is every reason to believe that the scene represents the king in the ritual drama known from the Edfu temple more than 2000 years later: The Triumph of Horus.[8] The king is here officiating in temple ritual and at the same time imitating the mythical role of Horus. Essentially the same motif is found on a seal as early as the first dynasty.[9] Both are examples of the divine access (of type a) of the **living** king, who could ritually act as Horus, his divine prototype.

It would certainly be interesting to collect the complete evidence on temple ritual in the Old Kingdom, but for our present purpose we shall content ourselves with the conclusion that, not surprisingly, the king has all kinds of divine access in the Old Kingdom. This was the natural outcome of his ritual and mythological status which, again, reflected his social and political position.

In the same period, the tombs of the officials are decorated with representations of the life of the deceased at work and leisure, and of the preparations for his funeral. Inscriptions describe his career, the high esteem in which he was held by the king, and sometimes also the quite extraordinary funeral bestowed on him by the king. The only **ritual** text that occurs in these private tombs is the *htp dj nsw* formula. No hereafter and no gods are represented, described, or invoked in private tombs. The idea that the current representations of daily life refer to a concept of the hereafter as entirely similar to earthly life is, to the best of my knowledge, unfounded in contemporary evidence. Although such a concept may have existed, the current scenes of daily life are best interpreted in the light of the current auto-biographical inscriptions, which deal with the earthly life and the funeral. Even in the case of representations of the funeral, only the preparations, the bringing and slaughtering of animals for sacrifice, the production of funerary furniture etc., are depicted. Funeral **rites**, like the Opening of the Mouth and the Ritual of Embalming, are never represented, and neither are the texts of such rituals inscribed on the walls of Old Kingdom private tombs.

We cannot deduce *e silentio* that such rituals were not performed at private funerals. In fact, we have evidence to the contrary: "For me are performed all rites by which one becomes *akh*",[10] one inscription has it, and quite a number of such allusions to mortuary rites exist.[11] But the fact remains that they could not be **represented**, by ritual text or picture, in a private tomb. This was a royal privilege, implying in all probability, divine access of type (b): identification with Osiris and perhaps other kinds of imitation of mythical roles.

The private deceased could, however, occasionally claim religious knowledge (type c). As a lector priest, the governor Harkhuf is quite justified in calling himself a well-equipped *akh* who knows his spell.[12] When others[13] claim knowledge about secret things and religious matters, the knowledge in question is likewise a **ritual** knowledge - of *ḥk3w*, 'ritual formulae'. *mdw nṯr*, 'divine words', and *jḥt*, 'rites'. Some of them were, like Harkhuf, lector priests and could thus regard their professional knowledge as a counterpart of the religious knowledge claimed for the king in the Pyramid Texts. That such private claims to religious knowledge were a conscious approach to the religious status of the king, is suggested by the following variant: "I know all the secret ritual formulae of the court (*ḫnw*), any secret, by which one becomes *akh* in the necropolis".[14]

Even though the private deceased may thus have divine access of type (c), it is important to note that the secrets of the court are not betrayed in the private tomb. The religious knowledge is a royal knowledge, which the private official may verbally claim to possess, but cannot expressedly demonstrate. The private claims to religious knowledge are only a tiny breach of the decorum, and like the autobiographical assertions of a close familiarity with the king, they rather serve to emphasize the fundamental dependence of the individual upon the king.

Due to the same decorum, the private deceased has no divine access of type (a) and (b), by officiating in temple ritual or by imitating mythical roles. Yet some of the higher dignitaries of the sixth dynasty had themselves depicted at a hippopotamus hunt. In his excellent study of hippopotamus hunting as a religious motive, Säve Söderbergh[15] points out that Old Kingdom representations in private tombs never show the deceased spearing the hippopotamus, but only watching the hunt. Later representations in New Kingdom private tombs frankly show the deceased harpooning the hippopotamus all alone and even wearing the royal *shendit* loincloth, i.e. in direct imitation of a royal, ritual scene like the one of Pepi II (Fig. 1). The Old Kingdom hippopotamus scenes are kept within the framework of private tomb decoration; the deceased watches or inspects the hippopotamus hunt, as he inspects the collection of taxes, the harvest, or the delivery of goods. Yet it is difficult to imagine that hippopotamus hunting was a favourite passtime of the higher officials or a part of their official duties. And even if it was, this calls for explanation. Private hippopotamus hunting was meaningful only as an imitation of the mythical prototype, the victory of Horus over Seth, i.e. as an approach to the ritual status of the king. The Old Kingdom representations are thus the beginning of a development which culminates in the New Kingdom representations of the deceased spearing hippopotamus, dressed in the royal *shendit* loin-cloth.

Thus for the king, Old Kingdom funerary monuments show divine access of all kinds; for the private officials, divine access is thoroughly limited and indirect, in fact only attainable **through** the king. Yet in non-ritual contexts the private deceased may claim religious knowledge and have himself depicted in imitation of the ritual and mythological victory of Horus. In the sixth dynasty, a period of royal decline and decentralization of economic and political power, we are already at the fountainhead of that democratization of divine access which follows the collapse of the Old Kingdom. Certain ritual limits are respected, but private autobiography and other non-ritual parts of the private tomb program absorb themes of divine access which used to mark the royal socio-religious status.

The age of the Coffin Texts

With the collapse of the Old Kingdom also disappeared the ritual limits we have just mentioned. As it is well known, the Coffin Texts of the First Intermediate Period and the Middle Kingdom represent what is currently called the democratization of funerary literature. With these texts, the whole ritual and mythological repertoire of the Pyramid Texts are at the disposal of private coffin owners, and each page of the Coffin Texts has examples of divine access of type (b) and (c): the deceased is identified with Osiris and other gods, imitates mythological roles, and claims knowledge of gods, of mythical events and names.

For our present purpose it is important to get an idea of how this spectacular breach of the decorum was experienced. The Middle Kingdom political lamentations of *Jpw-wr* list it among other signs of social **anomie**:

"Lo, the private chamber, its books are stolen
the secrets in it are laid bare.
Lo, magic spells (*ḥk3w*) are divulged,
spells are made worthless through being repeated by people ..."[16]

Others will have experienced the freedom to use the royal spells differently, but to *Jpw-wr* it obviously constituted a kind of value crisis. The spells of the Pyramid Texts become worthless when used by everybody, i.e. their efficacy is conceived as somehow linked to the former state of things; when they are no longer secrets of the court, they loose their power. This is evidence that religion was, as the invitation for this symposium has it, "integrated in society": Deprived of their institutional basis and uprooted from the royal exclusiveness they denoted, ritual formulae become worthless. While the coffin owners were probably enthusiastic about their newly gained divine access and the approach to royal status it implied, *Jpw-wr* faced a process of secularization.

Thus in the funerary literature of the First Intermediate Period and the Middle Kingdom there is no **textual** mark of a royal status in terms of divine access. This does not mean that every private official had a royal funeral or a mortuary cult, only that there were no limits to the use of royal funerary **texts**. The rituals actually performed for the private deceased may still have been subject to the limits of some decorum. It is important to notice, also, that the once exclusively royal funerary texts take the form of "magical formulae": Each spell of the Coffin Texts has a heading stating its purpose. This might be taken to mean that texts which were once part of the official cult had been turned into private **grimoires**. Non-royal persons had no claims to a funeral or a mortuary cult on a national scale; what they had acquired was only divine access of type (b) and (c) on a purely **textual** level, detached from its original institutional basis. Very much in the spirit of *Jpw-wr*, Kees[17] speaks of a "Degradierung der Pyramidentexte".

Divine access of type (a), by officiating in temple ritual, was still basically a royal prerogative. In the Middle Kingdom, however, private inscriptions allude to participation in the cult of Osiris at Abydos, sometimes as a wish to be there and see the rites, sometimes as an assertion that the deceased was actually there. The reference to the rites in Abydos may even take the form of a ritual title:

> "Kissing the ground for Khentamentes,
> beholding the *nfrw* of *Wp-w3wt*,
> traversing together with the great god
> to whereever he goes,
> by Generalissimo Antef."[18]

This is much more than just autobiography; placed on top of the stela of Generalissimo Antef these words do not only recount that he was in Abydos and took part of the processions. They **represent** his participation as a temple scene represents the worship of the king.

It is interesting to study in this perspective the famous inscription of Ikhernofret, our main source for the cult of Osiris in Middle Kingdom Abydos. Ikhernofret's account of the rituals of Osiris is part of his autobiography - in fact the central part. He recounts how the king sent him to Abydos to restore the cult, how he renewed the sacred barque, etc., and goes on to summarize his own active participation in the rituals in terms of divine access of type (b):

> "I celebrated the Procession of Up-wawet,
> when he went on to champion his father.
> I opposed those rebellious to the *neshmet*-barque,
> and I overthrew the enemies of Osiris.
> I celebrated the great procession, following the god in his footsteps ....
> I cleared the ways of the god to his tomb which is in Peker.
> I championed Wen-nofer on that day of the Great Fight,
> and I overthrew all his enemies on the flats of Nedit ....".[19]

Again, this is more than autobiography. The importance and delicacy of the task of restoring the cult of Osiris is already a prominent feature in the life of an individual, but Ikhernofret goes even further. Not only does he recount how he performed the ritual, but he speaks of this ritual in terms of the primeval events that it denoted and repeated: "I overthrew the enemies ...", "I championed Wen-nofer ....".

Thus, in this exceptional case, divine access of types (a) and (b) are combined within the framework of private autobiography. Much more than the take-over of the whole funerary literature by the class of officials, the case of Ikhernofret illustrates that drive towards

Fig. 2. The nomarch Khnumhotep spearing fish. (P. Newberry: Beni Hasan. Archaeological Survey of Egypt, 1. London 1893. Vol. 1, Pl. 34)

divine access which lay behind this "democratization" or "Degradierung der Pyramiden-texte".

The central concern of ancient Egyptian private autobiography is **status**. The career, the events, the deeds, and the lifestyle that it recounts purport to the social, moral, and religious status of the deceased. It is important to note that not only professional and moral qualities, but also the performance of temple ritual could contribute towards the status of the deceased. Just as a man may call himself strong, loyal, and diligent and refer to the important tasks he had, a Middle Kingdom priest may call himself a "breaker of the seal" and an "opener of the naos", referring to the opening rites of the daily temple liturgy.[20] And it is probably no mere coincidence that this liturgy is represented in priestly autobiographies by those rites which, in a most literal sense, gave access to the god.[21]

There are, however, still in the Middle Kingdom, limits to private divine access: a non-royal person could not have himself represented worshipping a god face to face. But there are **ritual** scenes in Middle Kingdom private tombs; the well known representations of the journey to Abydos begin to occur at this period.[22] Such a journey was hardly undertaken by every private deceased, but the representations may at least be taken as a mythological interpretation of private funerary rites, associating them with the rites of Osiris at Abydos.

The hippopotamus hunt is not found in Middle Kingdom private tombs, but Säve-Söderbergh[23] has pointed out that a scene in the tomb of Khnumhotep at Beni Hasan (Fig. 2) comes very close to it. The Scene in question shows the nomarch Khnumhotep spearing fish from a papyrus boat. In front of the boat, however, is a hippopotamus with its mouth turned towards Khnumhotep, as in the scenes of hippopotamus hunting from the Old and the New Kingdom, and the text above the scene states that he uses "his favourite harpoon on the day of harpooning the hippopotamus". This strange blend of a fishing and a hippopotamus scene probably represents a new approach to the theme of divine access through ritual imitation of mythical roles. "The day of harpooning the hippopotamus" must refer to some festival like "The Triumph of Horus" in Edfu. During this festival, when the ritual harpooning of the hippopotamus took place in the temple, people would tread down **fish** in the streets of the town as a more modest and a more public contribution to the annihilation of Seth.[24] Such a popular custom may have existed already in the Middle Kingdom. Anyway Khnumhotep could not have himself depicted spearing hippopotamus all alone. But he could have a not exclusively royal motive, the harpooning of fish, extended in a way which suggested the royal, mythological role of the triumphant Horus.

The facts we have surveyed till now permit, I believe, a few preliminary conclusions. The development which these facts illustrate may be - and has been - differently interpreted. When private people are, in increasing numbers, identified with Osiris, this may be taken as evidence of the increased popularity of Osirianism (whatever that is). When more and more people have ritual texts and religious scenes in their coffins and tombs, this may be interpreted as the rise of a more intense religiosity, or the like. Such interpretations, however, more or less construct historical circumstances which might have caused the changes we observe. Our formal thematization, divine access, makes us perceive a broader process in which distinctive marks of royal status become models or prototypes for the assertion of high private status. This process involved a gradual and manifold transgression of a decorum which originally reserved divine access for the king. The historical circumstances which account for this process need not be constructed. The decline of royal power at the end of the Old Kingdom, the collapse of the centralist state in the First Intermediate Period, and the still somewhat decentralized state of the Middle Kingdom are well known historical facts (although their causes are insufficiently understood). The process we have observed mirrors the increasing relative importance of non-royal persons, and the private autobiographies we have now and then consulted show that divine access could really be a matter of status.

But is this all? Did nothing happen to Egyptian religion during this process of "democratization"? Have we surveyed nothing but the snobbish pretentions of the **nouveaux riches**? Of course, something happens when the institutional basis of a religious tradition is changed, and when its social field of meaning is broadened. To *Jpw-wr* the process we have been studying meant a sort of religious inflation, a value crisis, or a process of secularization. This could hardly have been the average attitude of the coffin owners, but in their approach to royal status, the greater part of them must have been aware that they were not kings. This means that, for the first time in the world, there was something like a **religious status**, still defined within the framework of a social hierarchy, in a field of tension between royal and non-royal, still bound to social status, but nevertheless *in nuce* a religious status.

The New Kingdom - and later...

These preliminary insights will be useful, I believe, also in an attempt to understand certain developments during the New Kingdom and even later. For the socio-cultural process which began with the decline of royal power at the end of the Old Kingdom went on and on throughout the history of ancient Egyptian religion. As it is well known, the early New Kingdom in many respects reestablished the centralist state, and it also fostered a new, exclu-

Fig. 3. Hippopotamus scene from TT 155. (T. Säve-Söderbergh: On Egyptian Representations of Hippopotamus Hunting as a Religious Motive. Uppsala 1953, p. 7)

sively royal, funerary literature: the Am Duat, later to be followed by other Books of the Netherworld. These religious compositions had a predecessor in the Book of Two Ways found in Middle Kingdom coffins, but were essentially different from all other kinds of funerary literature. Both royal and non-royal funerary literature had always had the form of ritual texts; the Books of the Netherworld were **pictorial** compositions, and the texts found in them are comments on an autonomous sequence of pictures. As it is well known, this sequence describes a process of cosmic regeneration, the journey of the sun through the Netherworld from sunset to sunrise. It is important to note that whereas the king of the Pyramid Texts and the private deceased of the Coffin Texts were always mentioned by name as having divine access, the Books of the Netherworld seem to describe a process which takes place every night, with or without the king's participation. The king is not mentioned or depicted in the twelve hours of the night or the six caverns of the Netherworld. Yet it seems obvious that the king should somehow be thought to participate in the process of cosmic regeneration which is the topic of these books - but how?

One answer to this question may be found in the long title of Am Duat.[25] This title text repeatedly uses the word *rḥ*, 'know', to introduce its subject matter, e.g.:

> "Knowing the Bas of the Netherworld.
> Knowing the secret Bas.
> Knowing the gates and the ways
> along which the great god traverses...."

The Am Duat thus represents the religious knowledge of the king. But in contradistinction to the knowledge of divine names and mythological features we have found in Pyramid and Coffin Texts, the knowledge represented by the Am Duat and other Books of the Netherworld is a more complete and systematic knowledge. It is a whole piece of sys-

Fig. 4. 18th dynasty votive stela in two registers. (H.M. Stewart: Egyptian Stelae, Reliefs, and Paintings from the Petrie Collection. Part One: The New Kingdom. Warminster 1976, Pl. 41,1)

tematic cosmology[26] and eschatology, through which the king has access to the whole beyond and may participate in cosmic regeneration.

The novel features of the New Kingdom exclusively royal funerary literature are the pictorial form, the complete and systematic character, and the fact that it represents a religious knowledge formally detatched from ritual. These welldefined royal prerogatives were maintained throughout the New Kingdom. This does not mean, however, that there were no private attempts at imitating the royal funerary literature. The more luxurious private Books of the Dead were amply illustrated, and some of the illustrations were even variations on the theme of solar regeneration so prominent in the royal Books of the Netherworld. The Book of the Dead remained, however, a collection of ritual texts, most of which were already known from earlier Coffin Texts. It is also important to consider the way of divine access shown in New Kingdom illustrated versions of the Book of the Dead, i.e. the manner in which the deceased is made a participant in cosmic regeneration. As I have pointed out in another contribution in this volume, the classical New Kingdom illustrated Book of the Dead starts with a scene which resembles the representations on votive stelae: The deceased and his wife (or the deceased alone) in a posture of adoration, with a hymn to the sun written in front of them. This may be followed by a symbolic representation of sunrise as a solar and Osirian regeneration (counted by Lepsius as Chapter 16). It is thus through his hymn, through the perpetuation of his worship, that the deceased participates in cosmic regeneration. This ritual access is clearly distinct from the royal, direct access to a complete and systematic cosmology, represented by the Books of the Netherworld.

On the other hand both illustrations of Chapter 15 of the Book of the Dead and votive stelae involve a certain degree of divine access. Representations of non-royal persons in a posture of adoration before a god are a New Kingdom invention, and as a motif on votive stelae they undergo a development highly relevant to our subject. Representations of a person worshipping a god imply at least an approach to divine access of type (a), participation in the **culte divin**. From the beginning, however, it seems that the motif was subject to some

Fig. 5. Ramesside votive stela. (H.M. Stewart: Egyptian Stelae, Reliefs, and Paintings from the Petrie Collection. Part One: The New Kingdom. Warminster 1976, Pl. 27,1)

limits of decorum. The private person is never shown face to face with the god, and his worship takes the general form of hymnic adoration. In illustrated versions of Chapter 15 of the Book of the Dead, there is at least the hymn between the deceased and the god, and it may even be argued that he is not facing the god, since the symbolic representation of sunrise and Osirian regeneration is rather an illustration or a pictorial counterpart of the hymn.[27]

Votive stelae are often divided into two registers (cf. Fig. 3). In the lower register, the owner is shown in a posture of adoration; in front of him is a hymn or a ritual title indicating that he is worshipping the god. In the upper register the king is shown sacrificing to the god. This arrangement follows the scheme of the *ḥtp dj nsw* formula and respects the king as the *nb jrt jḫt*, the Lord of Rites, who alone could officiate in temple ritual and confront the gods.

Nevertheless, private votive scenes are an innovation which constitutes a further approach to divine access of type (a). The hymns on the stelae are hymns to the god in the upper register, and between the worshipper and his god there is only, for the sake of decorum, the king. Or, to put it the other way round: the king only has divine access of type (a), but the private owner of a stela is just behind him.

But were such approaches also approaches to the religious status of the king? Again, the hippopotamus theme and the precise observations of Säve-Söderbergh come to our assistance. Ten or eleven Theban tombs of the 18th dynasty had the deceased depicted in a scene of hippopotamus hunting.[28] In seven of the tombs the scene is accompanied by a text which states that the deceased is hunting hippopotamus to amuse himself (*r sḏ3 ḥr.f*), but which also somehow relates the hunting to the cult of the goddess *Sekhet*, the protectress of hunting and fishing in the marshes.[29] In spite of this endeavour to account for the representation within the private, non-royal sphere, the deceased is shown in superhuman size, wearing the royal *shendit* loincloth, and spearing the hippopotamus all alone; sometimes his wife is very unrealistically caressing his ankle during the fight with the hippopotamus (Fig. 4).[30] There can be no doubt that, on the pictorial level, this is a royal scene; and two of the tombs add a mythological text which expressly refers to the victory of Horus.[31]

Such representations which consciously, but discretely and equivocally, transgressed the limit between private and royal, show that the process towards full private divine access was still at work in the New Kingdom. This impression is strengthened when we consider the later development of votive stelae. Already in the 18th dynasty we find stelae, on which the deceased is shown worshipping a god face to face without the royal intermediary. And this is what becomes typical of votive stelae in the **Ramesside Period**: the deceased worships his god face to face with offerings and hymns (cf. Fig. 5). In the same period there is an increase in the use of religious scenes in tomb decoration. Early New Kingdom private tombs are still dominated by scenes of daily life and of the preparations for the funeral, but ritual scenes, e.g. the Opening of the Mouth, occur. In the Ramesside Period, however, scenes from the Book of the Dead, mythological scenes, and even scenes of the hereafter are a much more prominent part of the tomb decoration. All these well known features are aspects of divine access, and there is no doubt that in the Ramesside Period the private individual, as we know him above all from funerary monuments, had come very close to his god. This is, however, the outcome of a long process which began with the decline of royal power at the end of the Old Kingdom, but not necessarily the result of a more intense religious life. The culmination of private divine access in the Ramesside Period meant that religious traditions were detached from the social and political structure they had once denoted. This gave way, I believe, also to the literary expressions of "Personal Piety" collected by Breasted[32] from Ramesside hymns. Breasted saw the personal piety of the Ramesside Period very much as a heritage from the Amarna Period.[33] In a brilliant historical interpretation, Assmann[34] convincingly suggests that it was rather a reaction to the repression of traditional religion during the reign of Akhnaton. He quotes an inscription from the rock temple of Ay in **es-Salamuni**, in which the aged successor of Tutankhamon says:

"Ich habe das Elend beseitigt.
Ein jeder kann nun seinen Gott anbeten..."[35]

This was exactly what everybody did in the Ramesside Period, but if Ay's inscription points forward to the Age of Personal Piety, it certainly also points backwards, to the religious restrictions of Akhnaton. Assmann argues that the repressive measures taken by Akhnaton against traditional religion favoured an interiorization of religion, which meets us in Ramesside religious texts.[36] The use of our formal thematization, divine access, will yield a slightly different account of the process.

An important aspect of Akhnaton's reforms were the reestablishment and reformulation of the exclusiveness of the king's religious status. Religious knowledge was a royal monopoly, and so was all kinds of worship of Akhnaton's god. Mythological roles had ceased to exist, and the only divine identification is that between king and god. To non-royal persons, there was no divine access, except indirectly, through the king. The social distribution of divine access was that of the Old Kingdom. What remained of the old decorum, viz. certain restrictions on divine access of type (a), must, during the following time of restoration, have appeared as restrictions framed by "the criminal from Akhetaton". The almost programmatic statement of Ay, that everyone may now worship his god, cancels not only the restrictions of Akhnaton, but also a decorum still observed in the early 18th dynasty.

We shall question neither Breasted's nor Assmann's analysis of Ramesside testimonies of personal piety - nor the sincerity of Ramesside votive inscriptions and hymns. But we shall seriously doubt that personal piety was a Ramesside invention. If we are right that a decorum ruled and restricted divine access on private monuments, it follows that we cannot *e silentio* deduce that personal piety did not exist before the Ramesside Period - or even that a culmination of personal piety was reached in that period. What we can observe is that expressions of personal piety are regularly found on Ramesside private monuments. Viewed in the light of the broader socio-cultural process we have outlined, such expressions of personal devotion and personal religious experience are better taken as an aspect of increased private divine access. This process did not tend to make people more religious, but rather to deconstruct traditional bonds between religion and the central structure of Egyptian society. The development towards full private divine access could go hand in hand with the interiorization advocated by Assmann; both contributed towards an Egyptian religion less integrated in society.

A further reason that the process of "democratization" could continue throughout the New Kingdom is probably found in the fact that a new exclusively royal funerary literature, the Books of the Netherworld, was there to mark the particular status of the king. This royal literary monopoly, however, lasted only throughout the New Kingdom. In the theocracy of the 21st dynasty it was obvious that the Theban priesthood of Amun should approach the religious status of the king. It is probably no mere coincidence that two new types of funerary literature, Mythological Papyri and Am Duat-papyri, were first found with the mummies of members of that priesthood. These papyri represent a further progress towards full private divine access.

Mythological papyri[37] have many features in common with the Book of the Dead. They often start with a representation of the deceased in an attitude of worship, and they adopt many vignettes current in the Book of the Dead. But like the royal Books of the Netherworld they are pictorial compositions, in which texts play only a subordinate role. The pictures are mostly mythological variations on the theme of solar and Osirian regeneration, and the deceased is often shown as present at mythical episodes and cosmic sceneries. In short, the deceased has divine access, elaborated in pictures.[38]

Am Duat-papyri[39] are short versions of the royal Am Duat, comprising only the ninth to the twelfth hour of the night. The deceased has access to the cosmic and eschatological sceneries through the so-called **etiquette**, an introductory scene very similar to the votive scene introducing both the New Kingdom version of the Book of the Dead and the Mythological Papyri.

With these innovations in private funerary literature, the literary distinction between royal and non-royal was only a matter of standard. As it is well known, the royal standard was reached with the huge Saïte private tombs. The tomb of Petamenophis in Thebes, of which unfortunately no adequate edition exists, has virtually everything, from Pyramid Texts to Books of the Netherworld.

The process we have outlined and illustrated is only a perspective, and not even a new one, but rather an attempt to revitalize and formalize the old idea of a "democratization" of funerary literature. Throughout the investigation we have approached a **literary** (and pictorial) theme, divine access, but at the same time we have insisted that we were studying a broader socio-cultural process. We have argued that divine access is linked to social status. Originally denoting exclusively the royal status, divine access becomes, in times of royal decline, a mark of high private status. Thus a process of deconstruction can be followed throughout the history of ancient Egyptian culture and religion: the social limits to the various types of divine access are gradually but constantly transgressed in a process which tends towards full divine access for everyone. Instead of interpreting changes in form and function of funerary literature as evidence of a mental development, we have preferred to approach this literature formally and diacronically, always considering its changing social field of learning, i.e. its reference to the central structure of ancient Egyptian society. In this perspective two conclusions seem within reach:

> In private funerary texts and representations we should not, from the mere absence of motifs involving divine access, deduce that certain beliefs were not very widespread at the time in question. And accordingly, when such motifs occur, we should not, on this basis alone, conclude that certain beliefs or forms of religion had spread or become popular. In the long-term perspec-tive here proposed it is the degree of private divine access that develops and spreads; when a new way of divine access occurs in private funerary literature, this means that it has become socially possible, not that no one has thought of it before.

> On the other hand, this does not mean that nothing happened to Egyptian religion from Unas to Petamenophis. The process we have surveyed is a process of secularization, a process in which religious traditions which originally marked out the central structure of Egyptian society gradually lost their reference to a specific status. When a means of divine access which denoted royal status is taken over by high officials, it may still denote high private status, but royal status and religious status are now demonstrably two separate entities. When, in the end, almost everyone had all types of divine access, religion was no longer truly "integrated in society". It had become a particular, more isolated province of life, and the way was prepared for the **religio mentis** of the Hellenistic Period. In a certain sense the long process we have outlined is also the prehistory of the *synthema* of the initiates of Isis, as quoted by **Apuleius** in the second century AD:

"...*deos inferos et deos superos*   I approached close
accessi coram   to the gods above and
et adoravi de proximo."   the gods below and worshipped them
                                                      face to face" [40]

NOTES

1. JAMES HENRY BREASTED: *Development of Religion and Thought in Ancient Egypt*. New York 1912. Repr. 1959.

2. ibid. p. 369.

3. Pyr. 244.

4. Pyr. 281.

5. Pyr. 448-449.

6. Pyr. 855-856.

7. Wb. I, 124, 12.

8. T. SÄVE SÖDERBERGH: *On Egyptian Representations of Hippopotamus Hunting as a Religious Motive*. Horae Soederblomianae 3. Uppsala 1953, p. 20, Fig. 9.

- Cf. H.W. FAIRMAN: *The Triumph of Horus*. London 1974.

- E. CHASSINAT: *Le Temple d'Edfou*, VI, pp. 60-90 (text), X, Pls. 146-148 (line drawings), XIII, Pls. 494-514 (Photos).

9. T. SÄVE-SÖDERBERGH, op.cit. n. 8, p. 16.

10. Urk. I, 263, 14-15; cf. E. EDEL: Untersuchungen zur Phraseologie der ägyptischen Inschriften des Alten Reiches. *MDIK* 13, 1 (1944), p. 29.

11. Cf. EDEL, op.cit. n. 10, 24.

12. Urk. I, 122, 13 sq.

13. Cf. EDEL, op.cit. n. 10, 22-23.

14. Urk. I, 143, 2-3; EDEL, op.cit. n. 10, p. 23.

15. SÄVE-SÖDERBERGH, op.cit. n. 8, p. 12.

16. P. Leiden 344 Rto. 6, 6-7 - cf. ALAN H. GARDINER: *The Admonitions of an Egyptian Sage from a Hieratic Papyrus in Leiden*. Leipzig 1909. The translation quoted is from MIRIAM LICHTHEIM: *Ancient Egyptian Literature* Vol. I. Berkeley 1975, p. 155.

17. HERMANN KEES: *Totenglauben und Jenseitsvorstellungen der alten Ägypter*. Berlin 1956, p. 177.

18. OTTO KOEFOED-PETERSEN: *Les Stèles Égyptiennes*. Publications de la Glyptotèque Ny Carlsberg. Copenhagen. 1948, Pl. 9.

19. H. SCHÄFER: *Die Mysterien des Osiris in Abydos unter König Sesostris III*. Untersuchungen zur Geschichte und Altertumskunde Aegyptens; 4, Leipzig 1904, p. 21 sqq. The translation is Wilson's in *Ancient Near Eastern Texts Relating to the Old Testament*, ed. J.B. Pritchard, 1969, p. 329.

20. Cairo Cat. Gen. 20712, line 2-3 (*sw3d sjn, wn hr*) - cf. H.O. LANGE & HEINRICH SCHÄFER: *Grab- und Denksteine des Mittleren Reichs*. Catalogue Général des Antiquités Égyptiennes du Musée du Caire; 5. Bd. III, Berlin 1925, p. 337. - In line 6 also allusions to the rite *m33 ntr* in the daily liturgy. The rites here mentioned correspond to chapters 8 (*šd sjn* - breaking the clay seal of the naos); 10 (*wn ḥr* - opening the naos); and 11 (*m33 nṯr* - beholding the god) in the 22nd dynasty version of the daily liturgy of Amon in Karnak: cf. ALEXANDRE MORET: *Le Rituel du Culte Divin Journalier en Égypte*. Annales du Musée Guimet. Bibliothèque d'étude; 14. Paris 1902.

21. RUDOLF ANTHES: *Die Felseninschriften von Hatnub*. Untersuchungen zur Geschichte und Altertumskunde Ägyptens; 9. Leipzig 1928.: Gr. 17 (Pl. 16): *sw3d sjn, wn (ḥr)* Gr. 26 (Pl. 28): *wn ḥr, sw3ḏ sjn*.

22. Cf. *LdÄ*, I, 42 sq. with a convenient survey of the evidence.

23. SÄVE-SÖDERBERGH, op.cit. n. 8, p. 21.

24. Cf. INGRID GAMER-WALLERT: *Fische und Fischkulte im alten Ägypten.* Ägyptologische Abhandlungen, 21. Wiesbaden 1970, p. 72 sq.

25. ERIK HORNUNG: *Das Amduat. Die Schrift des verborgenen Raumes.* Vol. 1-3. Ägyptologische Abhandlungen, Bd. 7 & 13. Wiesbaden 1964-67.

26. Cf. JAN ASSMANN: *Ägypten. Theologie und Frömmigkeit einer frühen Hochkultur.* Stuttgart 1984, p. 77 sqq.

27. Cf. my interpretation in "Ancient Egyptian Thought...." (also in the present volume).

28. SÄVE-SÖDERBERGH, op.cit. p.5.

29. ibid. p. 10.

30. ibid. p. 6-12.

31. ibid. p. 36.

32. BREASTED, op.cit. n. 1, p. 344-356.

33. ibid. p. 346.

34. ASSMANN, op.cit. n. 26, p. 258 sqq.

35. ibid. p. 266.

36. ibid. p. 261 sqq.

37. ALEXANDRE PIANKOFF: *Mythological Papyri.* Bollingen Series, XL. 3. USA 1957.

38. Cf. my "Ancient Egyptian religious Thought .." (also in this volume) for an analysis of a mythological papyrus.

39. Cf. ABDEL-AZIZ FAHMY SADEK: *Contribution à l'étude de l'Amdouat; les variantes tardives du livre de l'Amdouat dans les papyrus du Musée du Caire.* Orbis Biblicus et Orientalis 65. Freiburg, Schweiz 1985.

40. APULEIUS: *Metamorphoses* XI, 23. For the Egyptian background, cf. also JAN BERGMAN: Per omnia vectus elementa remeavi. Réflections sur l'arriere-plan égyptien du voyage de salut d'un myste isiaque, in Ugo Bianchi & M.J. Vermaseren (eds.): *La Soteriologia dei Culti Orientali nell'Impero Romano.* Leiden 1982. The translation is that of Griffiths in *Apuleius of Madauros: The Isis-Book (Metamorphoses, Book XI).* Edited with an introduction, translation and commentary by J. Gwyn Griffiths. Leiden 1975, p. 99.

126

Lana Troy

Have a Nice Day!

Some Reflections on the Calendars of Good and Bad Days

The most well known expressions of Egyptian theology are oriented towards the explication and affirmation of the intimate interaction between the divine and mortal realms, the association between the mechanisms of generation, harmony and disorder found at work on the highest cosmic level, and the world of man. Texts relating to royal ideology and funerary ritual reiterate the integration of the divine and mortal realms, that they are interwoven in a network of interactions. The effects of this are many and are a common topic of study. The role of the *sp tpy* as a model for all generative events is, for example, a recurrent theme in the studies of Egyptian religion. The more banal effects of the intertwining of the divine and human worlds are, however, often ignored. The material which deals with this subject is more limited and less often incorporated into studies of the Egyptian world view. Nonetheless evidence of what Baines (1987) has called "practical religion" is of great interest. In general terms it provides another source for the manner in which the two realms are interwoven but more specifically it gives examples of what was seen by Egyptian theologians, as the immediate and prosaic response of the mortal world to the gods and their activities.

The presence of the gods in the same natural environment as man represented a number of problems for the Egyptians. It was necessary to recognize the divine influence, interpret it and finally formulate the most appropriate means of responding to it. There appears to have been a branch of Egyptian learning devoted to dealing with this problem. It is represented by the text genre which includes the Calendars of Good and Bad Days.

The texts associated with this genre date from the Middle Kingdom to possibly as late as the 20th dynasty (cf. Appendix I). The primary focus of these texts is the recognition of favourable and unfavourable days. Several of the texts are restricted to lists in which the portions of each individual day, commonly divided into three part, are designated as good (*nfr* in black ink) or bad (*ḏw*, *'ḥ'*, *'ḥ3* or *nfr* in red ink). Longer texts, particularly Cairo No. 86637 and the British Museum text known as Papyrus Sallier IV, attempt to explain the specific divine influences at work and the best way to respond to this influence. There are also pronouncements concerning the fate of individuals born on specific days.

The calendar texts are rich in information. Mythological tales, as well as individual cult practices, are documented. And all is placed in the context of the intertwining of the world of man and the gods. It is a source material worth examining with some care.

The Context of Calendar Texts

One of the main questions which arises in connection with these texts concerns the source of the information found therein and whether or not these texts emanated from the official and orthodox theology. The answer to this question is, I believe, best answered in the texts themselves.

A tradition of knowledge is referred to in the texts. Cairo Calender Book I, one of the feast lists, refers to the list as the writing of old (*sš n iswt*). Although less clearly expressed a similar reference may be found in the fragmentary first line of Gardiner 109. It is, however, the text of Book II of the Cairo Calender that is the most specific (Bakir 1966, p. 56, Pl. XLIX vs. XIX). The writing is said to be made (*ir*) by the gods and the goddesses of the shrine (*k3r*) and the assembly (*shwt*) of the Ennead. It is Thoth however who assembled (*dmd*) the text. This is said to have been done in the *pr wr* chapel of the temple, in the presence of the Lord of All (*nb r-dr*), that is Osiris. The text is said to be found in library (*pr md3t*) in the first office (*h3 tp*) of Ennead. The numerous references to temple geography, the *k3r* shrine, the *pr wr* chapel, the library, and the office, suggests that the author of this text is speaking of a specific occasion on which the text was both composed and then stored. One can speculate that the original text was composed or compiled in the *pr wr* in the presence of the shrines of the gods. The text appears then to have been stored in the library of a section of the temple allocated to the Ennead.

The exact origin of these texts is difficult however to determine. There is much to suggest that they come from the temples of Western Thebes. The Cairo papyrus, although purchased in Cairo, is said to come from Thebes and contains one reference to Karnak (III Peret 16). Bakir (1966, p. 1) would place the origin of these texts at Deir el-Medina. The ostracon published by Malinine (1938, p. 879 n. 1) has Deir el-Medina as probable provenance and Venus (1981, p.89) suggests that his wooden tablet originates from Deir el-Bahri. These general conclusions coincide with the elaborate description of the temple geography in the Cairo text, indicating a central temple archive, perhaps in Deir el-Medina or in one of the temple complexes of western Thebes active during the late 18th, early 19th dynasties.

These texts are thus very much a part of the temple environment. They appear to be compilations, from common or related sources. The variations in the texts, as to the designations of good and bad days, (cf. Bakir 1966, pp. 141-142) suggests, however, more than one source. At least one of the texts, Book II of the Cairo Calendar, was prepared for an individual with the title *h3ty-'*, although the copy, found on a papyrus containing other texts, was stored in the temple library. Papyrus Sallier IV appears to be a school text and was copied from a text closely related to that of the Cairo text. Shared characteristics, such as festival lists, or the terminology for good and bad suggest that these texts relate to a specific and well defined tradition.

Although part of temple traditions they lack the subtlety or metaphysical quality which so often characterize theological texts. Instead the content of these texts is directed towards the practical application of an elitist knowledge of the divine world. Here is a handbook for survival in an environment in which the activities of the gods influence the work-a-day world of man. The calendar texts prescribe the behaviour with which to counteract the disruption caused by the contact between the realms.

For the student of Egyptian religion these texts also give an insight into which of the themes, often encountered in more sophisticated contexts, are given priority in interpreting the day to day moments of harmony and disorder. It provides a catalogue of those mythic motifs regarded as most significant and powerful in shaping the features of each day.

Mythological Events

The premise of the calendar is that the gods co-exist with man, and share his natural environment. They live in the temple and sail the river. They are found in places such as Busiris, Heliopolis, Abydos and Letopolis, which have, not only mythic reference, but also a geographical reality. The events of myth take place in the here and now. These events are not, however, related in a tidy day to day sequence so that we can follow each episode and its consequences. Instead we find references to details, from what must have been familiar stories, scattered about through the year. The most important events, such as the victory of Re over the forces of chaos and the funeral preparations of Osiris, are referred to several times. And different versions of what is structurally the same myth (cf. esp. the story of the eye) appear in small fragmented allusions.

Many of these events are known from other sources. However, we are accustomed to meeting them in other situations, when they are called upon to endow validity to the rituals of temple and necropolis. In the calendar texts they are immediate happenings. The language used in ideological text context is intended to weave together as many influences as possible. The language of the calendars, however, is much more straight forward, describing the events as explanatory or prescriptive for certain reactions in the natural world, along with ways to counteract that action. And so the gods are met as contempories.

Re, King of the Gods

Re dominates in the world described by the calendar texts. It is Re who rises and sets and thus provides the temporal framework for the day. His journey from dawn to sunset takes place in a boat, which can sail with a sweet wind (I Akhet 24).

The imagery of the boat takes an important place in the calendar. Re is accompanied by a "crew" (*ḳdwt* I Shemu 18, II Shemu 2, IV Shemu 25) and followers (*imyw-ḥt*: I Akhet 20,21), who help the god in the destruction of his enemies, which takes place e.g. on I Akhet 20, II Akhet 9, 20 and I Peret 11. The enemies of the god are called the "children of Bedesh" (II Akhet 7, 24-25; IV Peret 22, III Shemu 24), the term *bdš*, commonly translated as weak or limp (WB I 488). This relates to the image of the defeated enemies of the Kadesh reliefs. Their status as foreigners is confirmed when on II Akhet 25 the children of Bedesh are found wrapped in a map and on their sides, the image of the dead and buried.

The success of this crew is celebrated during several days in the 2nd month of Shemu (days 2,3,8,9). On the 10th day the crew is rewarded by being allowed to catch birds and fish with the god.

Re is king of the gods. In times of crisis he gives orders that are read aloud by Thoth (IV Akhet 1) and even speaks before the gods (IV Akhet 9). He participates in the offering of Maat, both as recipient (III Akhet 22) and as officiant in offering to Atum (II Peret 10). Maat is brought to the shrine of Re in Heliopolis (III Shemu 16 cf. 18).

Shu is the son of Re (I Akhet 2, III Akhet 21), who plays the role of combatant, found in the solar bark (I Peret 16, II Peret 3) and as retriever of the Eye for his father (I Akhet 2, II Shemu 30).

The Court of the God

Re, as any king, has a court around him. The calendar texts place Thoth as the foremost among these gods and in an active administrative role. He reads aloud the orders of the king (IV Akhet 1). And on two days in Letopolis he establishes the nobles of Re (IV Akhet 26) and bestows the Red Crown on Horus (IV Akhet 24). As any good subject, Thoth takes an oath in Hermopolis (I Peret 28). The familiar scene in which Thoth is shown, scribe palette in hand, is recalled and he is said to be present when the count is taken (I Shemu 19). Thoth also assists Re in the defeat of Seth (IV Akhet 9).

The most important part played by Thoth however is that of the one who fetches and reestablishes the eye, a role played by several goddesses (II Akhet 21, I Peret 5, I Peret 29, II Shemu 30).

Thoth plays a specific role as administrative representive of the king. But the kingdom of Re is populated by many gods. There are the helpers of Thoth: Hu and Sia, Maat and even Ptah (IV Akhet 1, I Peret 5, I Peret 29). The texts describe the gods as the subjects of divine king. In some instances the gods are named as specific groups: the Enneads, Greater and Lesser, and the Great Ones, the *Wrw*. The Enneads and the gods in general often function as the celebrants of the victory of the god (cf. e.g. II Akhet 9). When things are good, they jubilate (e.g. I Akhet 19, II Akhet 1). The Ennead also sails the river (II Shemu 19) and, in the one reference to Apophis, it is the Ennead who kills him for Re at the beginning of the year (I Akhet 2). The Great Ones is a term apparently applied to the the children of Nut, as the *Wrw* are said to be born on the extra five days of the year (Bakir 1966, p. 49 vs. IX l. 11). They can appear, as can the Ennead, as a duality, called the Upper (*ḥry*) and Lower (*ḥry*) Great Ones when they arrive at Abydos to mourn Osiris (III Akhet 16, 17 in Pap Sallier IV). The *Wrw* are found in a hidden shrine (IV Akhet 21) and take an active role when they argue with the uraeus and force her to create the eye of Horus the elder (IV Peret 3).

The Pacification of Nun

Just as Re is the sun, Nun is the water on which boats sail (I Akhet 1). Nun possesses such power that the earth trembles under him (III Akhet 4). He lives in a cavern and goes to a place of darkness where the gods are and where those who are above and those who are below come into existence (I Peret 15, 17). Even those gods who are essentially beneficient can be reticient and so even Nun (IV Akhet 1, cf. IV Shemu 15). On one occasion it is necessary to coax Nun to come forth. This, it may be noted, coincides with the last month of the innundation. First the Greater and Lesser Enneads try by going to the cavern, but then when that doesn't work Thoth shows up with Sia and a copy of the decree issued by Re, which proclaims Nun's identity with every form of existence, beings (*irw*), lions, reptiles, gods, goddesses, Akhw, the dead and "those who came into being in the *sp tpy*". This evidently is enough to encourage Nun to come forth and complete the innundation.

The Revolt of the Gods

The world of the gods is not a place of automatic harmony. It shifts between festivity and disorder. Rebellion also occurs among the gods, even those found in the shrines (*k3r*) of the temple. The calendar texts refer specifically to a rebellion among the gods in the shrine (III Peret 15, III Shemu 10), apparently of a sufficiently serious nature that even Shu complained to Re about the "Great Ones of Infinity" (II Shemu 22). Dissension is created among them on III Shemu 10. The disturbance among these gods, which appears to begin late in the season of Peret, is resolved however during the last month of Shemu when the hearts of those who are in the shrine are happy (IV Shemu 12).

The Transformation of the Gods

The relationship between Re and the gods are not, as has been noted, always the best. On the 22nd day of I Akhet, Re calls the gods to him, devours them and then vomits them up, their bodies having been turned into fish and their bas into birds. Another reference to this tale may be found on I Shemu 21, in which Re appears to vomit something from his boat. And as noted above on II Shemu 10, Re and his crew goes hunting for birds and fish in his boat (cf. a study of the bird and fish motif cf. Hornung 1983 reference to this episode pp. 457-8).

The Story of the Eye

Certainly the most complex of the tales found reflected in the calendar texts is that of the eye. This story is known from several sources and can be traced in various ways as early as the the Pyramid Texts (cf. Troy 1986, p. 24) and surviving into the Roman period in Demotic (Spiegelberg 1917) and Greek (West 1969). Almost contemporary with the Cairo Calendar is the well known version from the Book of the Cow of Heaven, found in the tombs of Tutankhamun, Seti I and Ramses II (cf. Hornung 1982, pp. 1-9; 37-40). In this version Re's displeasure with mankind causes him to call upon his daughter Hathor who, changing into the raging lioness Sakhmet, almost destroys mankind. Thoth however tricks her into drinking beer. She becomes drunk and mankind is saved. Other versions of the story revolve around the daughter-eye that leaves her father Re and his efforts to regain her (cf. Junker 1911). The recently published Mut ritual, which the authors called *Le voyage de la déesse libyque*, further illustrates the central role of this myth (Verhoeven and Derchain 1985).

    There is a natural connection between the calendar texts and the story of eye. The transition between the old year and the new is regarded as a dangerous period, a time when one manifestation of the eye goddess, Sakhmet, roams the earth, spreading disease and disorder (cf. Säve-Söderbergh 1950, pp. 4 ff.). The most complete of the calendar texts, the Cairo Calendar, includes a spell appropriate for these days (Bakir 1966, p. 55 vs XVI). Even the

Deir el-Bahri wooden tablet concludes with reference to these days. But as the calendar texts indicate, it is not only during the transition period between the old and new years that the eye is on the loose. There are, throughout the year, periods of seeking and retrieving the goddess, periods of harmony and of disorder.

The story of the retrieval of the goddess is referred to numerous times in the calendar texts. It appears as details from what is evidently parallel versions of the tale. Several goddesses occur in the role of the eye. Bastet and Sakhmet are prominent in the role, with the goddess Wadjet and possibly Nekhbet, referred to with the epithet "White One", also appearing. There are references to the Upper Egyptian goddess, and the Upper Egyptian Merit. Even Neith and Maat occur in connection to the myth. Hathor is mentioned once, but the texts predates, it would appear, Tefnut's otherwise prominent status in this myth, as she does not occur in this context. Often the goddess is described quite simply as an "eye", the eye of Re, of Horus the elder, the *wḏ3t*-eye, the *3ḫt*-eye. The epithet "the Great Flame" (*nsrt wrt*) also occurs frequently.

Although the Cairo text, and its closest parallel Papyrus Sallier IV, give the greatest indication of the central role of the eye myth for the interpretation of the dangers of the year, even the less eloquent texts adds to that impression. Vernus' (1981, Fig. 1) wooden tablet only refers to the divine world in terms of the deities named as patrons of each month. The reader finds the *3ḫt*-eye as the patron of II Akhet, the Sovereign, Mistress of Great Fury (*ityt nbt nšny wr*) as patron of III and IV Akhet, Shesemet mistress of Punt as patron of I Peret, the Eye of Re, Mistress of the Two Lands for II Shemu and the *3ḫt*-eye, Mistress of Wine, Mistress of the Heavens for III Shemu. All of these names indicate an association with the story of the eye.

There are details from many episodes related in the calendar texts: the rage and blood thirsty character of the goddess, her flight, the gods, particularly Thoth, seeking her out and finally her pacification and return.

The idea of the angry goddess is found repeatedly in the texts. Bastet is so angry that the gods can't be around her (III Akhet 20). The Great Flame, who is in a secret shrine and kept there by Maat, Ptah, Thoth, Hu and Sia, rages at being confined (I Akhet 11; I Peret 5). Sakhmet is angry in Libya and pacing about (IV Peret 27). The Eye of Horus the Elder, being scrutinized by the Great Ones, is angry in front of Re (III Shemu 11). This anger leads both Hathor (I Akhet 4) and the Upper Egyptian Meret to go forth to slaughter (I Akhet 13) and Sakhmet to go off to the East to fight the confederates of Seth (I Akhet 25). The fury of the goddess, as one of her main characteristics is recorded in the wooden tablet as she is called mistress of great fury (*nbt nšny wr*).

The goddess escapes. "Her Majesty of Heaven" heads south on the II Peret 20. The "White One" however heads north I Shemu 10 to fight the enemy in the Delta. The departure of the goddess to the place from which she came makes the gods sad (III Shemu 5).

The eye is, of course, sought out. She is called at this point the *3ḫt*-eye (IV Akhet 20-21, II Peret 18), and the Great Flame (III Shemu 7). The ones doing the looking are Thoth (cf. above) the mysterious ones (IV Akhet 21) and the 7 executioners (II Peret 18). The gods get in a boat and sail after the goddess (III Shemu 7).

And the eye is found. Thoth guides the Great Flame into her house in the desert (III Peret 10). Shu goes forth to bring back the *wḏ3t*-eye (II Shemu 30). His retrieval of the Eye of Horus for his father Re is celebrated (I Akhet 2) in the text to Book I of the Cairo Calendar. Even Maat, much reproached, appears to have out wandering and she is returned to the shrine by Re (III Shemu 16).

The Eye has been pacified by Thoth, Hu and Sia according to the order of Re (II Akhet 3). The Eyes of Neith have helped him pacify and fetch the Upper Egyptian goddess (II Akhet 21).

The Eye, once returned, however, appears to be less than pacified and the Great Ones have to argue with her in her form as uraeus to force her to cause the transformation of the Eye of Horus the elder (IV Peret 3). The Great Ones even have to protect the *wḏ3t*-eye from Re (IV Peret 10).

Eventually, however, there is great jubilation because the Eye has returned whole (III Shemu 19). Its parts are even counted, using the system of fractions, 1/2, 1/4, 1/8, 1/16, 1/32 and 1/64, which the parts of the Eye are used to represent (IV Peret 8). The *3ḫt*-eye (II Shemu 25) and the *wḏ3t*-eye is pacified (1 Peret 1, IV Shemu 20). The Great Ones rejoice when they receive it (I Shemu 6). The gods are happy because Re is at peace with *3ḫt*-eye (III Shemu 9) and the *wḏ3t*-eye is behind the gods in their shrines (IV Peret 11).

And characteristically there is singing to celebrate this happy ending as the Upper Egyptian Merit goes forth in the presence of Atum and there are ceremonies of singing for Thoth (II Akhet 21). Wadjit (II Peret 10) and an unnamed goddess (IV Shemu 10) both go to Heliopolis to sing.

Burial of Osiris

The story of the funeral of Osiris is also embedded in the text of the calendar. In the description of this event there is an alternation between activities in Busiris and in Abydos. Anubis, the officiant at the embalming of Osiris is associated with the *w'bt*, the place of embalment. The calendar records the inspection of the *w'bt* (II Akhet 4, II Akhet 18). On one occasion, Anubis appears to be transformed into lizards (?) and emerges distraught to tell of what he has seen in the *w'bt*, presumably the body of Osiris. This upsets everyone and soon the entire assembly of gods are weeping (II Akhet 18). Ointment is made for the mummification (?) of Osiris (IV Akhet 19) and a ceremony for the preservation of the things used in the *w'bt* during the funeral is celebrated (II Peret 17).

On IV Peret 2 the text tells of Geb who goes to Busiris to see Anubis who "commands the council" (*wḏ ḏ3ḏ3t*) on business. What this business is, is uncertain. One may speculate that it concerned the official arrangements of the funeral.

Mourning is a natural part of the funerary activities and Isis and Nephthys have a given role as the mourners of Osiris. Surpisingly enough they are found weeping in Busiris (I Peret 14), Sais (III Akhet 17) and Abydos (III Akhet 16). The gods are sad because of the death of Osiris (III Akhet 14, II Peret 6).

Other ceremonies include the opening and closing of the windows (?) of the shrine in Busiris (II Akhet 19), a possible reference to building activities associated with the tomb. The raising of the Djed (II Peret 12) and the transformation into the Benu (IV Akhet 12).

The journey to Abydos for burial represents great danger for the god. And once again there is no sense of sequence in the events as they are described. IV Peret 13 is the day of conducting Osiris to his boat to Abydos. They look for the confederates of Seth ("don't be brave today"). But on III Akhet 13, a tale is told of how the boat carrying Osiris is attacked by creatures, the confederates of Seth, which are both reptile-like and which turn themselves into cattle. A ferryman also figures in the story as does a transformation into "an old man in the arms of a nurse".

The landing in Abydos and the establishment of Osiris in his tomb is the cause of great celebration. There are festivals of Wennefer (II Akhet 16) and of Osiris of Abydos in the Neshmet boat (IV Akhet 11), and of Osiris in Abydos and the raising of the *trty*-tree (III Peret 28). Isis and Nephthys jubilate (III Akhet 24, 26). Wennefer is pleased, the Akhw are joyful, even the dead participate in the festivities (II Peret 28). Osiris is happy in his tomb in Busiris (III Peret 6). The gods are satisfied adoring Wennefer (IV Peret 29) and Re sails to the West to see the beauty of Osiris (III Shemu 13). And finally, at the end of the year IV Shemu 1, every god and goddess spend the day celebrating the festival of of Wennefer.

Osiris' role as judge in the afterworld is not forgotten as it is confirmed in the text when the anonymous M is to be judged III Shemu 23.

Conflict of Horus and Seth

Among the many causes of uproar in the heavens described in the calendar texts, the conflict of Horus and Seth takes a particular place. One of the fascinations with this text is the manner in which the story of Re as king is interwoven with elements of the Osiris cycle. Horus and Seth can still, in Re's kingdom, struggle over the kingship of Egypt. Shu can, as Re's son, undertake to recapture the Eye of Horus.

The details from this myth come from four aspects of the story: the treachery of Seth, the conflict between the two gods, and the reconcilation and the division of the kingdom and triumph of Horus.

The treachery of Seth is described in terms of rebellion against the legitimate power. Seth, with his confederates, are the rebels against which the royal power must fight (I Akhet 25, 22 Akhet 12, II Akhet 20). Seth is found in the "Eastern" countries (IV Shemu 11) and rebelling against Re (IV Peret 16, IV Shemu 11) and against Wennefer (IV Peret 24). The battle between these gods are as much a battle between armies, as between individuals. Seth has his *sm3yt*, his confederates and Re his crew (IV Peret 16, IV Shemu 11). Seth's confederates, as noted above, attempt the take over of the boat to Abydos. And it may be these enemies of Seth which Thoth is said to have forced to kill themselves (IV Akhet 9). Seth is characterized by his loud voice in these texts. His voice being heard in heaven and on earth (III Peret 3). The name of Seth is associated in the texts with causing dissension and fighting at home (III Peret 17, 25, IV Peret 24). Speech is also a means of defeating Seth (II Akhet 12).

Seth is depicted as the archetypal rebel, the enemy of Re and Osiris. His counterpart Horus, is the archetypal hero. He enters the picture with a subtle reference to his birth as the text tells us that Re awakens Isis, and then Horus saves his father, and smites Seth (II Peret 16 cf. Coffin Text Spell 148). Another reference to Horus' birth is found on I Peret 10 which is the day on which Horus comes out the marshes together with the Great Flame, here associating the Great Flame with the role of Wadjit in the myth.

The most notable instance in the text, describing the conflict between the two gods, consists of the episode in which they are transformed into hippopotami (read "ebony" *hbny* in the Cairo text by Bakir 1966, p. 17 and "wolves" by Budge 1923, p. 35 in Papyrus Sallier

IV, but cf. Chassinat 1921, p. 91 and Griffiths 1960, p. 47 ff.), an episode occuring on I Akhet 26. Isis enters the picture and,attempting to hit Seth with her harpoon, she wounds Horus instead. The quarrel between mother and son is related here, as Horus orders her to attack Seth. Isis is left to contemplate the difference between love for a brother and love for a son.

The texts concentrate, however, on the reconciliation of the two rivals. III Akhet 26, Horus and Seth are judged and the fighting stopped. I Akhet 27,28 the peace of Horus and Seth, also called the children of Nut. The rule is divided between the two, Seth is given the desert and the red crown and Horus Egypt and the white crown (III Akhet 26, 29) and everyone is happy.

There is a triumph for Horus however. His heritage is established (III Akhet 8). He receives his father's throne (III Akhet 24), a will (*imyt-pr*) is even written on his behalf (III Akhet 28). And Horus acts the role of king, campaigning in a foreign country (I Shemu 7) and inspecting a sanctuary in Letopolis (I Shemu 20).

The Other Gods in the Calendar Texts

The myths mentioned above are those which dominate the contents of the calendar texts, either by their reoccurrence or by the length and detail in their telling. Other deities and myths do however appear in the texts. Apophis is killed by the Ennead (I Akhet 2) and displays an association with Sobek, who is characterized in the texts as a crocodile, waiting to slash his enemies (I Akhet 17, II Akhet 22, IV Peret 25, I Shemu 13). Many festival are celebrated in Sobek's name as well, appropriately in the first month of Akhet (1,7, 9, 11). The association between Neith and Sobek is preserved in these texts as Sobek goes forth to guide Neith in Sais, when writing material prepared for her was brought to her (II Peret 11). Towards the end of the year, when the flood waters are sinking, Neith is found treading on the flood, looking for the crocodile Sobek (II Shemu 26).

The Memphite gods Ptah, Nefertem and Sakhmet are represented as a family unit (I Akhet 24) and Ptah is celebrated with numerous festivals (e.g. I Akhet 3,14). The divine animals are also found in these texts, such as the Ram of Mendes, who on III Akhet 15 inspects the temple and the *Mr-wr* bull who is associated with the offering of Maat on II Peret 10. The texts assert the heterogenous population of the gods in the midst of man's world.

Predictions, Prohibitions and Ritual Behaviour

The state of affairs among the gods reviberates in man's world. The effects can be that of good fortune or catastrophe. At least four days every month, everything is good, the gods are in festivity, the *wḏȝt*-eye is pacified, or some other event brings a total harmony into the world. A holiday, like that of II Peret 2, can be proclaimed for the entire land.

Disorder can also, however, so pervade the land that the one for whom the manuscript is intended is advised to stay at home either all or part of the day. Over 40 days during the year have this admonition. Conflict among the gods is a typical cause of this admonition such as the day Shu complained to Re about the uproar among the gods on II Shemu 22.

The events of the divine world also affects the fate of the one born on a particular day. Seven days of the year bring death by old age. The one born on IV Akhet 10 will die of old age, with the offering of beer being poured onto his face. Born on II Shemu 16 gives one the opportunity to look forward to a career as a noble (sr). The reason behind this favor is to be found in the festivities of the gods (I Akhet 10), or a good day for Re's sailing (I Akhet 24) or the downfall of his enemies (II Akhet 10) to give some examples.

Deaths by the attack of an animal are also prophecied, most of them taking place in the season of Akhet: by crocodile (I Akhet 3, 16; II Akhet 23) by bull (I Akhet 6), and by snake (II Akhet 27). Death by crocodile, for example, could be caused by the gods out digging a canal. Sickness could also be predicted, such as that by blindness (I Akhet 13, IV Akhet 20), skinrash (II Akhet 4) or plague of the year (III Akhet 20). Death by blindness could be the result of one of the Eye goddesses, the Upper Egyptian Merit, roaming the land and slaughtering. Papyrus Sallier IV adds the proclamation of death by blindness to a text that refers to the day as the day of looking at the 3ḥt-eye. Skinrash is the result of Anubis' inspection of the w'bt for the protection of the limbs of Osiris. The plague of the year, appearing three months into the new year, affects those born on the day that Bastet goes forth in her rage.

Copulation (II Akhet 5) and drunkenness (II Akhet 6) can also be predicted as the cause of death. II Akhet 5, described as a day of offering to Montu and Hedj-hotep, predicts death by copulation (nk) for one born on that day. There is also a prohibition against union with a woman (sm3 m st-ḥmt) on this day. Borghouts (1981, p. 19-21), discussing this passage in connection with the publication of an ostracon text, remarks on the writing of the phrase irt ḥt m Ḥḏ-ḥtp r Mnṯw, noting that the preposition m is written with a phallus, suggesting the reading "it is the day of Hedj-hotep doing (certain) things against Montu", with the implication of either a homosexual assault or reference to adultery between Hedj-hotep and a wife of Montu's. Although this suggestion is tantalizing, creating as it does the possibility of discerning a new mythic theme, it is important to point out that the term ḥt which Borghouts translates as "(certain) things" does appear several times in the context of offering in the calendar texts (cf. I Akhet 17, IV Akhet 30, I Peret 1, I Peret 6, I Peret 9, II Shemu 28 and Appendix II). It is interesting to note that apparently to die of drunkeness is not a bad death, as it occurs on a day when the gods are having a good time.

A final example illustrates the way in which the violent tenor of an event can override its basically beneficient character. The defeat of the enemies of Re is a necessary prerequisite for harmony. The violence with which this is achieved however gives the dominate tone of the day, as the execution of the Children of Bedesh on II Akhet 7 occurs on a unfavourable day. One born on this day dies in a foreign country, like that from which these enemies came.

The calendar texts not only relate the divine influences of each day and predict their inevitable outcome in terms of the fate of those born on certain days, they also provide help in ameliorating those influences, by behaving in an appropriate way. Staying at home, during all or part of the day, was regarded, as noted above, an effective means of dealing with negative influences. Work (k3t) was also restricted because of the activities of the gods. Ten days of the year of Cairo Calendar's Book II (I Akhet 20, II Akhet 26, 27, I Peret 20, III Peret 15, IV Peret 20, 27, II Shemu 27, III Shemu 5, 19) have work prohibitions, primarily because of strife among the gods, but on one day (II Akhet 20) all forms of building, house and boat is prohibited because of the opening and closing of the windows at Busiris, a possible reference to a ritual associated with the tomb of Osiris. In contrast to the even distribution of work prohibition found in Book II, one may note that for Book I of the Cairo

Calender, with entries for I Akhet 1-15, there are eight days on which work is prohibited, and even said to be *bwt* (I Akhet 4).

Food is another area where prohibitions are put forth as a way of coping with negative influences. Fish is the food most frequently prohibited, occurring on five days in the season of Akhet. On I Akhet 17, it is associated with the offering to Sobek, taken from the mouth of the crocodile. The day on which Re transforms the gods into fish and birds (I Akhet 22) is also one on which one sustains from eating either fish or birds. Another, fragmentary, reference to the transformation into fish on IV Akhet 7, occurs along with a prohibition against eating fish. The goddess Hatmehyt, who takes the form of the *itn*-fish, goes forth on IV Akhet 28 and fish should not be eaten on that day. An association with the offering ceremonies of IV Akhet 29 makes fish an inappropriate meal on that day. Birds are prohibited as food on I Akhet 22 and 23 also in connection with the transformation of the gods. On IV Peret 25, Sobek is loose and nothing found on water should be eaten.

Other food prohibitions include milk (I Peret 25), which should not be "eaten" (*wnm*) indicating that it was considered a food rather than a drink. Instead one is told to drink wine and eat honey. The meat of a lion is also forbidden (II Shemu 18) as well as the funerary offers of bread and beer (II Akhet 17, IV Akhet 19, IV Shemu 23). One is urged to substitute wine for beer on one occasion (IV Akhet 19) when the embalment ointment is prepared for Osiris. Wine is to be drank instead until sundown. The avoidance of milk falls on the same day as the establishment of the Hesat-cow by Re, and of lion's meat on the day that the god Khenty, presumably in lion form, roams the mountains. Book I, containing the list of *prt*-festivals from the Cairo Calender, is much more eloquent with five of the fifteen days forbidding different kinds of fish. Very particular foods are to be avoid, *'ft*-herbs (I Akhet 2, 8) sugarcane honey (*bit d3is*) (I Akhet 8, 10), the head of an *'wt*-cattle (I Akhet 6), and a mouse (I Akhet 13).

Besides the texts prohibiting the eating of some animals, there are also prohibitions against killing others. A reptile called the *'nhy* was protected on three days. Killing it appears to disturb moments of reconciliation as one day is the peace of Horus and Seth (I Akhet 27) and another the day of the pacification of the *wd3t*-eye (IV Shemu 20). The third day (I Akhet 23) appears to be associated with events of the previous day, the transformation of the gods. Additionally, there is a prohibition against killing a bull (I Akhet 21). It is called a day of being on guard, and any contact with the animal, such as allowing it to pass you is to be avoided.

Other prohibitions concentrate on the elements of fire and water. Ten days give some form of prohibition against fire or light (I Akhet 22, 29, III Akhet 5, I Peret 3,7,10,11, III Peret 19,20 III Shemu 14). Very few give any motivation but III Shemu 14 connects the fire in the household with the glow on that day of anger of the Eye of Horus the elder. Seven days (I Akhet 4, 15, III Akhet 19, II Peret 24, II Shemu 10, II Shemu 20, III Shemu 5) forbid sailing in a boat. The most graphic motivations for this include the day of rage in the Duat (I Akhet 15) and the day when Re and his crew are on the river catching fish and birds (II Shemu 10). On III Shemu 5, the goddess journeys back to when she came from and the gods are sad ("don't use the boat on this day").

Sexual intercourse is forbidden on three days (I Akhet 11, II Akhet 5, I Peret 7). On two of these days there is an association with the Great Flame, an epithet applied to the goddess associated with the role of the Eye.

Some form of prohibition against speech is found on six days (II Peret 30, III Peret 17, 22, IV Peret 24, II Shemu 4, III Shemu 6). There is a general prohibition against talking on II Peret 30), without a reason being given. On II Shemu 4, there is a reckoning of what Geb and Nut has done, and the text states don't shout at anyone on this day. Don't fight in your house on III Shemu 6, not while the temple of the goddess is like that (*mi.s*). More specifically the name of Seth should not be spoken, fighting will go on forever if you do (III Peret 17) and it's the day of rebellion against Wennefer (IV Peret 24). Don't say the name of snakes either, it's the day of catching those who were born to him in Dep (III Peret 22).

Even ritual acts are the subject of prohibition. Water purification is to be avoided on II Akhet 22 when Sobek is on the river, nor is an offering to be made that day. And likewise when Nun goes forth to the place where the gods are on I Peret 17 there is a prohibition against water purification. A third prohibition is found on IV Peret 18 with the admonition don't approach when the Majesty of Re goes forth. Incense offering is not to be made on I Akhet 23, a day when the heart of the enemy of Re is evil, nor is singing to be heard that day. An avoidance of all ritual (*nt'*) is to be observed on III Shemu 11 when the gods look through the Eye of Horus the Elder and all are upset at what they see. Singing and chanting are not to be heard on I Peret 14 while Isis and Nephthys are weeping, mourning Osiris.

Prohibitions, together with the designation of the days as good and bad are essentially what is retained in the abbreviated texts found on papyrus fragments and ostraca. Most of them retain a reference reading "Don't do anything" (*imi.k irt ḫt*, cf. e.g. Posener 1951, p. 187 lines 7 and 12). This expression which is the negative correlate to the reassurance found at least four times a month that everything is good, is listed thirteen times in the Cairo Calender Book II (I Akhet 4, 26, II Akhet 7, 18, III Akhet 14, IV Akhet 3, I Peret 20, II Peret 29, III Peret 27, IV Peret 3, III Shemu 3, IV Shemu 6, 15).

Offering to the gods, an active religious rite, is also a way to interact with the influence of the gods. Some 30 days of the year contain references to offerings of some form, using Book II of the Cairo Calendar and Papyrus Sallier IV as a combined text (cf. Appendix II). The vocabulary used is varied as is the object of offering. In a few of the examples the reference appears to be, not to those ceremonies which the individual is admonished to perform, but to a ceremony being performed among the gods. On I Akhet 14, for example, there is the offering (*wdn*) of the great '*3bt*-offering in the southern heavens. On II Peret 10, the *wḏ3t*-eye sings in Heliopolis, while "Her Majesty of the *k3r*-shrine" is raised up by the *Mr-wr* bull and Re repeats the raising of Maat to Atum.

In many cases, however, the offering is to take place in the home. Such as on IV Akhet 4 when ritual (*nt'*) should be performed in the temple of Sokar and in the house (*pr.k*). Local gods and the Akhw are also the object of offering (II Akhet 14, 17, IV AKhet 30, I Peret 9, II Peret 4, 7, IV Peret 23, 29, IV Shemu 2). The importance of these offerings is underlined with the commentary that it is good to hear what is said to you (II Akhet 2, cf. II Akhet 17).

These offering ceremonies can directly coincide with the activities of the gods such as on IV Akhet 12 when Osiris is transformed into the Benu, and offerings are to be made to the Benu in the house. The connection can also be more diffuse as when the text records an unfamiliar myth such as on II Akhet 2 when Horus, majesty of Sais goes to his mother Neith, suffering (*g3y*) of his buttocks (*'ryt*). There is a *wḥm mswt*, repetition of birth, and celebration in heaven. This is accompanies by an admonition to offer to all the gods on that day.

The Festival Lists

A final commentary should be made concerning the festival lists found in the calendar texts. Several of the texts contain festival lists. Two of the texts of the Cairo Calendar, Books I and III, are festival lists. A certain correlation can be made among the range of festivals found in the different texts. Particularly Turin Ostracon 6415 provides a good parallel with the Cairo text. There are ,however, no readily visible relationship between these lists and those otherwise consulted for the study of festivals (cf. Schott 1950) . The terms *ḥb*, " festival" and *pryt* "the going forth", used in these text, may represent simple forms of celebration of the god, if indeed any specific ritual expression is involved at all.

Concluding Remarks

This extensive commentary of the contents of these texts has been intended to provide a background for a discussion of the practical and individual expressions of the Egyptian religious view. It takes us far afield from royal ideology and into an area not often covered by research. It reflects a world where the concerns are immediate: the dangers involved with leaving the house, whether or not it is propitious to work, or to travel on the river. Myths are not background to ritual, but real and present events bringing with them good and bad days.

The question remains, however, as to whether these text really represent the day to day life and state of mind of the Egyptian population. If so, we are dealing with an anxiety ridden community, continually consulting their knowledge of the behaviour of the gods in hopes of avoiding disaster.

Among the scholars that have treated the calendar texts, both pro and con opinions are found. Wresinski (1911, pp. 99-100), the first to present an overview of this material, concludes that there is no evidence that these texts were ever widespread or had any practical application. Drenkhahn (1972), presents an impression array of data demonstrating that the designation of days as good or bad, prohibitions against travel and work, is in no way reflected in the historical documentation. Only the epagomenal days, a part of the traditional period of the transition between the old and new year, were taken seriously as far as their dangerous nature was concerned. Brunner-Traut (1981) takes another view however, she calls the contents of the calenders *"fester Bestandteil im täglichen Leben"* (p. 31) and as an example of the power of myth in ancient Egypt.

Both views carry a certain validity. These texts, we should recall, although popular in terms of their intended audience, still emanate from the temple, and have, as their background, elitist knowledge of the divine world. They are, in nature, however technical texts. Describing a relationship of cause and effect. They do not call on the piety of the individual, nor is there an element of belief contra disbelief. These texts contain a description of the immediate world as seen from the perspective of the inner rooms of the temple.

The calendar texts are part of the Egyptian tradition of learning, going back, as we see from the Kahun papyrus, to the Middle Kingdom or earlier. But in at least one case, the most complete calendar, Cairo no 86637, the compilation was intended for a single individual, to be used, perhaps, for the duration of a single year. The possibility that the nature of each day, as described in these texts, had any influence on village life, must be discounted, by, if nothing else, the work journals of Deir el-Medina, which is the possible provenance of these texts, in which no indication of observation of work prohibitions is found.

Having said that, however, there is still the desire to support Brunner-Traut in at least the statement that these texts represent the power of myth in Egypt, illustrating as they do the contemporaneity between the conflicts and joys of the gods and the authors of the text. Such an awareness, if on a less pronounced level, must have existed among those who tended their altars, offering to the Akhw and saying the words of bread and beer to the dead.

APPENDIX I - The Sources

Kahun VII,3 (British Museum; Griffiths 1898, 62, Pl. 25)

The earliest of these texts dates from the Middle Kingdom and comes from the Kahun collection of papyrus. The text lists the 30 unnumbered days of an unspecified month with the *hrw* sign, with each day marked as *nfr* "good" or *dw* "bad".

An 18th Dynasty Wooden Tablet (Vernus 1981)

A wooden tablet published by Vernus and tentatively dated to the middle of the 18th dynasty, and with Deir el-Bahri as suggested provenance is stated to be a "menology" (*3bdyt*). Here each of the 12 months are listed with a divine patron and specific omens for each month and their interpretation. There are words to be said (*dd.hr.k*) when encountering these omens. There is also a reference to the epigomenal days on the wooden tablet which includes the admonition to the reader to identify himself as *w'b* priest who purifies "this goddess", suggesting that this text had a magic function in relationship to the epagomenal days.

BM 10474vs (Budge 1910, pp. XVI-XVII, Pls. 31-21)

The BM papyrus 10474vs, which is dated to the Ramesside period, is a list of 360 days from I Akhet 1, to IV Shemu 30. Each day is divided into three parts using the terminology *nfr* and *'h'*.

Cairo Calender (Cairo 86637; Bakir 1966)

The Cairo Calendar, dated specifically to year 9 of Ramses II, is the most complete of these calendars. It consists of a number of texts related to this genre.

A. Book II (recto III-XXX; verso I-XI)

The main text (called "Book II" by Bakir; rt III-vs XI) is a complete calendar which concludes with a magic text relating the events of the 5 epagomenal days and words to be said on each day. This concluding section of the text is largely parallel to Leiden I 346, dated to the early 18th dynasty. The description of each day is extensive in this text and many well known, and a few unfamilar, myths are reflected in the description of the individual days. Prohibitions, mainly focusing on when it is proper to "go forth", to travel and to sail are frequent. There is concern for when it is propitious to make offerings and when one should refrain from doing anything. Predictions concerning the fate of individuals born on specific days are also found in this text.

B. Fragmentary Calendar (verso XII-XIII)

An additional fragmentary calender is found on this papyrus covering the period of one unspecified month (vs xii-xiii). It is introduced by instructing the reader to throw black colour annointed with oil and perfumed with incense into the water for father Nun and mother Nut on the occasion of Re's birthday, which appears to correlate with the beginning of the innundation and which may be connected to the feast of Re-Harakhty described in Book II on I Akhet 1. An offering is to be made and the reader is to paint the eyes with green paint and annoint himself. Each day is given a single notation as good (*nfr*) or bad (*'ḥ'*).

C. Book I (recto I-II)

The calender papyrus includes two festival lists. The list which Bakir calls "Book I" is "an introduction of the manifestation festivals (*pryt*) of every god and goddess on their fixed days". It covers the period I Akhet 1 to 15, designating the day as good or bad and sometimes dividing the day into two parts, sometimes not. The feast of each day is named, and occasionally the reason for it is given. Warnings of a very specific nature conclude the text for each day. These are of a somewhat different nature than those found in Book II and include more references to what should or should not be eaten on specific days.

D. Book III (verso XXI-XXIV)

Bakir's Book III is a list of "festivals of divine words distinguishing good days from bad" (*ḥbyt nt nṯrw mdwt rḫ hrw nfr r 'ḥ'*). It covers the period I Akhet 1 to II Akhet 20. It is much more abbreviated that the *pryt* list, but there is a very close correlation between the festivals and when they occur on the two lists. An additional variation of this list is found on the Turin ostracon (cf. below). Each day is designated as good or bad, each day being given a single, double or triple notation. The admonitions here read for the most part either "do nothing" or "do everything" for each particular day.

E. Other Texts

E.1 Magic Spells for the Epagomenal Days (vs. XVI). In addition to the reference to the epagomenal days found in Book II, there is a list of spells for these days.

E.2 A notation of the names of the days said to protect the limbs (vs. XV) and a list of jars (vs. XVII), both texts have a strong association with the various forms of Horus.

E.3 A list of the hours of daylight and darkness of each month (vs. XIV).

E.4 A final text records the measurements of some of the rooms of an unnamed royal tomb, with the notation "damaged" for one of the rooms (vs. XX). The Cairo papyrus also names the scribe who is said to have "compiled" (*sḥwy*) the book for a *ḥȝty-'* whose name is unfortunately lost, although the date year 9 of Ramses II is retained.

Papyrus Sallier IV (BM 10184 = Sallier IV rto I-XXX, vs I- XXIII; Chabas 1870; Chassinat 1921; Select Papyri, Pls. 144-168; Budge 1923, pp. 34-38; Pls. 88-111)

A close parallel to the Cairo Calendar's Book II is found on Papyrus Sallier IV, also regarded as Ramesside. The text from this papyrus covers the period of I Akhet 18 to I Shemu 11. Here as in other Ramesside lists, the days are divided into three parts. The terminology employed, however, is more varied using both *'ḥ'* and *'ḥ3*. As *'ḥ3* is used only rarely, one may suppose that it has a stronger negative meaning than *'ḥ'*. It appears in connection with the most perilous mythological events. Papyrus Sallier IV, which also contains *The Instruction of Amenemhet I to his Son*, is generally regarded as a school text.

Papyrus Golenischeff (Moscow; Malinine 1938)

Evidence for other papyri of this kind can be noted in the survival of the fragmentary Golenisheff papyrus, which lists I Akhet 9, 15, 17, 19. This list, dividing the days into three parts, only uses the term *nfr*, written in black and red ink, Malinine (1938, p. 885) has interpreted the use of the red ink as equivalent to the negative terms *'ḥ'* and *'ḥ3*. A close comparision between these fragments and the Cairo Calendar could reveal a relationship, as the fragments clearly refer to the same elements as found in that calendar, mythological events, offering ceremonies, warnings against certain behaviour and festivals.

Papyrus Turin (CGT 54016 vs 2104 = 344/354; Unpublished, brief description in Roccati, 1975. p. 246, Nr. 15. Cf. Janssen, 1975, p. 98 for a suggested dating.)

An additional fragmentary unpublished papyrus in Turin is said to belong to this genre of texts. Also containing administrative texts, Janssen (1975. p. 98) has suggested dating this papyrus to the 20th dynasty.

Ostracon Malinine (Private Collection, from Deir el-Medina (?); Malinine 1938)

Three ostraca conclude the list associated with this genre. Malinine has published an ostracon which he states was purchased in Luxor and which he concludes had its origin in Deir el-Medina. Containing 10 lines of text, the period III Peret 1 to 30 appears to have been originally covered. The surviving texts gives commentary for 17 days from day 1 to day 28. As in the Golenischeff papyrus, also published by Malinine, the term *nfr* is used for both favourable and unfavourable days, the distinction between good and bad being made with the colour of the ink. Here too the days are divided into three parts. Only a few of the days have been given commentary, the majority recorded simply with the number of the day and the writing *nfr nfr nfr*, in black and/or red ink. The commentary of the days are given using formulae familiar from both the Cairo Calendar and Papyrus Sallier IV. The content of the extant commentary is not, however, always paralleled in the two more complete papyri. For day 4 or 5 one reads that anyone born on this day will die of drowning in the innundation of the Nile, a statement lacking parallel in the main papyri. Similarly a curious warning against looking at the *šps* star in the sky does not occur in the other lists. An unusual element in the writing of this list is the use of the expression *pr R' pr Ḥr pr Wsir* House of Re, House of Horus, House of Osiris. This occurs in both the Cairo and Papyrus Sallier IV lists, but placed consistently as the introduction to a new month. Here the phrase is used as a commentary to day 19.

Ostracon Turin 6415/57304 (Lopez 1980; Posener 1951)

Of the two remaining ostraca, it has already been noted that Turin 6415, which records I Akhet 1 to 12, is a close parallel to the festival lists found in the Cairo material, recording the same festival for each day, although with somewhat different descriptions.

Ostracon Gardiner 109 (Allam 1973, pp. 174-176, Pls. 40-41)

The remaining ostracon, Gardiner 109, deviates significantly from the other texts. Like the Turin ostracon, the Gardiner text records one month, a fact which is stressed in the introductory lines of the text. The text is also said to have been brought from "the land of Syria" (*p3 t3 n ḫ3rw*)(lacuna) to a place called possibly *Mnwt*. The text begins by stating that a good day to start (the calendar) is the "going forth of the moon". One may take this to to refer to the obviously lunar character of the calendar which is, interestingly enough, specified here. The terms used on this ostracon differ from those previously described. Each day is given one designation, *nfr*, written out, for good and *bin* for bad. Notation survives for 25 of the 30 days. Like the Malinine's Deir el-Medina ostracon, the majority of the days are only commented upon as good or bad. The form used to express warning against inappropriate behavior also differs on this ostracon. The normal form is *imi.k* + verb. Here one reads *m irt wdn n p3y.k nṯr m p3 hrw* "Do not offer to your god on this day". The phrase *m p3 hrw* also differs from the commonly repeated *m hrw pn* from the other texts. Also the formulation of certain stereotype warnings differ. Cairo for example can read *imi.k pr m pr.k m hrw pn* "You should not go forth from your house on this day". The Gardiner ostracon however reads *m dit prt rmṯ šmit* "Don't let people go or come" (line 8).

The Epagomenal Texts: Leiden I 346 (Stricker 1948, cf. Borghouts 1978, pp. 12-14).

Reference to the epagomenal days are found in a number of the calendar texts. Leiden I 346 concentrates on these days and their special character. It has been dated to the early 18th dynasty, thus predating many of the calendar texts. Rather than being a calendar as such it is a primarily an invocation intended to describe the events of the epagomenal days and magic formulae for avoiding the consequences of the negative influences of these days. There is a great similarity between this text and reference to the the epagomenal days found in the Cairo texts.

APPENDIX II - Terms for Offering

irt '3bt
"make '3bt-offerings to the gods" (II Peret 7).
"making '3bt-offerings of the followers of Re" (I Peret 21).
"make '3bt-offerings to the gods in the presence of Re" (IV Shemu 24).

irt nt'
One should perform the rituals in the temple of Sokar and in your house with all provisions in the necropolis (IV Akhet 4).
"As to any ritual, it will be good on this day" (III Peret 13).
Don't perform any ritual on this day (III Shemu 11).
"Maat (and all gods) perform rite as the one who is in heaven (IV Shemu 2).
"As for anything (or offering) any rite or anybody on this day, it is good throughout the year" (IV Shemu 30).

irt ḥt
"day of offering before Hedj-Hotep and Montu" (II Akhet 5).

ir sntr
"make incense of sweet herbs for his followers" (II Shemu 9).

w'b ḥt
"Purification of things" (II Shemu 28)

wdn
"offering to the gods" (I Akhet 7).
"offering of the great '3bt-offering in the southern sky" (I Akhet 14).
"offer to the followers of Re" (I Akhet 21).
"offer to all gods" (II Akhet 2).
"offer to the Benu in your house" (IV Akhet 12).
"offer to Ptah-Sokar-Osiris..Atum, lord of the Two Lands of Heliopolis..to all gods" (IV Peret 30).
"offer to your local gods" (II Akhet 13).

wdn '3bt
"offering of the great '3bt in the southern sky" (I Akhet 14).

wḏb ḥt
"return the offerings" (I Peret 9)

wḏb k3w
"repeat the k3w offerings" (I Peret 6)

prt-ḥrw
"Give up bread and beer...(burn incence) to Re and an innvocation offerings to the Akhw.

It is important so that your words will be heard by the local gods. (II Akhet 17).
"Make a *prt-ḥrw* to the Akhw" (IV Akhet 30).
"Make a *prt-ḥrw* to the Akhw in your house" (II Peret 7).
"...*prt-ḥrw* to the Akhw" IV Peret 23).
(Cf."It is great to hear what is said to you": II Akhet 2).

rdi sb
"give food" (IV Akhet 30).

ḥtpw
"offerings in Busiris" (II Shemu 28).

ḥnp snṯrw
"day of offering incense" (II Shemu 13)

ḥt
"day of (taking) Sobek's offering from his mouth" (I Akhet 17)
"offering of Sakhmet" (I Peret 9)

sm3' '3bt
"present the *'3bt*-offering" (I Peret 1).

swḏ '3bt
"transmitting the '3bt-offerings to those who are in heaven" (IV Shemu 1).

sm3' ḥt
"Offer to the gods and the assistents of the Ennead" (IV Akhet 30).

smn p3wt
"establish the *p3wt*-cakes" (I Peret 9).

snṯr ḥr ḥt
"incense on the fire of the followers of Re in the Mesektet and Andjet boats and for the gods" (I Akhet 19).
"Do not neglect them while incense is on the fire according to their list" (I Peret 30).
"Pay attention to the incense on the fire, smelling of sweet myrrh (IV Peret 7).
"Day of...putting incense on the censors of the gods" (IV Peret 23).
"incense on the fire and your local gods..." (IV Peret 29).

sht
"Appease your Akhw" (IV Shemu 19).

shtp
"Pacify your Akhw" (II Akhet, 13, II Peret 4).
"pacifying the heart of those who are in the horizon (I Akhet, 9).
"pacification of the *wḏ3t*-eye" (II Akhet 3).

"pacifiying the heart of the great gods with a festival" (II Akhet 13).
"Thoth pacifies and praises the Upper Egyptian Goddess" (II Akhet 22).
"pacifying the Two Lords" (III Akhet 26, III Akhet 27).
"pacifying Wennefer in the Necropolis" (III Akhet 28).
"pacification of Nun in the cavern" (IV Akhet 1, IV Shemu 15).

k̲3b ẖt
"double the offerings" (I Peret 1, 6).

BIBLIOGRAPHY

ALLAM, S., 1973. *Hieratische Ostraka und Papyri aus der Ramessidenzeit*. Urkunden zum Rechtleben im alten Ägypten, Band 1. Tübingen.
BAINES, J., 1987. "Practical Religion and Piety." *Journal of Egyptian Archaeology,* Vol. 73, pp. 79-98. London.
BAKIR, A., 1966. *The Cairo Calendar No. 86637*. Antiquities Department of Egypt. Cairo.
BORGHOUTS, J.F., 1978. *Ancient Egyptian Magical Texts*. Religious Texts Translation Series. Vol. 9. Leiden.
- 1981. "Monthu and Matrimonial Squabbles." *Revue d'Egyptologie* Vol. 33, pp. 11-22. Paris.
BREASTED, E., 1930. *The Edwin Smith Surgical Papyrus*. University of Chicago Press. Chicago.
BRUNNER-TRAUT, E. 1981. "Mythos im Alltag." *Gelebte Mythen*. pp. 18-33. Darmstadt.
- 1985. "Tagewähleri" *Lexikon der Ägyptologie*, Band VI, cols. 153-156. Wiesbaden.
BUDGE, E.A.W., 1910. *Facsimiles of Egyptian Papyri in the British Museum* (1st Series). London.
- 1923. *Hieratic Papyri in the British Museum* (2nd Series). London.
CHABAS,F. J., 1870. "Le calendrier des jours fastes & néfastes" reprinted in *Bibliothèque égyptologique*, Vol. 12 1905, pp. 127- 235.
CHASSINAT, E., 1921. "Sur quelques passages du de Iside et Osiride de Plutarque." *Recueil de travaux*, Vol. 39, pp. 84-94 esp. pp. 91-92.
DRENKHAHN, R., 1972. "Zur Anwendung der 'Tagewählkalender'." *Mitteilungen des Deutschen Instituts fur Ägyptische Altertumskunde in Kairo*, Band 28, pp. 85-94. Cairo.
GRIFFITHS, F. Ll., 1898. *Hieratic Papyri from Kahun and Gurob*, London.
GRIFFITHS, J. G. G., 1960. *The Conflict of Horus & Seth*. Liverpool.
HORNUNG, E., 1982. *Der ägyptische Mythos von der Himmelskuh*. Orbis Biblicus et Orientalis 46. Freiburg & Göttingen.
- 1983. "Fisch und Vogel: Zur altägyptischen Sicht des Menschen." *Eranos Yearbook*, pp. 455-496. Ascona.
JANSSEN, J.J., 1975. *Commodity Prices from the Ramessid Period*.
JUNKER, H., 1911. *Der Auzug der Hathor-Tefnut*. Berlin.

LOPEZ, J., 1980. *Ostraca Ieratici N 57093-57319*. Catalogo del Museo egizio di Torino. Serie Seconda-Collezioni Volume III. Fascicolo 2. Istituto editoriale cisalpino. La Goliardica.

MALININE, M., 1938. "Nouveaus Fragments du calendrier Egyptien des jours fastes et néfastes." *Mélanges Maspero*. Mémoires publié par les membres de la l'Institut français d'archéologies orientle du Caire, Vol. 66:2, pp. 879-899. Cairo.

POSENER, G., 1951. "Ostraca inédits du Musée de Turin (Recherches Littéraires III)." *Revue d'Egyptologie*, Vol. 8, pp. 171-189. Paris.

ROCCATI, A., 1975. "Scavi nel Museo di Torino VII. Tra i Papiri Torinesi." *Oriens Antiquus*, Vol. 14, p. 246 Nr. 15. Rome.

SÄVE-SÖDERBERGH, T., 1950. "Några egyptiska nyårsföreställningar." *Religion och Bibel IX*, pp. 1-19. Lund.

SCHOTT, S., 1950. *Altägyptische Festdaten*. Mainz

SELECT *Papyri in the Hieratic Character*, 1841. London.

SPIEGELBERG, W., 1917. "Der ägyptischen Mythus vom Sonnenauge in einem demotischen Papyrus der römischen Kaiserzeit." *Sitzung. der phil.-hist. Klasse*. pp. 876-894. Strasburg.

STRICKER, B.H., 1948. "Spreuken tot beveiliging gedurende de schrikkeldagen narr Pap. I 346." *Oudheidkundige Mededelingen uit het Rijksmuseum van Oudheden te Leiden*, Vol. 29, pp. 55-70.

TROY, L., 1986. *Patterns of Queenship in Ancient Egyptian Myth and History*. Boreas 14. Uppsala.

VERHOEVEN, U., and DERCHAIN, P., 1985. *Le Voyage de la Déese Libyque. Ein Text aus dem "Mutritual" des Pap. Berlin 3053*. Rites Egyptiens V. Bruxelles.

VERNUS, P., 1981. "Omina calendérique et comptabilité d'offrandes sur une tablette hiératique de la XVIIIe dynastie." *Revue d'Egyptologie*. Vol. 33. pp. 89-124. Paris.

WEST, S., 1969. "The Greek Version of the Legend of Tefnut." *Journal of Egyptian Archaeology*. Vol. 55, pp. 161-183. London.

WRESZINSKI, W., 1913. "Tagewählerei im alten Ägypten", *Archiv für Religionswissenschaft*, Band 16, pp. 86-100. Leipzig.